Apartheid
Terrorism

CHANGING SOUTHERN AFRICA

Published in association with
the Commonwealth Secretariat

PHYLLIS JOHNSON
& DAVID MARTIN

The Destabilization Report

**APARTHEID
TERRORISM**

Paper 0-85255-339-0
Cloth 0-85255-340-4

The Financial Sanctions Report

**BANKING
ON APARTHEID**

Paper 0-85255-341-2
Cloth 0-85255-342-0

JOSEPH HANLON

**SOUTH AFRICA:
THE SANCTIONS REPORT**

Documents

Cloth 0-85255-338-2

Report available from Penguin

Apartheid Terrorism

THE DESTABILIZATION
REPORT

Phyllis Johnson
& David Martin

The Commonwealth Secretariat
IN ASSOCIATION WITH
James Currey
LONDON
Indiana University Press
BLOOMINGTON AND INDIANAPOLIS

The Commonwealth Secretariat
Marlborough House, Pall Mall, London SW1Y 5HX

James Currey Ltd
54b Thornhill Square, Islington, London N1 1BE

Indiana University Press
10th and Morton Streets
Bloomington, Indiana 47405

Southern African Research and Documentation Centre
Box 5690, Harare, Zimbabwe

ISBN Cloth 0-85255-340-4 (James Currey)
     Paper 0-85255-339-0

ISBN 0-253-33133-1 (Indiana University Press)

Typeset by Opus 43, Cumbria, UK
Printed in England by Villiers Publications
London N6

Contents

Acknowledgements

At their summit in Vancouver, Canada, in October 1987, the 48 Commonwealth Heads of State and Government established the committee of Commonwealth Foreign Ministers on Southern Africa (CFMSA). The eight members of this group are the Foreign Ministers of Australia, Canada (chair), Guyana, India, Nigeria, Tanzania, Zambia and Zimbabwe.

The group, supplemented by members of the Commonwealth Secretariat, personal staff and expert advisers, first met in the Zambian capital, Lusaka, in February 1988. Thereafter, they met in Toronto, Canada, in August 1988 and Harare, Zimbabwe in February 1989. Their final meeting, preceeding the next Commonwealth summit in Kuala Lumpur in October 1989, occurred in Canberra, Australia, in August.

During the course of their deliberations the Ministers requested three specific studies: on South Africa's financial links to the international community; on the present and future impact of sanctions against South Africa as a positive and peaceful means of ending apartheid; and, on South Africa's aggression against the Frontline States.

The Southern African Research and Documentation Centre (SARDC), an independent regional research foundation, was requested to undertake the last of these studies, and a preliminary report was presented to the CFMSA meeting in Harare in February 1989.

Although it was a preliminary document, the Ministers, recognizing the gravity of the situation and the need to inform the international community, immediately released the report.

Further, the meeting asked us to update and finalize the study as a matter of urgency for publication as a book as part of a Commonwealth trilogy, the other two being the financial links and sanctions studies. Thus, this final report is substantially expanded and updated and is now in manuscript form for publication prior to the Kuala Lumpur summit.

The objective of this study is to give an overview of South Africa's policy towards it neighbours and to provide examples of the pressures it exerts on the Frontline States, individually and collectively. The report has no theoretical pretensions as far as analysis of the South African regime is concerned or its apartheid policy. Rather the purpose is to present, in an accessible format, evidence of the consistent and continuous economic and military pressure to which these states have been subjected.

Apart from some historical information, which gives depth and perspective to the report, it focuses on events since 1980 and, in particular, the years 1986-1988. The earlier period has been well documented elsewhere.

In reaching conclusions as to human and economic costs we have, at all times, been guided by the need to err on the side of caution, with statistics and assertions that can stand up to objective scrutiny. Some target states may feel that we have been too cautious.

The facts of the southern African holocaust are horrifying enough, calculated at minimum: 1.5 million war-related deaths and US$45 billion economic costs. These figures tell their own story as to the magnitude of the shattered dreams of the region.

To thank all of those who assisted us in the production of this report would mean adding a list almost as long as the report. To all of you, we are grateful and look forward to working with you in the future.

To President Kenneth Kaunda we are especially grateful for the foreword he has written and for his encouragement.

Finally, we must thank the staff of SARDC who laboured tirelessly to meet requests for yet another set of statistics, more explanations, updated chronologies, and so on. While we, as the authors, take responsibility for the contents and presentation, the report reflects a collective effort.

Phyllis Johnson and David Martin
Directors, SARDC
July 1989

Abbreviations

AECI	African Explosives and Chemical Industries
Agricom	Agricultural Marketing Board
ANC	African National Congress
BDF	Botswana Defence Force
CFM	Mozambique Ports and railways
CFMSA	Commonwealth Foreign Ministers on Southern Africa
CIA	Central Intelligence Agency
CIO	Central Intelligence Organization (Rhodesia)
CONSAS	Constellation of Southern African States
EPG	Eminent Persons Group
ESCOM	Electricity Supply Commission (South Africa)
FAM	Mozambique Armed Forces
FIR	Flight Information Region
FNLA	National Front for the Liberation of Angola
FPLM	Peoples Forces for the Liberation of Mozambique
FRELIMO	Mozambique Liberation Front
IMF	International Monetary Fund
JMC	Joint Ministry Commission
MNR	Mozambique National Resistance
MPLA	Peoples Movement for the Liberation of Angola
NOCZIM	National Oil Company of Zimbabwe
NRZ	National Railways of Zimbabwe
OAU	Organisation of African Unity
PIDE	International Police for the Defence of the State
PLAN	Peoples Liberation Army of Namibia
PTA	Preferential Trade Area
RENAMO	An acronym of MNR above
SABC	South African Broadcasting Corporation
SACU	South African Customs Union
SADCC	Southern African Development Coordination Conference
SADF	South African Defence Force
SARDC	Southern Africa Research and Documentation Centre
SAS	Special Air Services
SATS	South African Transport Services
SWAPO	South West African Peoples Organisation
SWATF	South West African Territorial Forces
TANU	Tanganyika African National Union
TAZARA	Tanzania-Zambia Railway popularly called The Great Uhuru Railway or The Freedom Railway
UDI	Unilateral Declaration of Independence
UN	United Nations
UNHCR	United Nations Commission for Refugees
UNICEF	United Nations Childrens Fund
UNITA	National Union for the Total Liberation of Angola
ZANU	Zimbabwe African National Union
ZNA	Zimbabwe National Army

Annual Average Exchange Rates for FLS Currencies to US$

Year	Angola kwanza	Mozambique metical	Botswana pula	Tanzania shilling	Zambia kwacha	Zimbabwe dollar
1988	30.01	461.00	1.82	96.76	8.14	1.82
1987	29.50	289.10	1.68	63.43	9.56	1.65
1986	29.91	40.68	1.88	31.56	7.52	1.66
1985	29.91	43.15	1.89	17.40	3.24	1.67
1984	30.14	42.45	1.36	15.40	1.79	1.31
1983	30.21	30.27	1.08	9.63	1.18	.97
1982	30.21	30.29	1.03	9.21	.93	.77
1981	27.84	29.33	.84	8.19	.87	.69
1980	27.36	28.93	.77	8.23	.78	.66

Sources: Africa Research Bulletin, African Economic Digest.

**Foreword
By Kenneth Kaunda**

When I was asked to write a foreword to this report prepared for the Commonwealth Heads of State and Government Meeting, I wondered which of the several hats I should wear.

Would it be as a President of one of the victim states; or as the Chairman of the six Frontline States for which this report is about; or as a member of the Commonwealth or simply as an ordinary mortal appalled by the contents of this report being made to this Summit for the first time.

After some soul-searching, I chose to wear all the hats, firstly, because of the moral outrage evoked by the human and economic cost the system of apartheid has wrought upon the Region of Southern Africa as a whole and, secondly, because of the need to dismiss the fallacy prevalent in some international quarters that the evil ideology of apartheid afflicts only the population inside South Africa. Indeed, because to all fair-minded human beings the ideology of apartheid invites total condemnation. This report before you lays bare the facts.

Beyond the vicious violence and oppression inside South Africa, there is an equally vicious violence and oppression inflicted by apartheid on the peoples of neighbouring countries bringing untold social and economic destruction and shattering of hopes for rapid development in the region. The ideology of apartheid is hitting the neighbours back into the stone age.

As an ideology that erodes the humanity of man, apartheid has international ramifications feeding its diseased thought into the thought, words and actions of leaders of other systems using kith and kin, gold, capital, profit and other open leverages.

Humanity has no boundaries. The diseased sentiments, thought, word and action of the apartheid ideology has no boundaries, if not checked. Apartheid's declared policy of "total strategy" is directed at all countries always striking at their soft underbellies.

In reading this report on the devastation of Frontline States by apartheid, I accept the assertion of the authors that their figures for these states are conservative. In Zambia, we have no doubt at all that the economic cost to us resulting from apartheid aggression and destabilization from the day of our independence in 1964 is far greater than the US$7 billion cited in this report.

I, however, respect the view of the authors that they could only base their report on the evidence the Frontline States provided in the brief interval of the preparation of the report. They are correct in rejecting statistics which they could not at this time verify on their own and therefore be able to defend. This makes their report a tough indictment indeed against apartheid in these Frontline States.

The facts they represent are appalling. And in this context, I would like to draw your attention to the reported comments in Maputo last year of a senior officer of the United States of America State Department, Mr Roy Stacey. What was occurring, he said, "was a systematic and brutal war of terror against innocent Mozambican civilians through forced labour, starvation, physical abuse and wanton killing . . . one of the most brutal holocausts against ordinary human beings since World War II".

I am sure that none of us can miss the point of Mr Stacey's reference to World War II as clearly pointing to the mass slaughter of the Jewish people by Adolf Hitler and his Nazis. We are, and we remain, ashamed by that disgusting episode in human history — that holocaust.

After that holocaust by the Nazis, there were people who argued quite lamely that they did not know what Hitler was doing. They were lying. The truth of the matter is that they knew what the Nazis were doing even if they did not know the exact figures and statistics of the holocausts.

Today, dear Commonwealth colleagues, you have to accept that you know what apartheid is doing in Southern Africa. About this there can be no doubt on the part of any leader. To Commonwealth leaders, apartheid is not a remote happening. Apartheid is not an abstract debate. Already more than two decades ago South Africa was expelled from the Commonwealth because of the doings of apartheid.

Apartheid is a horrendous physical reality. None of us will be able to plead in the future that he or she did not know. If we do not speak out and act now; or if we hedge about with fine but meaningless sentiments; or push our heads deep into the sand for any convenient reason, then we shall be as guilty as the direct perpetrators of this heinous crime against humanity.

Couched again in conservative terms, the authors of the report have put the war-related death toll in the six Frontline States at 1.3 million people killed by apartheid in the ten years only since 1980. A staggering figure! But I have seen estimates higher than this for this same killing. I have seen some estimates 50 per cent higher than this figure.

Surely 1.5 million apartheid deaths in the six Frontline States of Southern Africa is enough to electrify the Commonwealth and the international community into action! Indeed, were these apartheid deaths occurring in Europe or in North America, would these communities not have reacted with a deafening outcry of indignation at such an unwarranted and savage holocaust?

The United Nations Children's Fund (UNICEF) told us in a recent report that in one of the Frontline States covered by this report, a child under the age of five dies every three and a half minutes in an apartheid death. Children die in this way because health facilities have been destroyed, vaccination campaigns halted by strife and war generated by apartheid.

When a Jumbo jet is sabotaged over Scotland with the sad loss of all on board, there is an international outcry of indignation and millions of dollars spin out to hunt the killers. We in the Frontline States share that indignation.

Yet, what is taking place in the Frontline States under aggression by apartheid is the same as one Jumbo jet filled with frontline children crashing without survivors every day!! Surely, even if you fail to share, you must at least understand our indignation when confronted with this level of apartheid terrorism.

It is totally impossible for us to put a human or economic cost on such total loss of young life. Indeed, for the hundreds of thousands of adults maimed and mutilated by apartheid aggression. How do you calculate the value of a lost arm, or a lost leg, cut away ears and a mutilated nose, lips and plugged-out eyes and annihilated eye-sight of living people? How do we calculate the loss of our war-traumatized people who will never again be able to play a normal role in our societies which they would otherwise have played if not stopped in their tracks by apartheid aggression?

In Mozambique alone, as many as six factories to produce artificial limbs have been set up to assist those mutilated by war. Young Mozambicans are being sent overseas for crash programmes to train in plastic surgery to help rebuild the faces, noses, lips and ears of those of their countrymen and women who have had them savagely hacked out by apartheid bandits.

Angola, today, has the highest per capita number of limbless people in the whole world. These are the victims of the landmines used by apartheid South Africa against the civilian population of Angola. By the way, some of these landmines are specially manufactured by apartheid South Africa to cut off limbs and maim victims while they leave their victims alive. Apartheid wants the victims to go home and report. A beastly level of cruelty of man to man.

The rest of the Frontline States, Tanzania, Zambia, Zimbabwe and Botswana are continuously subjected to cross-border raids by these surrogate apartheid forces. Well over 1,000 of our people have been kidnapped and murdered.

Apartheid South Africa tries to fool the world by claiming its cross-border action has been aimed at the African National Congress (ANC). And yet we in the region know only a tiny fraction of the victims have been South Africans. The apartheid Government of South Africa claims that the ANC are "terrorists". We in the Frontline States know the apartheid military forces and their surrogates are in truth the marauding terrorists in Southern Africa.

It will be recalled that at the Nassau Commonwealth Summit in 1985, we established the Commonwealth Eminent Persons Group on Southern Africa. Their mission, to terminate the suffering and killing in Southern Africa, was brought to an abrupt end by apartheid's simultaneous military attacks on three Commonwealth capitals — Gaborone, Harare and Lusaka — on 19 May 1986. This naked aggression illustrated apartheid's contempt for the Commonwealth and for the international community as a whole.

I am further appalled by another, though yet again minimally stated statistic in this report, that the total economic cost to the Frontline States has been at least US$45 billion over the past ten years since 1980. This cost is double the external debt of the six Frontline States.

Had this US$45 billion not been dissipated by apartheid and instead remained available to us for our positive development in the exploitation of our immense economic potential, where might we have been today? One thing is clear, we would not have had the level of external debt that we now have. We would have invested directly US$27 billion of our own resources in the development of our own economies fulfilling the aspirations of our people.

This is but a glimpse of the ugly devastation of apartheid upon Southern Africa outside South Africa which a little peep into the past ten years by this report makes possible. The ugliness of destroyed all-round development, lost opportunities and shattered hopes is far wider and deeper than this throughout the region.

However, horrendous as this is, it is only a spill-over of the devastation inflicted by apartheid on the black population inside South Africa. Apartheid which is directly linked to Hitler's warped race ideas and expanded Nazism is a monumental evil. General Jan Smuts, as Prime Minister of South Africa at the time of Hitler's racist power in Germany, arrested and detained in prison as Nazis some of the founders of apartheid.

As we meet, therefore, in Kuala Lumpur, let us once again rise together and face this contemporary disgrace to the human race. Though ostracized, South Africa is still a Commonwealth area. The blot South Africa brings to the race of man is of direct concern to the Commonwealth of Nations.

We, the millions of black people in Southern Africa including South Africa who suffer apartheid directly look to the new day when apartheid will not only be dismantled but will be stone dead, buried and no more.

Before that new day, we want to say we have no respect at all for the utterly mean argument that apartheid should be treated with due consideration, due care and due respect and be wooed to move on its own accord away from its victims. Be cajoled to love that for which it is the ideology to oppress, exploit, torment, kill and destroy.

It is a diabolic view to say to resist apartheid, to halt apartheid, to hurt apartheid is to resist, halt and hurt the welfare of its victims. The people who have created this line of thought are not black. Those blacks prevailed upon to think in this way are mentally dead victims of apartheid. This sadist view is an expression of naked racism and open approval and defence of apartheid. It is biting racism because it is spiteful. An ugly deception.

That is why that esteemed man of God and Nobel Peace Prize Winner in the fight against apartheid, Archbishop Desmond Tutu said "for goodness sake, let people not use us as an alibi for not doing the things they know they ought to do. We are suffering now [from apartheid] and this kind of suffering seems to be going on and on and on. If additional suffering is going to put a terminus to our [apartheid] suffering then we will accept it".

And I want to add, it is stupid to think the suffering inflicted by apartheid on the victims will end without the victims inflicting suffering on apartheid. To survive, apartheid inflicts suffering. To stop it surviving, suffering has to be inflicted on apartheid. This is the natural flow of corrective forces.

Every kind of suffering that can be put on apartheid to stop apartheid, must be put on apartheid to stop apartheid. Apartheid has to be shown that it does not pay to be apartheid. Apartheid has to be shown that it pays not to be apartheid.

The black population inside South Africa who are the reason and direct victims of the apartheid ideology has risen to resist apartheid, to halt apartheid, to dismantle apartheid law and physical structures.

So has the black population of Southern Africa and the African continent. So has the international community worldwide. And increasingly today, so is some of the white population inside South Africa down to the Afrikaans community itself. Indeed, down to the circles of the Nationalist Party and its government and still further down to the Broederbond.

It is not just an echo of the resistance against apartheid that is heard today but the tremor of resistance is shaking the foundations of all these bastions of the ideology up to apartheid's spiritual citadel and guiding light of the Dutch Reformed Church. Apartheid's moment of truth has arrived.

This internal and external, local, regional and international pressure on apartheid should not be lessened now that apartheid is beginning to move back. This movement back is not yet strong or decisive enough. So this pressure on apartheid should not be levelled out but increased manyfolds more. The greatest service at this point in time all of us can render to end apartheid is to increase the pressure on apartheid.

Apartheid will yield to this mounting pressure because apartheid is political. It is politically imposed from the top upon the people of South Africa in the face of the strong biological and social process accelerating the integration of the population where already for every two white persons there is one coloured person who is the offspring of the biological love between white and black. And, indeed, many whites passing as white today are coloured persons. Not even the apartheid army will hold apartheid together. Apartheid is bursting already. It must not be mended or shielded.

Intense and decisive pressure on apartheid will make apartheid crack and yield politically long before any great damage to the economy. It is the weak, wavering and unsure pressures on apartheid that work to strengthen apartheid politically, prolonging it and in the process damaging the economy while apartheid persists.

The history of Southern Africa shows dramatically that sanctions work. We in the Frontline States know sanctions work. We live here. Sanctions against apartheid work. This report proves it. Sanctions applied by apartheid on its neighbours work too. Either way sanctions work.

Sanctions are very much at work inside South Africa now. Sanctions are at work on the apartheid military might. Apartheid suffered historic defeat in Cuito Cuanavale early 1988. That defeat triggered the apartheid military retreat in the region. Military sanctions had a share in that defeat.

More sanctions including disinvestment will make apartheid easier to manage for dismantling by the emerging new white and black leaders in South Africa. These new leaders need a weakened apartheid for faster and more decisive action by them.

The white and black population need a weakened apartheid for them to work together more decisively to dismantle the system and lay down new political foundations. All-round sanctions must therefore be applied and intensified. Strong apartheid intimidates. Apartheid should not in any way be strengthened or be given the hope for strength.

We in the Frontline States know the Commonwealth of Nations is in a unique position to lead Western Europe and North America, in this matter of apartheid, to rise above considerations of kith and kin, gold and profit in the struggle to bring to a speedy end apartheid as an insult against the race of man.

There will be confusion in Western Europe and North America if the Commonwealth sends confused signals on the quick eradication of apartheid. This confusion will in the end damage the efforts of Western Europe and North America by weakening its practical action against apartheid, prolonging the evil and inviting the penetration of apartheid trading by Japan and other elements of Eastern Europe and Asia and in that way increase the apartheid confusion in Southern Africa. The Commonwealth should provide Europe and North America a clear perspective on apartheid.

The survival of our people of all races in Southern Africa, the realization of our beautiful potential and the preservation of our environment, a deeply disturbing new factor of apartheid aggression dealt with for the first time in this report, are paramount. The misplaced sentiments of kith and kin and the irrelevant interest of gold, capital and profit should and must come secondary at the present ominous time for the final grapple with apartheid.

Those who advocate to prolong apartheid under whatever guise and for whatever motive will be remembered for the injustices to which they are making themselves accomplices.

Given the weakened condition of apartheid both economically and militarily, I ask, is this the moment for us to adopt the wait and see attitude or the moment to tighten the screw when even the limited sanctions which have been imposed are so obviously working?

Clearly, this is the hour to tighten the screw and not to be dragged into believing that South Africa, still promising "reform" and not abolition of apartheid, will of its own volition abandon its ideology and end the carnage in our region in good time.

If we do nothing to increase the pressure now, apartheid will read from us a false hope for the future and work not to diminish but to increase its strength. I fear then that in the years to come apartheid will still continue to occupy a dominant place on our Commonwealth agenda when we should be devoting our attention and energies to other more forward-looking and constructive issues.

I for one want to see apartheid dismantled immediately and removed permanently from our agenda.

Dear colleagues, to end as I began, I commend this valuable report to your attention and to the attention of the international community everywhere.

I commend the Ministers and the Commonwealth Secretariat who commissioned it for us. We, the neighbours of apartheid, have up to now done too little to publicize in concrete terms the sufferings of our region. Let this be the beginning, not a terminus.

Kenneth David Kaunda
President of the Republic of Zambia and
Chairman of the Frontline States of Southern Africa

State House, Lusaka
19 July 1989

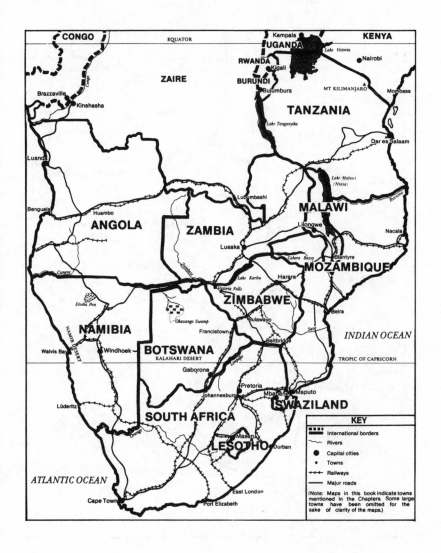

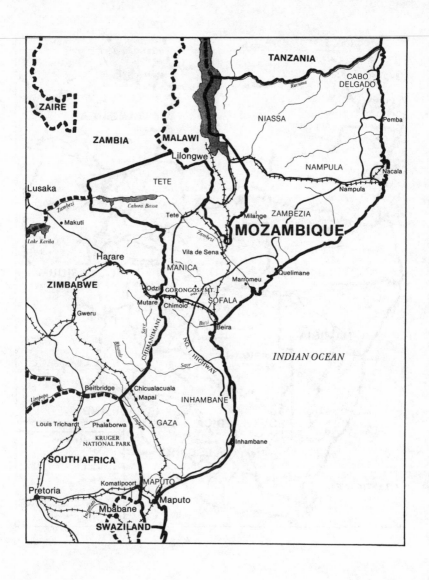

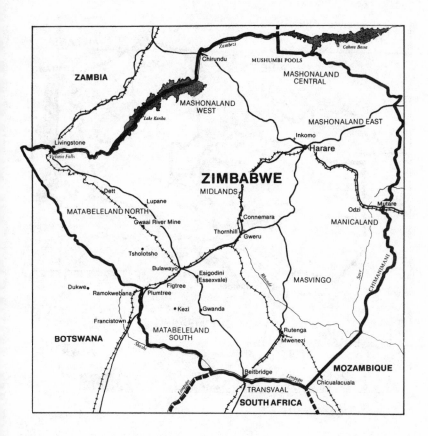

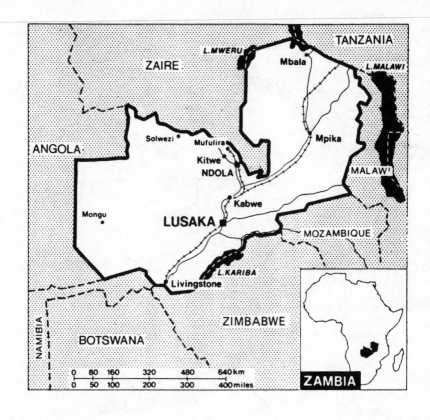

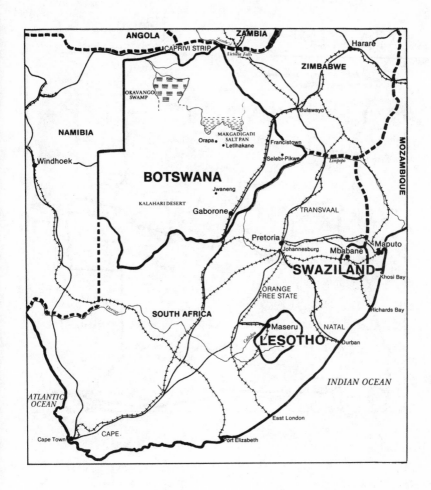

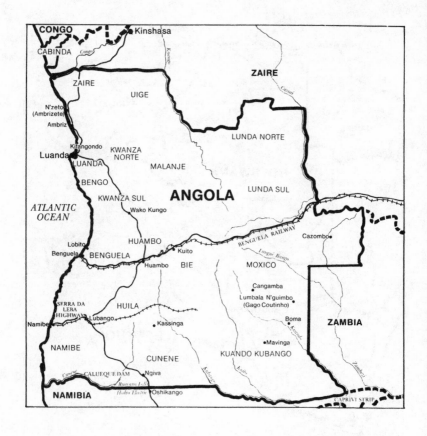

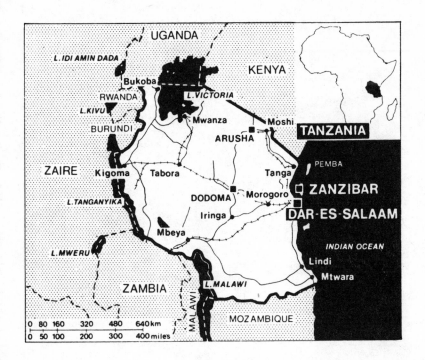

Introduction to South Africa's Regional Policy

South Africa remained apart from the "wind of change" that swept most of the rest of the continent to majority rule in the 1960s. Protected by a ring of colonial buffer states, Pretoria concentrated its regional policy on strengthening economic and military ties with those states and on thwarting the activities of liberation movements in the region. The coup d'etat in Portugal on 25 April 1974, caused by military opposition to the far-off African wars, changed the face of the region virtually overnight, bringing independence to Mozambique and Angola in 1975.

Attempts at "detente" and "dialogue" by the South African Prime Minister, B.J. Vorster, collapsed with the invasion of Angola by the South African Defence Force (SADF) in 1975, Pretoria's first large-scale military intervention in the region, and with the vicious repression of the uprising in Soweto in 1976. The South African military, embarrassed by their humiliating withdrawal from Angola, began to reformulate regional policy by choosing a theme first presented in a Defence White Paper in 1973.

Perceiving the threat to its safety in terms of an externally organized "total onslaught" conceived by the Soviet Union, rather than in terms of democratic opposition to apartheid, South Africa's response was drawn from the ideas of a French General, André Baufre, who developed a theory of "total strategy" based on his experiences in wars in Europe, Algeria and Indochina. The South African concept of "total strategy", detailed in a Defence White Paper in 1977, encompasses economic, military, political and diplomatic tactics toward the region, and uses military means to achieve economic ends.

South Africa's regional policy has as its goal the extension of South African hegemony over the subcontinent through the creation and maintenance of a dependence that is economically lucrative and politically submissive, and acts as a bulwark against international sanctions. That is the regional dimension of a strategy which also encompasses the internal situation in South Africa through preparations for sanctions-busting and military self-sufficiency, tough repression of popular political leaders juxtaposed with attempts to widen divisions and give credibility to other non-white leaders who can be co-opted to work within the existing system or a "reformed" version of it.

The internal dimension is outside the scope of this paper, which will concentrate on the regional context. However, there is a focal point at which the internal and external aims of South Africa's "total strategy" merge and that is in relation to the African National Congress (ANC). As well as ensuring the economic dependence of its neighbours, South Africa seeks to persuade or force them to abandon material support and sanctuary for the ANC, and has been reasonably successful in removing any substantial presence from contiguous states.

The Goal: A Co-prosperity Sphere

When P.W. Botha became Prime Minister of South Africa in 1978, he revived Vorster's proposal for a "co-prosperity sphere" in the region, calling it a Constellation of Southern African States (Consas). This "constellation" would depend upon South Africa economically, militarily and technologically. Any hopes Pretoria had for easy acceptance of this approach were shattered in the space of 27 days in early 1980, with the results of the independence election in Zimbabwe announced on 4 March and the formation of the Southern African Development Coordination Conference (SADCC) on 1 April.

Since Zimbabwe occupies an important position on South Africa's northern border, commanding trade and transportation routes to the hinterland, Pretoria would have preferred a pliable government there. Despite vast sums of money poured into the Zimbabwe election campaign by South Africa, their candidate lost and Robert Mugabe became Prime Minister, taking his place at the inaugural meeting of SADCC in Lusaka.

SADCC members include the Frontline States — Tanzania, Zambia, Botswana, Mozambique, Angola and Zimbabwe — and three other independent states in the region — Lesotho, Swaziland and Malawi. South Africa is not included, nor are the "homeland" leaders whom Pretoria envisages as part of its Praetorian guard. SADCC's mandate is to strengthen regional cooperation and reduce dependence, particularly on South Africa. Each country has responsibility for a specific development sector but, in a grouping of states predominantly landlocked and heavily dependent on trade routes to the sea, transportation is top priority.

Transportation routes bind the region together, a legacy of the economic planning of a century ago. Although the main road and rail network was affixed to the South African hub, shorter and cheaper regional routes were also developed to ports in Mozambique and Angola. These routes are the key to reduction of regional dependence on South Africa, and have formed the primary economic target for Pretoria's "total strategy".

The southern African region is thus bound together by geography, history and economic reality but torn apart by the moral effrontery of apartheid.

After 1980, the Botha administration began to effect interventionist policies towards neighbouring states, turning South Africa's posture around, from the defensive to the aggressive, in a highly coordinated manner. The objective was, and still is, the creation of a safe, dependent and profitable region for a South African "superpower". At a tactical level, Pretoria's main problem is the maintenance of a balance between safety and profitability. A devastated region would be safe but not very profitable in market terms. On the other hand, economically successful but politically independent and racially integrated states on its borders would be profitable but threatening ideologically as an alternative model of social relations.

These interventionist policies, under the rubric of the "total strategy", have had a mixed success, from Pretoria's point of view, in the 10 years since they were adopted, and have been costlier than anticipated, largely due to international pressure through sanctions. However, there is little indication that the mixture of military might and diplomatic manoeuvre has been abandoned at a strategic level, however adjustment has been necessary tactically. From Pretoria's standpoint, "total strategy" has enabled it to weather 10 years of increasingly severe internal and international pressure without toppling, while battering neighbouring states into a greater understanding of its military-economic power.

International negotiations and other diplomatic forays that have arisen out of this strategy are another part of the process, giving implied recognition of Pretoria's authority and power – and thus legitimacy. This is not intended to suggest that these manipulations are completely within Pretoria's control (although in its interest), rather to illuminate the strategic format against which its responses are formulated. Although the prospect of a new President, without the military background of his predecessor, may hint at a reduction in direct regional military aggression, an economic and diplomatic offensive can be anticipated under Baufre's theory of integrated warfare.

The three basic elements in South Africa's regional approach have been as follows:

- the construction of a regional alliance held together, despite its members' opposition to apartheid, by joint economic projects;
- the conclusion of formal agreements on security;
- the elevation of the "homelands" to regional acceptance.

To achieve these objectives, and to bully those neighbouring states which were unwilling to cooperate, Pretoria resorted increasingly to threats and to illegal and violent measures which have had an enormous social and economic cost for the region.

The combination of tactics that South Africa has used against each of its neighbours depends on their individual political, economic and military vulnerabilities, from open military aggression against Angola and a surrogate war in Mozambique to sabotage of regional transportation routes, customs delays and tariffs manipulation as well as direct attacks, incursions, sabotage and car bombs in Botswana, Zimbabwe and Zambia, economic pressure and assassinations in Lesotho and Swaziland.

South Africa has used economic sanctions to effect against its neighbours, by causing congestion at border posts, destroying alternative transportation routes or withholding railway rolling stock; and its economic blockade of Lesotho in early 1986, despite unique geographical conditions, shows how effective sanctions can be when seriously enforced.

The economic and military tools for constructing the regional aspects of South Africa's "total strategy" were already available in the region and merely needed to be gathered up and coordinated. These included the transportation network and shipping companies, the South African Customs Union (SACU) and the Rand monetary zone, as well as import-export dependences and other economic linkages. The SACU groups Botswana, Lesotho and Swaziland into a common customs union administered by South Africa which distributes the revenue and which has used this as a pressure point for joint security agreements and to try to force inclusion, and thus recognition, of the "homelands". Lesotho and Swaziland rely on the customs union for well over half of government revenue. Lesotho and Swaziland (and Namibia) remain part of the Rand monetary zone, in which the South African reserve bank performs all central bank functions, thus limiting the control of those capitals over their own monetary policy and increasing their vulnerability to economic pressures.

Some of the joint economic projects date back to colonial days and others are new developments. The giant Cahora Bassa dam for generating electricity was a joint project of Portugal and South Africa, and set up in such as way that Maputo would receive its power from Cahora Bassa via the South African grid. The Highland water scheme in Lesotho is a new joint project signed recently and including security clauses. A very few projects are double-edged, in the sense that the dependence created for South Africa may be greater than that of the host country. One such project is the new Sua Pan soda ash project in Botswana.

One of the most ambitious of Pretoria's future plans to consolidate economic control over the region (and beyond) is its grand design for an electricity grid ultimately linking the 15 member states of the Preferential Trade Area (PTA) as far north as Somalia and Rwanda.

The plan envisages three transmission routes within the next decade: west through Namibia and Angola to Zaire, central through Botswana, Zimbabwe and Zambia, and east through Mozambique and Malawi to Tanzania. However, the chief executive of Escom, South Africa's power authority, acknowledges that neither Angola nor Tanzania have been approached, and that Zambia and Zimbabwe are "taking a little longer" to co-operate.

A Tool: Regional Surrogates

Of great importance in the context of the current military and diplomatic situation in the region is the fact that, during the colonial wars, the Portuguese and Rhodesian administrations created or co-opted groups to use as surrogates against the nationalist parties, groups which were later inherited by South Africa. The historical evidence of this is confirmed by those who created, armed and directed these groups, and the support they have received from Pretoria is now a matter of public record.

The Mozambique National Resistance (MNR or Renamo) was created by Rhodesia's Central Intelligence Organization as a cover for its intelligence-gathering activities in Mozambique and was later used to disrupt road and rail links — and as a cover for Rhodesian sabotage operations. MNR personnel and equipment were moved out of Rhodesia in March 1980, on the eve of Zimbabwe's independence, to the South African Department of Military Intelligence.

Under South African tutelage, with closer coordination and better equipment, the MNR became an important vehicle in Pretoria's regional policy, enabling the portrayal of the conflict in Mozambique as a "civil war" while in fact it is an undeclared and covert war with external backers. The evidence of this is now well documented, and senior South African officials have admitted SADF involvement with MNR prior to 1984, although previously they had denied this. There is no indication that this support has ceased; on the contrary, there is mounting evidence that it has not, and the US ambassador to Mozambique has stated publicly that, "There continues to be conscious support from South Africa for Renamo."

In Angola, letters and documents published in a new book, *Operation Timber*, reveal that when UNITA was supposedly fighting against Portuguese colonialism, it was in reality an adjunct of the Portuguese armed forces with its own area of operation to fight against the MPLA. Senior Portuguese military officers who were in Angola in the pre-independence period have confirmed that these letters and documents are authentic. They say there was a "gentlemen's agreement" to provide ammunition, medical and other assistance to UNITA, and they speak highly of its work on their behalf. One of the main areas of operation, which continues to the present, was the disruption of the Benguela railway, a main artery not only for the Angolan interior but for trade from Zambia and Zaire. UNITA's subsequent acceptance of South African military support is public knowledge, as are utterances and appearances in support of South Africa by the UNITA leader, including his presence at the swearing in of P.W. Botha as President, where he took his place alongside the "homeland" leaders.

Thus the two main contra groups used by South Africa as cover for its regional designs were inherited from Rhodesia and Portugal, the last remnants of the colonial buffer zone. Other groups have been created, co-opted or supplied by South Africa to cause destruction in Lesotho, Zambia and Zimbabwe, but the main thrust of ensuring regional dependence has been the disruption of transport links to the ports in Angola and Mozambique. Captured documents, prisoners and ballistic tests have identified South Africa as the source of training, weapons and strategy for the destruction of economic targets and have mentioned particularly those relating to SADCC.

In many ways, the vigilante groups operating within South Africa resemble these regional surrogate groups, using similar tactics of violence and terror against individuals or groups who oppose apartheid. Details have also emerged from Mozambique and Angola of small regionally mixed military units containing nationals of different countries, and of black and white instructors from South Africa and Angola, particularly for heavy weapons training.

The Phases of Total Strategy

South Africa's regional policy has encompassed several phases since its revision following the Portuguese coup in 1974. The periods 1974-1978 and 1978-1980 are covered at the beginning of this introduction, but in the period since 1980 patterns have also emerged in the dimension and scope of the particular mixture of economic and military tactics toward the region. It will be useful to give a brief outline here of these phases, and some examples, although actions are presented in more detail in country sections. 1980 was a US presidential election year and it is noteworthy that the broad phases of South Africa's "thump and talk" chronology has continued to align to US political phases.

During the period from mid-1980 to 1982, South Africa launched a concerted offensive against the region involving direct incursions as well as sabotage, assassinations, kidnappings, bombings and espionage, particularly against the newly independent state of Zimbabwe. In Mozambique, captured documentation revealed the extent of re-deployment of MNR, their source of supply and their instructions to destroy or disrupt economic targets. There was also evidence of direct sabotage by SADF, and an open commando attack into Maputo. In Angola, SADF reoccupied part of southern Angola in an invasion in August 1981 and remained for the next four years. Sabotage of the Benguela railway closed it to all transit traffic. Two brazen commando attacks against regional capitals, Maputo and Maseru, in this period killed 33 South African exiles,12 nationals of Lesotho and a Portuguese technician. Further afield in the region, a South African-initiated coup d'etat failed in the Seychelles in late 1981.

The period 1983-1985 saw an escalation of this activity in a more systematic implementation of "total strategy" but using a more subtle tactical approach. Beginning with a period of heightened military activity followed by the diplomatic offensive of 1984 and then a rapid return to the former posture, these rapid changes characterized in the South Africa press as "thump and talk" were also likened to the sudden downpour of a Transvaal thunderstorm.

The sabotage of a main pumping station on the pipeline in the Beira corridor in late 1982 had brought the Zimbabwe National Army into Mozambique to protect its lifeline to the sea, and the escalation in 1985 brought Zimbabwean combat troops into Mozambique. The Cahora Bassa power lines were put out of operation through sabotage in 1983, and the Limpopo and Nacala railways were similarly halted in 1984. Two attacks in Maputo in 1983 killed three ANC officials and six others, only one of whom had ANC connections, and damaged a jam factory. In Angola, the SADF launched "Operation Askari" in December 1983, and were surprised by new and sophisticated Soviet weaponry.

This period saw the conclusion of a military agreement for the withdrawal of troops from Angola, and a security agreement with Mozambique called the Nkomati Accord, both in early 1984. It was revealed that Swaziland had signed a similar agreement two years earlier. South African troops withdrew and then re-entered southern Angola in 1985, and, in Mozambique, the capture of the main MNR base at Gorongosa revealed massive violations of the Nkomati Accord by South Africa.

Economic and military pressure against Botswana escalated in this phase, in the form of bombings and raids as well as withholding of SACU revenue payments and border congestion. In a massive SADF attack into Gaborone in June 1985, ten houses and an office block were destroyed and 12 people killed, only four of whom had any form of connection with the ANC. Despite the pressure, Botswana has continued to refuse to sign a security agreement saying its territory is not used for aggression against its neighbours.

The period 1986-1988 saw a massive escalation of military action across the region, directly and through surrogates. 1986 began with the economic blockade of Lesotho that prevented movement of migrant labour, food and other essential supplies, and led to the coup d'tat on 19 January; the year ended with the death of President Samora Machel of Mozambique in a still unexplained plane crash in South Africa. In between those events were the 19 May raids on three Commonwealth capitals in the region, an increase in economic pressure on Mozambique, Zambia and Zimbabwe, and a massive invasion of the centre-north of Mozambique aimed at taking and holding towns and cutting the country in two. Tanzania committed a brigade of combat troops to northern Mozambique, as well as its earlier offer of military training facilities, and Britain increased its training of Mozambican military units in eastern Zimbabwe.

A further escalation through 1987 was signalled with the 25 April SADF commando attack on Livingstone, Zambia, 11 days before the South African general election showing, as is often the case, that these events are timed for internal consumption. Cross-border attacks into eastern Zimbabwe and Zambia began in mid-1987 and escalated through 1988, killing and kidnapping nationals and destroying property. Commando attacks and bombings in Maputo and Harare killed and wounded nationals, and Botswana continued to be a target for bombings and cross-border raids. In May, on the Botswana border, South Africa staged Iron Eagle, its largest ever airborne commando exercise, delivering a message of military power not dissimilar to that a year later, in September 1988, when it staged its largest ever naval exercise off the coast of Walvis Bay.

South African-trained forces continued their economic destruction in northern Mozambique and, and following a massive infiltration from South Africa of men and equipment in April and May, a new wave of terror began in the south. There were several large massacres, including one of over 400 people at Homoine and another of over 100, and vicious attacks on civilian convoys. As 1987 drew to a close, attacks on the main roads around Maputo increased, isolating the capital by making its main access roads unsafe to normal commercial traffic.

Malawian troops entered Mozambique in this period to protect railway workers repairing the Nacala line, the country's shortest and cheapest route to the sea and out of operation since 1984. Mozambicans continued to flee into southern Malawi swelling the ranks of the displaced to well over 600,000 by late 1988.

A South African offensive in south-eastern Angola in late 1987 led to the siege of Cuito Cuanavale, the commitment of Cubans to the fighting in the south for the first time since 1976, and subsequently to the agreement a year later on South African and Cuban troop withdrawal, and Namibian independence.

South African car bombings, assassinations and kidnappings escalated sharply in 1988, particularly in Botswana, Zimbabwe,

Mozambique, Zambia, Swaziland and Lesotho, as well as against ANC representatives in Europe. In the diplomatic offensive, P.W. Botha visited Songo near Cahora Bassa but, as shown in the section on Mozambique, the military situation deteriorated rapidly after the meeting. Having destabilized the region, however, South Africa now claimed to be the "stabilizer". The deputy minister of defence, delivering "non-lethal" equipment to Mozambique for the rehabilitation of Cahora Bassa power lines, said, "South Africa is the stabilizer of the region and would like to expand this role."

However, lest the region forget South Africa's military might and its "superpower" aspirations, a new intermediate-range ballistic missile — capable of delivering a nuclear warhead as far north as Angola and Tanzania — was test launched in early July 1989. The missile is a modified version of Israel's Jericho II IR BM and has been developed, with assistance from Israel, since 1987.

Namibia

Namibia is not covered by this study but deserves mention as part of South Africa's regional strategy. An arid, mineral-rich territory with vast potential for economic prosperity, Namibia presently relies on South Africa as its main supplier and its main market. Its close financial and economic ties with South Africa are among the various constraints which could inhibit optimum development of economic potential, and this is reinforced by the domination of South African firms in the mining, import and distribution sectors. Pretoria has left no doubt that it will use economic influence as leverage over an independent government in Namibia. Pretoria's main fear, born out by its own intelligence sources, is that an open election in Namibia would be won by the South West Africa Peoples Organization (SWAPO), which launched a guerrilla war against South African occupation in 1966 and which maintains an effective international lobby.

The United Nations (UN) assumed responsibility for Namibia by resolution in 1966, but South Africa refused to relinquish control and has clung to Namibia, dallying from time to time with internationally organized negotiations, while seeking to establish and strengthen an "internal" administration through civilian, military and security structures. In 1977, Pretoria issued a proclamation annexing Walvis Bay, Namibia's only deep-water port, and maintains a military base there. Since 1978, when the UN Security Council adopted Resolution 435 outlining the process for a transition to independence, Pretoria has put in place the means for future control, and if necessary destabilization, of another independent neighbour.

Since the purpose of South Africa's "total strategy" has been to maintain, and where necessary create, a regional dependence to contribute to its own survival, and since the military aspects of destabilization are only a means to economic control, there is little need in the foreseeable future for military destabilization of Namibia, even if it were to become independent in 1990 under a Swapo government. However, the structures are already in place, should that become necessary, and the proximity of the South African military base in Walvis Bay would make the supply and command very easy indeed.

Cost to the Region

The full cost to the region of South Africa's "total strategy" may never be known. It is an accumulation over the past 13 years of war damage, extra defence expenditure, higher transport and energy costs, lost export revenue, greater import costs, lost production and reduced economic growth, the displacement of people, destruction of rural environment and infrastructure, even smuggling. The implications for the future, in terms of the health and educational impact on the youth and the cost of economic recovery, are unquantifiable.

Estimates as to the cost to the Frontline States vary, and because human costs are inestimable, figures tell but a part of the story. Nevertheless, calculations of the cost of defence, damage and lost development now begin conservatively at US$45 billion to the end of 1988, and some costs are still missing from this equation. Given current rates of exchange and the scale of hidden amounts of resources spent on the purchase of arms, through soft and long-term loans to be repaid in years to come, the figure could be considerably higher.

This figure includes total costs, quantified and estimated, to Angola at $22 billion and to Mozambique at over $12 billion. In the case of Zimbabwe, the quantifiable costs only, not including other estimated costs, amount to almost $3 billion, while for Zambia these costs are $7 billion. For Botswana, which did not have an army prior to 1977, defence spending alone has been almost 0.5 billion, and for Tanzania, military costs and maintenance of refugees have reached several hundred million.

In addition, South Africa's regional wars have cost 1.5 million lives since 1981 and, as with the cost estimates, the figure may be much higher. These deaths were caused directly by war or occurred as a result of war, through the destruction of rural medical clinics and emergency food supplies, dislocation of communities and loss of food production.

The UNICEF report, *Children on the Frontline*, updated in early 1989, has estimated that war-related deaths of children in Mozambique and Angola to the end of 1988 is 825,000, and concludes that a child under the age of five is dying in those two countries every three and a half minutes. This is equivalent to a Jumbo jet full of children crashing every day — deprived of immunization and rudimentary health facilities destroyed by war — as directly war victims as if they had been shot.

"The state of the 15 million children under the age of five who live in countries bordering on the Republic of South Africa is grave, and getting worse," the Unicef report says. "They are caught up in externally supported civil conflict and economic destabilization which they are too young to understand or counter."

This now means that with other direct and indirect war deaths in both countries, as a result of war or war-related famine, the toll from South Africa's military action in human terms over the past eight years is 1.5 million dead.

As a result of South Africa's actions, almost four million people are displaced from their homes in the region bordering on South Africa, and twice that number are reliant on emergency food aid. Over 2.2 million of those displaced are within their own national boundaries, having fled from their land in fear of their lives, losing relatives and belongings. At least 1.5 million others have fled across international boundaries, stretching support systems for food and clothing, health and education. And behind those numbers lies the suffering of individual people, displaced and bereaved and often hungry.

There is one further aspect of South Africa's regional policy which has not been included in previous studies. This is the impact on the ecology, and in many cases it is irreversible. US satellite pictures show the once great southern Angolan teak forests have been stripped, the timber carried off to South Africa to pay for the war against the Angolan government. A 1988 US Congressional sub-committee hearing was told that 100,000 elephants had been slaughtered in southern Angola, the ivory again carried to South Africa to pay for the war.

In MNR bases overrun in Mozambique in 1987, a total of 19,700 elephant tusks were recovered, 7000 beside a bush runway waiting for a South African transport plane to pick them up. Because of the influx of people fleeing the security situation in the rural areas, Maputo city now needs ten tons of fuel firewood per day. As a result, the closest fuel firewood to the city is now 30 km.

An international ivory study has shown that South Africa exported 50 tons of in 1988, despite records which indicate 14 tons. Yet Pretoria is able to use its position as the hub of regional ivory smuggling as another lever for international contact and recognition through its presence at meetings to resolve this problem.

The impact of apartheid on the region, in economic, human and ecological terms, represents a holocaust that few people outside the region know about or can comprehend. The mental and physical scars are deep. The human cost is on a staggering scale in some countries and, for a generation that has known nothing but war, this is a cost to be carried forward for decades. The economic and military costs to the Front Line States amount to almost three times their total foreign debt.

With peace instead of war, and some of these human and economic resources available for development instead of defence, these countries could be prosperous and self-sufficient; but for the region's ecology, apartheid has exacted from it a price from which it can never recover.

1 🌐 Mozambique

On 12 September 1988, at the tiny Songo airport near Cahora Bassa dam, Mozambique's President, Joaquim Chissano, introduced South Africa's President, P.W. Botha, to the crowd which had gathered following a meeting between the two men. Addressing the crowd, President Chissano said, "Do you know what he [Botha] came to do here? He came to cooperate and improve the situation. Now he must deliver, right?"

A young man shouted back in Portuguese, "Vamos ver se é verdade" — "Let's wait and see if that's true." It was a perceptive comment from one member of a nation brutalized by broken South African promises. Equally perceptive was the reaction of children at Songo airport when Botha's delegation was introduced. "Which one is General Malan?" they asked officials. South Africa's Defence Minister was a curiosity even for the children of Songo.

These two seemingly trivial incidents provide an insight into the perceptions of ordinary Mozambicans, who have learned that South African promises and practice are two different things.

At Songo, President Chissano reiterated his country's opposition to apartheid and made a number of specific demands. These included maximum usage by South Africa of Maputo port, which had been built a century earlier for that specific purpose; an end to the cutbacks in recruitment of Mozambican labourers for South Africa's mines; an end to South African support for the "bandidos armados", which Pretoria had undertaken to stop four years earlier; and the restoration and utilization by South Africa of power from the Cahora Bassa dam.

The income from ports/railways and the remittance of migrant labourers were essential props of the Mozambican colonial economy bestowed upon an independent nation 13 years earlier. The giant Cahora Bassa dam complex had been initiated during colonial times specifically to supply South Africa with electricity, and supplies to southern Mozambique were to flow through the South African grid. The sale of that electricity held the promise of substantial foreign exchange earnings for Mozambique, unfulfilled since the first sabotage in 1982.

Verbally, Botha acceded to these demands. His undertaking covered the same four points: increased usage of Maputo port; an end to cutbacks in recruitment of Mozambican migrant labour; cessation of support for the MNR; and restoration and usage of Cahora Bassa electricity.

What followed, however, revealed an all too familiar pattern.

Deception and Deceit

Cahora Bassa

The Songo meeting occurred in part as a result of another meeting three months earlier in Lisbon involving the partners in the Cahora Bassa dam project: Mozambique, Portugal and South Africa. A tripartite agreement reached at the earlier meeting committed the signatories to repair and secure the power lines.

While the Lisbon meeting was to be the prelude to Songo, a much publicized event in Beira in December was to be the postscript. Three South African deputy ministers visited the port to hand over US$4 million worth of "non-lethal" military aid for the protection of the Cahora Bassa transmission lines. The international and South African press attended the ceremony in large numbers and Pretoria scored a propaganda victory.

President Chissano did not know at the time that, between the Lisbon and Songo meetings, a further 886 Cahora Bassa pylons covering a distance of 130 km had been simultaneously destroyed in a remote area near the Zimbabwe border. South Africa's "generous" donation of vehicles, uniforms and rations represented only 0.7 per cent of the cost of infrastructural damage and electricity exports lost as a result of the systematic destruction carried out since 1982 — a fact which escaped the international press. If lost industrial output and exports are taken into account, the benefit to Mozambique is even smaller.

The Cahora Bassa dam, a highly controversial project at the time, was constructed between 1969 and 1974 on the Zambezi river in Tete province. Although the dam is located in Mozambique, and its power lines traverse 890 km of Mozambican territory, the interests of that country were secondary. The principle objectives of the project were to supply South African industry with additional electricity and to resettle in Tete one million peasants from Portugal, Europe's most impoverished nation.

However, there was to be one major benefit to Mozambique. South Africa was to pay convertible currency for electricity from Cahora Bassa, while the power routed to southern Mozambique through the South African grid was to be paid for in local currency, then the escudo, now the metical. Thus, Cahora Bassa was potentially an important foreign exchange earner for Mozambique.

That potential has been destroyed since 1982 when the line was first sabotaged. Diaries of the Mozambique National Resistance (MNR or Renamo) retrieved when their Garagua base was overrun in December 1981, contained the following explicit order conveyed by their South African liaison officer at a meeting in a South African training base the previous year:

"DESTROY THE CABORA [sic] BASSA POWER LINES TO SOUTH AFRICA TO COVER THE IDEA OF SOUTH AFRICAN SUPPORT."

In 1983/84 the sabotage of pylons and transmission lines continued on a comparatively small scale — 10 to 12 pylons a year. This prevented the supply of power to southern Mozambique and to South Africa, saving vital foreign exchange for Pretoria and withholding the potential earnings from Mozambique.

In May 1984 — and it is important to note the pattern which now becomes obvious — the three partners in the hydroelectric project met in Cape Town, where they agreed to repair the power lines and resume generation of electricity. That agreement came two months after the late President Samora Machel signed the Nkomati non-aggression agreement with P.W. Botha.

Soon afterwards, in late 1984 or early 1985, 530 pylons were simultaneously sabotaged. It is difficult for the Mozambican authorities to establish the exact date as no power was flowing along the line and thus there was no interruption of service. The pylons have four legs and the bolts holding them to the ground were removed on one side. Then, at strategic intervals, some pylons were blown up with explosives. The weight of the transmission lines brought down the pylons over a 100-km distance stretching from the Buzi to Save rivers in southern Manica province. The timing and sophistication of the sabotage suggested its perpetrators were more than "armed bandits".

Thereafter, sabotage was sporadic, until the three partners met again in Lisbon in June 1988 and again agreed to repair the line and resume electricity generation. Three months later President Chissano met P.W.Botha at Songo, unaware that a further 886 pylons had been sabotaged south of the Save river down to the Limpopo railway line in Gaza province. That means that 25 per cent of the Cahora Bassa pylons have now been damaged.

Because no power has flowed along the lines running south from Cahora Bassa since 1982, it is not possible to establish exactly when this massive sabotage occurred. Only the perpetrators would know for certain. However, according to Cahora Bassa officials, who have flown over the area, it was definitely between these two meetings.

The method of sabotage used on the Save/Limpopo section of the Cahora Bassa transmission lines is not known. This is a particularly inhospitable area, notable for its lack of water and arid terrain. As a result, few people live in the area and, for the same reason, there is little presence by the army or the MNR. Italian engineers who supervised the building of the power lines through this section admit the difficulties they had during that period, when special water bowzers had to be used to carry water to the construction crews. It is an area where it is impossible to live off the land and a sabotage of this nature — over a 130-km distance — would necessitate outside support.

Mozambican officials raised the matter of this massive sabotage with the South Africans in a joint security meeting and, following the meeeting, a SADF Brigadier suggested to them that it had been done by Zimbabwe as a sign of disapproval of contacts between Maputo and Pretoria! However, the officials recognized this as deliberate disinformation by those responsible for the sabotage.

The cost to Mozambique, in this single sector of the economy, is in the region of $560 million, comprising lost Cahora Bassa export sales, actual physical damage, and foreign currency imports of electricity from South Africa. Apart from the unquantifiable items, such as lost industrial output and exports, must be added the cost of sabotaged power lines in southern Maputo province which carry the imported electricity for Maputo.

Cahora Bassa provides a micro-study of South Africa's "total strategy" and the scale of its aggression. Instead of earning money from the dam's output, Mozambique is forced to pay hard currency to import electricity from South Africa.

A logical question which arises is why would South Africa, a partner in Cahora Bassa, participate in talks and agreements, and then destroy something which it partially owns? The explicit instructions to the MNR in the Garagua documents provide part of the answer — "to cover the idea of South African support".

Beyond that, there is a much more important consideration. Since 1982, when sabotage of the pylons began, the South African economy has been in recession. Cahora Bassa power is not necessary at present to sustain the growth of the South African economy. Instead, sabotage of the pylons has resulted in a financial gain to South Africa of almost $500 million since 1982 — through monies not spent on electricity imports and revenue gained from electricity sales to Mozambique. The earliest date the line can be repaired, security permitting, is 1991.

Beyond the immediate consideration of the Frontline States there is an addendum. Portugal, as majority partner in Cahora Bassa, is also paying a price. The dam must be maintained if it is to function at some future date, and that maintenance is costing Portugal about $10 million a year, some $80 million since 1982. That figure does not include what Portugal might have earned had Cahora Bassa generated the revenues its planners anticipated.

One final point puts into perspective the cynicism of South African propaganda. South Africa had committed $26 million in loans to repair of Cahora Bassa lines under the Lisbon agreement and had given its "generous" $4 million donation in Beira. However, once Pretoria "learned" of the 1988 sabotage, the loans were suspended on the grounds that the security situation made it impossible to proceed with repairs.

Maputo Port

Another of Botha's commitments in September 1988 was to maximize usage of Maputo port and the rail system connecting it to South Africa, directly and through Swaziland. However, the sabotage of those two routes resumed following the Songo meeting, as did the destruction of rolling stock belonging to Mozambique ports and railways, after a period of some months without attack.

Following are some examples of post-Songo sabotage of the Goba and Ressano Garcia railways, both of which were out of service for most of December 1988.

Goba line via Swaziland:

- 16 November 1988: train derailed, injured the driver and damaged 50 metres of track;
- 4 November: locomotive detonated a landmine 30 km south-west of Maputo, interrupted traffic;
- 30 October: locomotive detonated a landmine near Chitevele, armed men hidden nearby fired on the train, damaged 150 metres of track, interrupted traffic;

Ressano Garcia line/direct to South Africa:

- 17 February 1989: attack on a train on route to Maputo, killed 8 people, injured 51, near Movene, only 15 km from the South African border, 55 km from Maputo city;
- 5 February: ambush of another passenger train near the same spot resulted in 11 dead and 16 injured;
- 19 January: train partially derailed after detonating a landmine near Movene; 4 people killed, 14 injured, and the train looted;
- 14 December: passenger/goods train hit a landmine near Movene, 2 people killed, 33 injured, one wagon and 100 metres of track damaged;
- 10 November 1988: at least 6 people killed in attack at Pessene railway station, line damaged, several people abducted, including railway workers;
- 3 November: railway bridge sabotaged at Secongene, interrupted traffic;
- 2 November: passenger train attacked between Pessene and Maguanza, 9 people killed, 39 injured.

The sabotage of these railways linking Maputo port to South Africa and Swaziland rendered meaningless the promise to maximize usage of the port. Although traffic increased from South Africa in the first six months of 1989, 85 per cent of the cargo was coal.

A massive attack on the border railway town of Ressano Garcia on 27 April 1989, in which four locomotives valued at $6 million were destroyed or damaged, was carried out with direct South African military assistance, according to some of the witnesses.

The five-hour attack began after 10 p.m. when the first 15 armed men were unloaded from what witnesses described as an open-topped South African armoured vehicle called a "Pincher". About 250 armed men were involved, divided into three groups which attacked the military headquarters, the immigration post and the foreign exchange shop, where the estimated value of goods stolen was $30,000. One witness said that South African soldiers shot at people who tried to flee across the border. Seven vehicles were destroyed, cattle were shot, and windows broken in the firm that recruits miners to work in South Africa. Over 20 miners returning home from the mines had all of their belongings stolen. Ten civilians were killed and 22 injured in the attack.

Three locomotives were set on fire, and a fourth was dynamited. The latter was still burning two days later and is unlikely to be put back into service. Rail traffic to Maputo was disrupted until the following day.

Migrant Labour

The number of migrant labourers from Mozambique working under contract in South Africa's mines dropped by 10 per cent in the three months after the Songo meeting. By December 1988, according to the Ministry of Labour in Maputo, there were only 46,242 Mozambican labourers employed in the South African mines, a reduction of over 5,000 men since September. By February 1989, the figure had dropped to 46,068, suggesting that cutbacks in recruitment had not ceased. The number of Mozambicans working in the mines in South Africa peaked at just over 66,000 in mid-1986 and has been dropping steadily ever since.

In the first three months of 1989, according to South African police figures, 8,000 "illegal" Mozambican agricultural migrant workers were expelled from the Transvaal.

These migrant workers face a hazardous journey before and after their contracts, whether they travel by road or rail. Both options are risky due to ambushes, and belongings are often plundered. Returning miners are particularly lucrative targets since they spend their salaries on goods to carry home. Their "take home pay" contributes little to the Mozambican economy: the miners earn and spend their money in South Africa.

MNR Support

The final undertaking given by Botha at Songo was to abide by the March 1984 Nkomati Accord between Mozambique and South Africa under which South Africa agreed to cease supporting the MNR.

In December 1988, more than three months after Songo and shortly after the presentation at Beira of "non-lethal" assistance, Mozambique's Minister of Defence, General Alberto Chipande, added a footnote to Botha's promises. He told the People's Assembly (Parliament) in Maputo that there had been a resurgence of military activity in Mozambique since the Songo meeting, and that military equipment and logistical support continued to flow to the MNR from outside the country. They "are continuing to use some neighbouring countries as a launching pad for combat actions inside Mozambican territory", he said, by infiltrating across land borders as well as by sea and air, and there is a "network of sophisticated communications equipment" through which they receive instructions and transmit information.

Six months later, in June 1989, the US embassy in Maputo confirmed that the MNR was still receiving support from South Africa.

The State Department's most senior official on Africa, Herman Cohen, Assistant Secretary of State for African Affairs, had spoken a few weeks earlier of "evidence that a certain amount of assistance is coming into Mozambique to the MNR bandits from South Africa". Answering questions from six African capitals in May, via satellite, Cohen said: "As you know, RENAMO was originally aided by the white regime of Ian Smith. After the independence of Zimbabwe, assistance to RENAMO was taken over by the South African defense forces. The accords of 1984 at Nkomati, which were mediated by my predecessor, Mr. Chester Crocker, were designed to stop this aid. Unfortunately, the South African government did not implement that accord as far as aid to RENAMO was concerned."

Cohen's deputy also stated in early 1989 that Washington knew of MNR bases within 16 km of the South African border, and knew that supplies were coming across that border.

The security deterioration in the post-Songo period has included sabotage of the railways and other transportation routes, and electricity supplies, as mentioned above, as well as villages, towns, shops, factories, even warehouses and trucks containing food and other relief supplies. The attacks have become larger, more daring and more destructive, resembling the tactics used during the massive invasion of late 1986. The upsurge in activity has been noticeable in all parts of the country, and in some areas of the north large numbers of people have died of starvation or disease because the security situation prevented food and medicine from reaching them.

Security has deteriorated rapidly in the southern border area adjoining South Africa, where villagers have reported seeing groups of armed men with new uniforms and weapons. Attacks have increased in the southern province of Maputo, particularly around the capital city and on the routes connecting it to the rest of the country. The electricity supply to Maputo city was sabotaged five times in the last three months of 1988, each time in broad daylight, by destroying a single pylon less than 5 km from the South African border. Hostages who witnessed the saboteurs on one occasion said they used a telescopic ladder to avoid mines planted around the foot of the pylon and placed explosives halfway up the structure so the explosion caused the pylon to split, making repair difficult.

The area 35-75 km north of the capital has been a regular target, especially along the Limpopo railway and the main highway, but the attacks have become bolder. In April 1989, the town of Marracuene, 30 km north of Maputo, was attacked for the first time, inmates from the local prison were abducted and a locomotive in the station was partially destroyed.

An example of the scale of post-Songo economic destruction in this province is the three attacks on the sugar-producing town of Xinavane, 100 km north of Maputo, in December 1988 and January 1989. The hospital was wrecked, including medicines and surgical equipment, sugar processing equipment was damaged and the power station was blown up. Several shops and the hotel were destroyed, fuel tanks were damaged, and vehicles and houses burned. Preliminary estimates of the cost of the destruction begin at $1.6 million. At least 26 people were killed. Technicians, mechanics and other skilled personnel fled, and many were afraid to return. Their services are essential to the Incomati Sugar Company whose mill is the main productive centre in the area with some 5,000 employees and one of only three sugar factories operational in the entire country. The population now sleeps in the bush outside town at night and many families have gone to stay with relatives in Maputo, joining almost 300,000 other displaced people who have sought sanctuary in the city. A nearby plantation which produces raw sugar cane was attacked in March, 27 people were killed and 40 abducted.

More than 250 buildings (shops, huts, houses, warehouses) were destroyed or looted in Maputo province in the first four months of 1989, as well as over 30 cars and trucks and at least three buses.

Inhambane province, on the south-east coast, was likened by Mozambican officials to "the Wild West" as a result of new landings by sea in late 1988. The population of Inhambane city swelled to

100,000, almost half of them people displaced from rural areas. The city has suffered severe water shortages since the pumping station and most of the equipment was destroyed in January, after a group of 500 MNR, freshly infiltrated, split up into three groups and moved into the north, west and south of the province. They are believed to have used a regular infiltration route from South Africa through the Kruger National Park crossing Gaza province into Inhambane.

At least one Western embassy in Maputo advised its aid workers to evacuate Gaza province in late 1988, and in mid-February the town of Manjacaze was reduced to ashes. Though not as bloody as an earlier attack in which 90 people were massacred, this one was costly in economic terms. The shops had been filled with consumer goods to encourage peasants to collect and market cashew nuts, and the value of goods and shops destroyed is estimated at several million dollars. The town of Chibuto, headquarters of the provincial military command, has been a target in recent months. It is also President Chissano's home town, and attacks on home areas of government leaders have been common in this period.

The pattern in the south extends to the central provinces of Manica and Sofala. In October 1988 there were 16 sabotages of the Beira-to-Zimbabwe railway, the highest number for some time. On 11 November, 200 metres of the oil pipeline to Zimbabwe were blown up — the most serious sabotage for several years and probably no coincidence that it occurred on the anniversary of Rhodesia's 1965 unilateral declaration of independence. These attacks on the railway and pipeline suggest a resupply of explosives, which had appeared to be in short supply in the previous 12 months.

The port city of Beira was without electricity for two weeks in October and its power supply was sabotaged again in December and February. The city has been without electricity for a total of 650 days since 1981, almost two years out of eight. The railway town of Inhaminga, 150 km north of Beira, was overrun and destroyed in mid-October.

MNR attacks in Manica province, along Zimbabwe's eastern border, are largely against villages, which are burned and looted, although there has been considerable activity in Gondola district, where two saboteurs were killed and several wounded in May when they were caught — with weapons, ammunition, spades and picks — planting explosives to sabotage a pipeline station.

In Tete province, attacks on the agriculturally rich Angonia and nearby Moatize districts sent thousands of refugees fleeing into Malawi. The provincial governor said in June 1989 that the military situation had deteriorated in the previous three months, with the approach of the Frelimo Fifth Congress in July.

From October 1988 until February 1989, at least 360 civilians were killed and 331 injured in 40 MNR attacks south of the Zambezi river. Roughly one third of the tabulated attacks and fatalities, and almost half of the injuries, occurred in January and February. In a further 12 attacks in March and April, over 100 civilians were killed and 76 wounded.

Further north, Zambezia province, which once provided over half of Mozambique's export earnings, faced a massive offensive similar to the one in 1986 aimed at cutting the country in two. The important tea-processing centre of Gurue, where plantations and equipment were destroyed in early 1987, was occupied again briefly in late 1988 in an attack in which an unidentified white man leading one of the MNR groups was killed. The value of goods stolen and destroyed was estimated at almost one million dollars.

The resurgence of MNR activity in the densely-populated province put over one million lives at risk as ambushes on main roads prevented food and relief supplies reaching people displaced by the war. The number of aircraft available, and the landing conditions, have been insufficient for a sustained airlift.

Visitors to the town of Gile in December found 38,000 displaced people alongside the airstrip. Another 19,000 were homeless at Alto Molocue, after fleeing 180 km on foot, and many died on the way to safety. In January and February, 3,800 people, mainly children, died in a measles outbreak in Gile district, in an area which had been under MNR control for two years and children had not been vaccinated. An airlift of food to Gile was interrupted in late April when a plane carrying supplies detonated a landmine planted at the airstrip. Only a few days after an announcement in April, in Lisbon and Johannesburg, of a "unilateral ceasefire for humanitarian reasons", 15 lorries were destroyed in Zambezia, seven of which were carrying relief supplies.

Over 5,000 people starved to death in the first 10 weeks of 1989 in one district of Nampula province because emergency supplies could not reach them safely. Four officials of the International Committee of the Red Cross, who went to assess the situation, were abducted on 16 March and later released.

Two hundred metres of track on the Nacala railway through Nampula province were destroyed in November, as well as a loco-motive and several wagons. The security deteriorated sharply, with food being a major target — for theft or destruction. Agricultural Marketing Board (Agricom) warehouses containing emergency food supplies were looted, and food that could not be carried was burnt or otherwise destroyed.

An important town on the Nacala railway line was destroyed in March, along with 2,000 tonnes of food destined for emergency relief. The attackers, who numbered about 800, systematically wrecked every building in the town of Iapala, using explosives. Clothing, agricultural implements, consumer goods and even the sports facilities at the local railway club were destroyed. Twelve people were killed, 220 abducted and, on the outskirts of the town, almost 1,000 dwellings of peasant farmers were burnt down. Although they had surplus crops in this district, what was not destroyed will be difficult to move, since warehousing facilities were wrecked. Peasants will be left with unsold crops, and may be discouraged from producing a surplus next year.

The cost to Agricom of the destruction of food and warehouse facilities was estimated at $640,000. Two weeks later, a group numbering 2,000 attacked the district capital of Nacaroa, again looting or burning food in warehouses of Agricom and the emergency relief office. Health and administration facilities were destroyed, and installations for water and sanitation were mined, as were the approaches to some residential areas.

In the two northern-most provinces of Niassa and Cabo Delgado, there was increased activity, and growing threats to Tanzania's border area across the Ruvuma river. Reports to the end of March 1989 show that 235 people died of starvation in one district recently affected by MNR actions in Cabo Delgado. Grasshopper swarms damaged crops in parts of the north where spraying could not be done because of MNR activity.

Officials of the Catholic and other churches have suffered at the hands of the MNR, which often claims to be fighting for freedom of worship, and casualties have recently increased. Between March 1982 and March 1989, the MNR murdered 10 Catholic priests — two Mozambicans, four Portuguese and four Italians. Four of the ten were killed during the first three months of 1989, in the northern provinces of Zambezia and Cabo Delgado. A priest and two Franciscan nuns were abducted in separate incidents in the same period, and later released.

A further indication of the scale of escalation in recent months is the improved ability of the Mozambican army to respond. Despite this the incidents are increasing. Mozambican special forces of Green Berets, trained by British and Zimbabwean instructors, and Red Berets, trained by the Soviet Union, are now posted in strategic locations near the Nacala and Limpopo railway lines, and the main highway. These are well-disciplined, well-equipped forces with rapid and effective responses. The Zimbabwe National Army is stationed in defence of the Beira, Tete and Limpopo transportation routes, and Malawian army units along the Nacala railway. This has freed the Mozambican regular army for offensive operations, and many MNR bases have been destroyed in different parts of the country in recent months.

Evidence of South African Involvement

Destabilization of Mozambique is carried out in the name of the MNR or Renamo, which was created by Rhodesia's Central Intelligence

Organization in 1976. A senior officer involved in early training said "the MNR gave a cover for Rhodesian operations and, from initial intelligence-gathering, moved on to getting recruits and then on to the offensive, disrupting road and rail links." In March 1980, just before Zimbabwe's independence, MNR personnel and equipment were moved out of Rhodesia to South African Military Intelligence.

In the Rhodesian era, the activities of these "bandidos armados" were confined to the central provinces of Mozambique, but from 1981, under South African tutelage with fresh armaments and trained personnel, the war escalated dramatically. The disruption began of the main rail routes to the sea for the land-locked hinterland, and new fronts were opened in the southern provinces bordering on South Africa.

There are at least six types of evidence available to show South Africa's involvement in destabilizing Mozambique. These include documents found at MNR camps, statements by South African government officials, evidence of prisoners released from South African jails, statements by former senior MNR officials, eyewitness accounts given by former MNR members or others, and verified direct attacks and sabotage.

Documentation

Two sets of documents in particular reveal some examples of directives to the MNR from the South African Defence Force (SADF). The first set of documents, found when a large MNR base was overrun at Garagua in eastern Mozambique in 1981, contains minutes of a meeting held at an MNR training camp in South Africa, Zoabostad, on 25 October 1980. The MNR delegation was led by Afonso Dhlakama, appointed by Rhodesian intelligence after the death of his predecessor. The South African delegation was led by a military intelligence officer, Charles van Niekerk, then a colonel, who had been the SADF liaison to the MNR in Rhodesia.

These minutes emphasize the need to close road and rail traffic on certain routes, to open a new southern front, and to establish a base near the South African border. One of the main targets identified was the highway linking Maputo with the centre of the country and it soon became unsafe to travel on this road, except in armed convoys. The minutes of a later meeting at Zoabostad, on 5 November 1980, say: "Destroy the Cabora Bassa power lines to South Africa to cover the idea of South African support."

As the war escalated, Mozambique tried to negotiate. On 16 March 1984, the late President Samora Machel met P.W. Botha at Nkomati on their common border to sign an agreement of "non-aggression and good neighbourliness" under which both sides agreed not to provide from their territory to opponents of the other: military bases, training, armaments, command, communications, propaganda, etc. and to refuse transit or recruitment to individuals planning acts of violence against the other. The accord itself was an admission by South Africa of its support for the MNR — as was the fact that the MNR radio propaganda station, Africa Livre, purportedly located in Mozambique, stopped broadcasting the day before the agreement for "technical reasons" and never resumed.

Mozambique scrupulously implemented the agreement, but South Africa did not. Sabotage and other military activity escalated, and the piles of incriminating documents found the following year clearly revealed that South Africa had not, and never intended to, abide by the agreement.

More than 200 kg of documents were recovered when the main MNR base at Gorongosa, in central Mozambique, was captured in 1985, and among these were the diaries kept by Dhlakama's secretary. One of the entries refers to a meeting in Pretoria which began on 23 February 1984, three weeks before the Nkomati Accord. The objective of the meeting, says the diary, was "planning the war in the face of the situation taken up by South African Republic". The SADF team at that meeting was extremely high-powered, including the head of military intelligence and the commander of Special Forces, both members of the State Security Council.

The diary for that day notes that the SADF committed ongoing support, adding, "Machel can only fall immediately through a cut in the economy and communications routes."

The meeting continued for a further two days, and involved the "definition of targets that force Frelimo to talk to Renamo". Such targets were defined as railways, Cahora Bassa, foreign aid workers and "other targets of an economic nature, SADCC".

Some of the other diary entries include:

24 February
11. The 100 men should enter Maputo in small group via the Libombos, with predetermined aims and targets for each group;
12. Joan and Eurico will go only with the authorization of the Minister of Defence, General Magnus Malan;
13. Two RNM men will be trained in ultra-secret communications between RNM and Pretoria;
14. The general will ensure resupply even after the agreement by SA with the communist Machel, especially ammunition and radio transmitters;

25 February
7. Communication by radio or physically between Renamo and the SA soldiers;

8. Apologies for the release of the Russians without the complete agreement of Renamo — pressure from the USA.

The documents also show that, before the signing at Nkomati, the SADF had moved into Mozambique enough armaments and other supplies to cover MNR needs for at least six months. Their communications continued despite the agreement, using new radio frequencies, as did supply drops and training.

Statements by South African Officials

South African officials often deny that they are currently supporting the MNR, although they now admit their involvement prior to 1984 — which was also denied at the time.

General Constand Viljoen, who was then SADF commander, confirmed that the documents found at Gorongosa were genuine, and the Chief of the Operations Directorate, Major-General Jan van Loggerenberg, admitted that the SADF had become "tainted by its support for Renamo". He told a South African newspaper, "We were helping Renamo overthrow the Frelimo government. They were attacking military and strategic targets."

The South African Foreign Minister, Pik Botha, told parliament on 25 April 1985, a year after the signing at Nkomati, that, "There was of course a time when we helped to train Renamo and assisted it . . . Renamo requests for aid were acceded to. I wish to confirm today that in similar circumstances in southern Africa, we should do it again."

A few months later, on 6 February 1986, after publication of the diaries found at Gorongosa, Pik Botha told parliament that the documents were genuine. "One can go through all those entries in the diary . . . the information tallies with the flights undertaken by the air force. That is true. The times of our meetings [with MNR] in Pretoria are correct. The times that they indicated I had been present, are correct." He claimed that violations of the Nkomati agreement, including construction of a clandestine airstrip in Mozambique, were "technical".

Evidence of Released Prisoners

Further details have been established since the release from prison in South Africa of some members of a group who were collecting information about assistance to the MNR.

One of those was Trish Hanekom, a Zimbabwean citizen released after three years imprisonment. In late 1987, she gave details of the case against herself, her husband Derek, and a friend, Roland Hunter, who had worked as an assistant to van Niekerk, the MNR liaison officer. Hunter, who is still in prison, had photocopied documents and memorized file numbers. He "handled large amounts of money on behalf of the military, paying Renamo rebels, including one of its leaders, Afonso Dhlakama. The leaders were very well paid and also received free board and lodging."

She said that Hunter had witnessed new weapons being loaded into aircraft at Voortrekkerhoogte, the South African military head-quarters, "destined for Mozambique, and was told by his superiors that this operation, code-named Mila, was successful and cost effective. They admitted their plans for Zimbabwe's destabilization were not going as well as expected."

Statements by Former MNR Senior Officials

Another source of inside information is the statements given by former senior MNR officials such as Paulo Oliveira, the representative in Western Europe, who returned to Maputo in March 1988 under the government amnesty. He spoke publicly about the training camps he had visited in Mozambique and South Africa which "enabled me to see the degree of control that the South Africans had over the MNR".

Oliveira confirmed that South Africa was still giving material support to the MNR at the time he left the organization in late 1987, and said van Niekerk had visited Lisbon while he was there and "installed sophisticated communications equipment" to communicate with the main camp at Phalaborwa in South Africa.

Oliveira gave the names of other officers whom he dealt with, and said he was told by one of them that the objective was "not to put the MNR into government, but to create massive confusion and difficulty for the Mozambican government".

The MNR's head of mobilization for Europe, Chanjunja Chivaca Joao, who returned home under the amnesty in late 1988, said the organization's response to the Chissano-Botha meeting at Songo was to strengthen ties with South African military intelligence.

Eyewitness Accounts by Former MNR Members and Others

Many former MNR members and others have given detailed descriptions of South African resupply of armaments, medicines, uniforms, communication and other equipment. Since this assistance is of a clandestine nature, the evidence takes time to emerge and may be difficult to substantiate because planes are often unloaded in remote areas by peasants who are unable to give dates or technical descriptions.

Such incidents have been reported from various parts of the country, and more information is trickling in with people who have escaped from MNR captivity, surrendered under the government amnesty, or been captured. From this information, it seems that the main sea landings of equipment and supplies are along the lengthy coast of Inhambane province in the south, and near the mouth of the Zambezi river in the centre-north, that resupply by air occurs in many parts of the country, and that armed men and supplies are also infiltrated across the land frontier.

These accounts are too numerous to record here in full, but the following are a few examples from different areas of the country. Most accounts given below are from MNR members who left the bush in 1988 to accept the government's amnesty, and most refer to the years 1984 to 1988.

A former MNR military intelligence officer, Luis Tomas, described the landing on the coast near the mouth of the Zambezi river of freshly trained men and the unloading of anti-aircraft equipment from South Africa. He also told of the death of a South African soldier in an airforce bombardment of a base in Manica province, both incidents in 1987. He said that three other South African military personnel, who intended to erect a radio transmitter, were evacuated. Three years earlier, a week after the Nkomati accord, he had witnessed six South African soldiers unloading material — mortars, AK-47 rifles, ammunition and uniforms — from a boat on the same stretch of Sofala coast. Tomas said that people kidnapped from nearby were made to carry the equipment overland to the main base at Gorongosa.

- Alexandre Manuel, former secretary at an MNR base in Manica, said he had seen white South Africans in the area, who came and went by plane to sabotage bridges and carry out other operations;
- A 14-year-old former MNR combatant, Felisberto Chilenga, witnessed a plane dropping military supplies at a base in northern Gaza province;
- Anuario Macume, aged 18, transported ammunition from a coastal base in Inhambane, which he was told had come from South Africa by boat;
- Clopes Sitoe, a former MNR military intelligence operative, said that weapons and personal goods for MNR leaders came across the land border from South Africa, arriving at a "provincial base" at Goba near the frontier with both South Africa and Swaziland;
- Neva Benison, who surrendered in Manica province, told of his training in South Africa and said the MNR had been supplied with anti-aircraft missiles in early 1987;
- Jorge Valoi, captured in Maputo province in 1985, said that pilots of aircraft and helicopters dropping supplies are white;
- Laurinda Vira, who fled from an MNR base in early 1988 after being held captive for a year, said she saw two South Africans with MNR leaders in Gorongosa, and witnessed South African planes

overflying bases to drop military equipment;

- Abilio Jangane said he saw eight black South African soldiers at an MNR base in Tete province who were giving military instruction and planning operations;
- Augusto Goncalves, who worked as a radio operator, said heavy weapons training is done by South Africans and Angolans, black and white;
- Diogo Domingos Toni, who spent many years as an instructor on heavy weapons for MNR, confirmed South African supply of arms and ammunition and infiltration of men, both black and white, as well as smuggling of ivory and gemstones;
- Alberto Rendicao and Horacio Taimo, former bodyguards to MNR commanders, said that large quantities of precious stones, ivory and hardwood are transported to South Africa from Gorongosa national park in the same military aircraft that offload weapons and ammunition.

A commander in a women's detachment, Isabel Jorge, who surrendered at the end of November 1988, said that at her base in Manica province when she left the previous week, there were 17 "South African boers" training "recruits" who had been press-ganged after raids on villages. She said she had been kidnapped in 1982, at the age of 13, and received military training the following year from South African instructors at the main MNR base in Gorongosa. She said she had travelled to Gorongosa in October 1988 with others to collect supplies and that South African planes unloaded military equipment, uniforms and combat rations.

A common theme among older MNR operatives who are captured is that they went to South Africa seeking work in the mines, were detained by police and taken for training, then given a gun and sent back across the border. The following are examples of another recruiting technique.

- Four men detained in South African border towns in August 1988 said that while under arrest they were taken to a white caravan where Portuguese-speaking people tried to recruit them to join MNR and offered them money to "fight for their land".
- Another group of Mozambicans who fled across the the border in December 1988, after an MNR attack on their village, told of police harassment and of attempts to recruit them. Some were taken to Skukuza, in the Kruger National Park and one, Eduardo Tivane, spent some days at an MNR base near there. He was held for five days during which time he was beaten and offered money to work with MNR. He described the centre near Skukuza as very large, with a lot of South African soldiers and armed black Mozambicans.

A report released in March 1989 provided a further insight into MNR recruitment. "The Mozambican National Resistance (Renamo) as Described by Ex-Participants", prepared by US academic William Minter, is based on interviews with 32 former MNR members.

Minter's principal conclusion is that it is probable "that at least 90 per cent of the Renamo rank-and-file are recruited by force". They have been abducted, or they have been forced into joining the MNR after being caught working illegally in South Africa. They remained in the MNR, before escaping or accepting the government amnesty, out of fear after threats of execution.

Another important finding in Minter's report is the extent to which South Africa, despite claims to the contrary, continues to be the movement's inspiration and command, identifying targets to be attacked, providing a communications channel through South Africa and supplying armaments, medicine and other supplies by air, land and sea.

"The author's interviews and Mozambican eyewitness reports, together with South Africa's well-documented past record of deception," make it difficult to accept the assertion that Pretoria is not backing the MNR, Minter concludes.

Direct Attacks and Sabotage

The SADF stages open attacks into Mozambique, claiming the target is ANC guerrillas, but more often destroying Mozambican property and killing civilians. There have been several attacks in the capital, Maputo, which is very near the South African border and easily accessible by land, air or sea.

- ANC offices in Maputo ransacked on Christmas Day, 1988;
- South African soldier killed by Mozambican troops in July 1988 "in direct confrontation in an incident close to the border of the two countries south of Maputo". Foreign Minister Mocumbi said Mozambique initially believed clash was with MNR, but "South African authorities asked us to return the body of a dead soldier and the material we had captured";
- Car bomb explosion in April 1988 maimed prominent South African lawyer and writer, Albie Sachs, who worked in the Ministry of Justice;
- Three Mozambicans, including a senior government official, shot dead in commando attack in May 1987;
- Shortly after that attack, a South African passport-holder was arrested and confessed to being a member of a commando unit responsible for a bomb earlier in the year in Matola, near Maputo;
- Car bomb explosion in April 1986 injured 50 people, and

damaged a blocks of flats in Maputo residential area near the city centre;
- SADF commando unit bombed ANC diplomatic offices in Maputo in October 1983, wounding 5 people;
- Suburb of the capital rocketed in May 1983, 6 people killed, only one of whom had ANC connections; the main damage was to a creche at a jam factory;
- Ruth First, Director of the Centre of African Studies at Eduardo Mondlane University in Maputo and a member of the ANC, killed in her office by a parcel bomb in August 1982;
- 13 ANC members killed in attack in January 1981;
- Petrol storage tanks in Beira sabotaged twice, first in March 1979 by a Rhodesian military unit landed from a South African submarine, causing $2 million damage; and again in a similar operation in 1982 when, if Rhodesians were involved, they were by then working for SADF special forces.

Targets

The Economy

Mozambique has had three distinct economic phases since independence in 1975. In the first phase, from the transition in 1974 through 1978, Mozambique was confronted with the neglect of 500 years of Portuguese colonialism and the departure of all but about 15,000 Portuguese citizens, abandoning thousands of rural stores, farms, businesses and factories. Mozambique's inheritance at independence was a population 93 per cent illiterate, about $1 million in gold and foreign reserves, 100 secondary school teachers, and some 80 doctors, only one of whom was outside the main centres. The vulnerable economy rested on income from ports and railways, and from migrant labour working in South Africa with partial remittance for their labour in gold.

The second phase from 1978 to 1981 saw a marked improvement in the country's socio-economic outlook and, despite the difficulties caused by inheriting an incredibly underdeveloped economy, considerable progress had been made by 1981, just six years after independence. The medical system, oriented to primary health care, was hailed as a Third World model and school enrolment had tripled. Agricultural and mineral exports had increased and the economy was expanding. The mood in the country was buoyant, future prospects bright.

Then South Africa unleashed the surrogate force inherited from Rhodesia which systematically disrupted or destroyed railways and roads, farms and agro-industrial complexes, foreign aid projects, schools, health clinics and rural shops. Even the people who live and farm in rural areas became an economic target, their massive displacement part of the disruption of rural infrastructure; the disruption which destroyed self-sufficiency in the countryside. This economic and human destruction is the picture of the third economic phase, since 1981, which has seen the destruction of the young nation's economic base, its social system and at least 900,000 lives.

The ferocity of the onslaught mounted since 1981 by South Africa and its surrogates took Mozambique by surprise, but they gradually regained the upper hand in the southern provinces. South Africa then extended the war in the centre-north to Mozambique's "bread basket" provinces which produced over half of its export earnings.

October 1986 was a turning point, in terms of regional resolve as well as international awareness. The centre-north provinces of Tete and Zambezia were invaded in September and the MNR appeared to be sweeping to the coast, thereby easing South African resupply and raising the danger that they would try to declare a provisional government in the northern part of the country. Prior to this, Pretoria seemed content with a level of destabilization that caused economic and social damage and disrupted the transportation system, thus maintaining regional dependence on southern routes with considerable benefit to the apartheid economy. The invasion of 1986 signalled a substantial escalation.

Part of the apparent objective of this escalation was to disrupt elections at the urban, provincial and national levels taking place over a three-month period from 15 August to 15 November. But South Africa's real intentions were broader.

Following the attacks in May on three Commonwealth capitals and prior to the mini-summit set for August to consider tightening sanctions — and decisions taken in September on limited sanctions by the US Congress and the EEC — Pretoria warned Zimbabwe through indirect channels that such action would lead to further retaliation. This retaliation would involve orders to the MNR to take towns and hold them, to make the countryside ungovernable, and to disrupt the Beira corridor. The large numbers of armed men who entered Mozambique in the centre-north in September began to carry out these instructions, and relations between Mozambique and Malawi reached their lowest point.

Coinciding with the military pressure was an economic squeeze. On 8 October, four South African ministers signed a note cutting off recruitment for the mines, declaring that "no further recruitment of workers from Mozambique will be allowed as from today." Threats from both sides over violations of the Nkomati Accord became so heated that the Mozambican news agency said, in a story on 16 October, that "assassination of the Mozambican leader appears to be in the minds of the South African generals".

General Malan said that President Machel "appears to have lost control of the situation" and threatened that, if he "chooses terrorism and revolution", South Africa would act accordingly. Mozambique had accused South Africa of resupplying the MNR and sending a commando unit into Maputo, and Pretoria had claimed that land mines which killed six South African soldiers in the border area were planted by ANC guerrillas operating from Mozambique.

On 19 October, President Machel and some of his key advisers died in a plane crash just metres inside South African territory. Mozambican authorities believe the crash was caused by a false radio beacon which lured the plane off course, causing it to turn away from Maputo instead of towards its destination and crash into the hills near Mbuzini. South Africa blamed the crash on the Soviet crew.

The new President, Joaquim Chissano, began to implement an economic and military recovery programme mapped out under his predecessor. Some of what had been lost was regained, with military assistance from neighbouring Tanzania and Zimbabwe, and increased British and Soviet training of Mozambican army units. But the agricultural and industrial base of the economy was devastated and vast sectors of the rural population displaced. Production in virtually every agricultural sector was reduced to less than one quarter of its 1981 level, and commercial trade patterns between rural and urban areas were disrupted.

A general escalation of military action against the SADCC region in 1987 was characterized in Mozambique by large-scale massacres and bloody attacks on convoys. A large infiltration of armed men across the border from South Africa was reported in April and May. These were joining up with groups filtering south from Sofala province — after the successful offensive by Frontline forces in the first half of the year — and attacking in large numbers.

On 8 July, a Maputo newspaper, *Noticias*, reported that passengers on a coastal ship, *Chiloane II*, had seen an "unidentified" submarine inside Mozambique's territorial waters south of Beira. At the same time, there were reports from Inhambane province of several hundred newly trained men landed by sea, and of military supply parachutes retrieved from a lake in the area.

On 18 July there was a massive attack on the lush agricultural centre of Homoine in Inhambane in which 424 people were slaughtered, including 44 children and some patients in the local hospital where pregnant women were bayonetted in the stomach. The attackers wore new uniforms and were well equipped. A US Mennonite agronomist, Mark von Koevering, who survived the massacre, said, "This is not a war to win land or support. It's a war of terror. The bandits have absolutely no support from any person or group I have met."

Homoine was the bloodiest massacre, but not the last. The nearby town of Manjacaze was attacked a few days later and almost 100 people were killed. Ambushes increased on commercial convoys in Maputo province, especially near the capital. In one such attack 96 trucks were destroyed, in another a busload of people were burned to death.

As 1987 drew to a close, attacks on the main roads around Maputo increased, further isolating the capital by making its main access roads unsafe to normal commercial traffic. These attacks seemed to be aimed at cutting off main roads and preventing the reopening of the Limpopo rail line.

Attacks on economic targets during 1988 were primarily on power transmission lines, railways, villages and towns, and the pipeline to Zimbabwe, with a general escalation following the Songo meeting between Presidents Chissano and Botha.

Transportation

The transportation system through Mozambique, which is a key to its economic survival and to reducing the region's dependence on South Africa, has been the major target. Three railway systems serving the hinterland traverse Mozambique but the only lines now operational are those which also run through South Africa or which are defended at massive military cost.

In the south, the port of Maputo is the natural egress to the sea for the northern Transvaal province of South Africa, for Swaziland, and for Zimbabwe's bulk exports such as sugar and steel. The railway through South Africa to Maputo is operating, but the direct route from Zimbabwe via the Limpopo railway — rehabilitated with assistance from Botswana, Zimbabwe, Britain, Canada and the Non-Aligned Movement's Africa Fund — cannot reopen along its full length due to security and Zimbabwe's traffic to Maputo must transit South Africa.

In central Mozambique, the port of Beira is a natural outlet for other trade from Zimbabwe and Malawi. Zambia, Zaire and Botswana can also use this route. The rail link to Malawi is not operational but the route to Zimbabwe is open, guarded by Zimbabwean soldiers and — with international development assistance — slowly increasing traffic.

Nacala, further north, has the deepest natural harbour on the east African coast. The Nacala railway is Malawi's shortest route to the sea and also serves Zambia, but that too has not been fully operational for over four years due to sabotage. The rehabilitation of this line is one of the largest regional projects in the transport sector — financed by Canada, France, Portugal and the EEC. The first phase, 192 km from the port to the provincial capital of Nampula, is complete but the second phase is longer and more difficult. Repair work is semi-paralyzed due to the attacks in some parts of the province accessible only by air. Britain has promised to send military engineers to help to clear landmines along the track.

Mozambique Ports and Railways (CFM) divide pre-1986 losses into two phases. The first period begins in 1976 — when Mozambique closed its border with Rhodesia in compliance with UN sanctions — to Zimbabwe's independence in 1980. The loss in this phase, mostly from lost rail and port revenue, was $510 million.

The second phase encompasses 1982 to 1985, the years when South Africa and its surrogates intensified destruction of the Mozambican routes. Losses in this phase are broken into two categories: $82.5 million (direct) as a result of destruction, and $260.5 million (indirect) as a result of lost transit traffic.

The third phase, beginning in 1986, has been by far the most destructive, in terms of both direct and indirect losses, totalling $139.4 and $415.30 respectively. The revenue lost as a result of South Africa's diversion of traffic away from Maputo port since 1982 is given as $534 million.

Thus, in the 13-year period to the end of 1988, CFM losses totalled $1.94 billion, a figure almost 20 times in excess of the country's 1988 exports.

The following illustration gives a breakdown of losses since 1976.

Losses to Mozambique Ports and Railways, 1976 to 1988 (in millions US$)

	1988	1987	1986	1982-85	1976-80	Total
Sanctions/Rhodesia	—	—	—	—	510.0	510.0
Direct: destruction						
Action on Railways	8.7	11.8	36.5	11.1		
Locomotives	14.4	23.6	12.0	46.0		
Wagons and Cars	4.2	2.1	6.3	24.0		
Bridges	6.1	7.5	2.2	1.4		
Stations	1.0	1.0	1.0	—		
Telecommunications	1.0	—	—	—		
	35.4	46.0	58.0	82.5	—	221.9
Indirect: lost transit traffic	151.0	137.2	127.1	260.5	—	675.8
SA reduction in usage Maputo port since 1982				534.0	—	534.0

TOTAL $ 1,941.7

Source: Mozambique Ports and Railways

Added to this is the human cost — 1,867 railway workers and passengers killed or wounded from 1982 to 1988 — as shown below.

Wounded and Dead on Mozambique Railways, 1982 to 1988

	1988	1987	1986	1985	1984	1983	1982
RAILWAY WORKERS							
Wounded	59	68	150	50	88	42	30
Dead	16	33	18	20	16	20	11
PASSENGERS							
Wounded	284	153	142	93	108	66	82
Dead	112	71	11	39	20	43	22
TOTALS							
Wounded	343	221	292	143	196	108	112
Dead	128	104	29	59	36	63	33

Source: Mozambique Ports and Railways, April 1989.

Major sabotage in 1984 stopped external traffic on the Limpopo and Nacala railways, and the following chart illustrates the level of continuing non-utilization in 1987 as a result of this and other sabotage on the southern, central and northern systems. The white parts of the chart indicate the small amount of usage in relation to capacity, thus illustrating how South Africa has imposed economic sanctions on Mozambique.

Non-Utilization of the Rail Routes as a Result of Sabotage, 1987

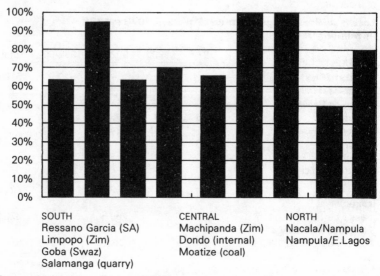

SOUTH	CENTRAL	NORTH
Ressano Garcia (SA)	Machipanda (Zim)	Nacala/Nampula
Limpopo (Zim)	Dondo (internal)	Nampula/E.Lagos
Goba (Swaz)	Moatize (coal)	
Salamanga (quarry)		

Source: Mozambique Ports and Railways.

A comparison of the above chart with a previous one for 1985 shows an improvement on some routes, while others have deteriorated.

However, the overall picture improved, largely due to increased security and rehabilitation.

On Mozambique's southern system the only route where there was an improvement over the three years was from Salamanga quarry, which provides raw materials for Maputo's cement plant. However, the quarry was sabotaged in March 1989 and all the equipment destroyed, so the line is not working because there is nothing to transport. The two routes to South Africa, direct and via Swaziland, remained much the same — highlighting Pretoria's sanctions against Maputo port.

The Limpopo railway, Zimbabwe's most important potential route to the sea, remained closed to through traffic although there was some internal movement. The line has been rehabilitated and, security permitting, could reopen in 1989. However, guarding the route, located close to the South African border, will be a formidable task. The Limpopo line was targeted in early 1989 and a small section damaged by explosives detonated with a sophisticated remote control device.

The central system provides Zimbabwe's other vital route to the sea at Beira, as well as three important internal routes for Mozambique. The situation on the route from Beira through Machipanda to Zimbabwe improved over the three years, but with trains running only in daylight hours and the line guarded by the Zimbabwe National Army. Usage of this route would be higher if it were not necessary to have daylight traffic restrictions.

The three internal routes provide a further insight into the destruction within the country. The line to the important Sena sugar complex on the Zambezi river was not utilized at all in 1985 due to sabotage. That has remained the case and CFM have deleted Sena from graphs in later years. The railway bridge nearby, at Mutarara — 3.6 km, the longest bridge in Africa — was sabotaged in the MNR offensive of September 1986 and two 90-metre spans were damaged. Other internal routes to the important coal mines at Moatize and to the quarry north-west of Beira, which previously supplied raw materials for the Dondo cement plant, also dropped to zero usage in 1986 and 1987.

Only on the northern railway system, from the provincial capital of Nampula to the port of Nacala, has the situation really improved. Growth usage on this route rose by 30 to 50 per cent due to rehabilitation and improved security. However, the increased level of usage is from internal traffic, as links to the landlocked hinterland are not yet secure.

Ports

The charge that South Africa has been applying sanctions against Mozambique through systematic sabotage of the revenue-earning communications routes, as shown above, is further illustrated by the port handling statistics, as contained in the chart below.

Port Handling of Transit Cargo (unit: 1,000 tons)

Year	Zimbabwe			South Africa	Swaziland	Malawi	Others
	Maputo		Beira				
1988	314.6	1616.3	1274.7	419.9	497.9	47.3	105.6
1987	396.6	1600.1	1203.5	479.7	585.0	68.1	89.7
1986	312.2	1032.9	720.7	619.0	504.4	5.4	30.8
1985	403.5	1191.5	788.0	587.5	601.2	76.6	44.7
1984	527.5	1259.4	731.9	785.3	524.5	221.9	14.2
1983	454.6	1190.1	735.5	1512.2	575.1	335.7	0.7
1982	825.2	1183.7	358.5	2295.9	748.8	662.4	24.8
1981	531.1	656.2	125.1	2295.9	708.7	892.7	0.0
1980	194.3	199.4	5.1	2922.3	1189.1	886.8	0.0
1979	0.0	0.0	0.0	3267.5	1741.5	1013.7	0.0

Note: Information related to 1988 corresponds to the quantity actively handled, and for the other years, to what was taxed during the year.

Source: Ports and Railways, Ministry of Transport.

The above chart reveals a number of particularly important points. The first is the dramatic impact of this one sanction against Mozambique, that is, the drop in tonnage through Maputo. From the 1979 high of 3,267,500 tons the figure of South African traffic through Maputo has consistently dropped to only 419,900 tons in 1988. Thus, Maputo port — developed a century ago as a trade route for the Boer Republics to reduce their dependence on the British authorities in Cape Town — has been increasingly and tightly squeezed, and the revenue has dropped accordingly.

Due to South African sabotage of routes used by other countries in the region, their usage of Mozambican ports has also decreased, as revealed by the above statistics. A slight increase in traffic from Malawi and Zimbabwe since 1986 reflects rehabilitation and increased security, both very costly procedures. The slight increase in usage by "others" reflects in part the portion of Zambia's copper now transiting Beira.

The major positive input into the Mozambican economy through its transport infrastructure came from Zimbabwe. From zero throughput in 1979 due to the border closure, Zimbabwean traffic, direct and indirect, rose steadily to a peak of 1,616,300 tons in 1988.

The above, somewhat bland statistic, disguises Zimbabwe's reality over this decade. In 1982, as an example, 825,200 tons of Zimbabwean trade transited the Limpopo line to Maputo. Thereafter the tonnage fell dramatically, to less than half the peak figure by 1988. Yet even this figure disguises the reality. All of this traffic was passing through South Africa to reach Maputo because the Limpopo line had been destroyed, thus the benefit of shipping costs was accruing to South Africa's coffers.

Another insight into the regional war comes from the volume of Zimbabwean trade through Beira, all of which is direct. As in the case of Maputo, this trade was zero in 1979. By 1982 it had risen to 358,500 tons, coinciding with the beginning of serious South African and surrogate sabotage. As throughput on the Limpopo line ceased and dependence upon South Africa increased, traffic on the Beira route rose dramatically to 1,274,700 by 1988. Inevitably attacks increased, but the ZNA increased its presence and this vital trade route has remained open with minimal disruption.

Trade

Mozambique's fertile land is traversed by many rivers, and its mineral wealth is virtually untapped, so there is great potential for economic growth. But the destruction of marketing and transport systems has hampered the internal distribution of goods and prevented the movement of exports to the coast. Tea worth almost $14 million deteriorated at Gurue in Zambezia province, and production halted at the Moatize mine in Tete due to a stockpile of coal worth $25 million. The railway wagons that moved the coal now give shelter to families displaced by the war.

It is not intended here to try to provide a detailed study of the economic impact of South Africa's destabilization and sanctions against Mozambique. Rather, some examples are cited to give an insight into the economic effects.

In October 1988, when President Chissano toured Nampula province, he visited Texmoque, a textile factory completed in 1983 with a capacity of 12 million sq. metres of cloth per year. He found that it was operating at 10 per cent capacity due to a shortage of electricity caused by the war. Yet the production of cotton increased in 1988, reaching 20,000 tons (still only half the level of 1981). About 80 per cent of the factories in that province have been attacked, some several times, and when repair work on the Nacala railway slowed down due to security, the factory producing concrete railway sleepers reduced output by one third.

The situation in Nampula sheds some light on the ripple effect caused by the destruction of one economic target. Cement is another example:

- A quarry which supplied the cement factory at Dondo, near Beira, was forced to close because of the security situation;
- This led to the closure of the cement plant itself, then of an asbestos roofing factory, and finally an asbestos mine;
- Mozambique, which became a significant post-independence cement exporter, has been forced to import clinker from South Africa, spending precious foreign currency to produce any cement at all;
- Meanwhile, South African companies have taken over Mozambique's cement export markets, and more Mozambicans are without jobs or means of livelihood.

The final value of export earnings for 1988 was expected to be just under $100 million, showing an inrease over the previous three years but covering only 13 per cent of the cost of imports. The projected 1989 budget shows a 22 per cent increase in exports to $121 million wile imports are expected to increase 10 per cent to $850 million. In presenting his budget to parliament, the Prime Minister said that 80 per cent of imports would have to be covered by donations and credits and that, to avoid a reduction in imports which could compromise the economic recovery programme, other forms of financing would have to be sought and reductions in debt repayment would have to be negotiated. Foreign debt at the end of 1988 had reached $4.8 billion and Mozambique is seeking almost $1.4 billion (only 60 per cent of which is pledged) to cover its financial needs for 1989.

Health and Education

Health and education facilities have been targets in this war, and the social sector, which showed vast improvement in the first six years after independence, was devastated during the second six years. This destruction of facilities, and the constant movement of hundreds of thousands of families, have disrupted their access to education and health care.

There were 5,886 primary schools open in Mozambique in 1983 but 2,655 of these were closed by the end of 1987, either because they had been destroyed or because of the security situation in the area. Primary school pupils and teachers affected numbered 448,530 and 7,154 respectively. In addition, 22 secondary schools and four teacher training colleges had been destroyed and over 400 teachers — one of the main targets of the MNR — had been murdered or mutilated. In 1988, Mozambique was 99 per cent dependent upon foreign donations or credits for equipment for its schools.

Statistics from the northern Niassa province bordering on Tanzania, one of the least affected by the war, provide an insight into the assault on Mozambique's educational system:

- In 1983, the year before the MNR offensive began in the province, there were 65,000 pupils attending 508 primary schools;
- By late 1988, the number of pupils had been reduced by one half and the number of schools by almost two-thirds: 34,645 pupils attending classes; 223 primary schools left;
- Under normal circumstances, the provincial education system should now cater for 90,000 primary pupils.
- Six of the 15 secondary schools have been forced to close and three others moved with their teachers and pupils to more secure areas.
- At least 16 teachers have been murdered in the province and nine kidnapped.

The following table gives a national perspective on the destruction of schools, and shows the escalation that followed immediately after the Nkomati accord, by comparing figures for 14 November 1983, four months before the accord, with those of 15 December 1985, two years later.

Primary School Population Affected by Armed Banditry, 1983 to 1987

Province	Schools Open in 1983	Schools Closed to 1987	Pupils Affected	Teachers Affected
Gabo Delgado	542	18	3,884	59
Gaza	546	95	14,026	213
Inhambane	506	151	33,565	431
Manica	225	88	12,919	189
Maputo Province	339	190	22,463	466
Nampula	1,116	372	57,134	1,006
Niassa	508	285	30,355	552
Sofala	386	231	41,134	607
Tete	479	391	44,822	509
Zambezia	1,130	834	188,226	3,122
Maputo City	109	—	—	—
TOTAL	5,886	2,655	448,530	7,154

Source: Ministry of Education.

Across Mozambique, over 800 health posts have been destroyed or seriously damaged. Of the 27 rural hospitals existing in 1981, only 17 were still functioning in 1988. Tete province, to give only one example, had 977 hospital beds available in 1985, but by early 1989, destruction had reduced that figure to only 60 beds for a total provincial population of one million.

Six artificial limb factories have been established to deal with war victims and a special employment programme has been started for the physically handicapped. Doctors have been sent overseas to train in plastic surgery, to help mutilated victims. Health spending has dropped:

- In 1981, Mozambique imported $12 million worth of medicines. By 1987, the figure had fallen back to $10 million and this amount would purchase far less than six year earlier. The medicine purchased amounted to only half of the country's requirement and 87 per cent of this came through donations.
- From 1975 to 1981, with the emphasis on primary health care, health spending as a portion of total budget rose from 4.5 per cent to 12 per cent. By 1988 it had fallen back to 4.4 per cent. In 1981 the equivalent of $5.40 was spent on the health of each Mozambican. By 1988, the figure was less than $1.

The reconstruction of health and educational facilities has been increasingly hampered by the need to give budget priority to defence and security. On 20 March 1989, Mozambique's Minister of Finance, Magid Osman, told a meeting of non-governmental organisations that "40 per cent of our national budget is [now] for defence and security". In contrast, the allocations for education and health, priority areas after Mozambique's independence, has plumeted to 9.9 per cent and 5.4 per cent respectively.

"The need to allocate increasing financial resources to the country's defence has inevitably resulted in a dramatic reduction in the resources available for social services," Prime Minister Mario Machungo told parliament, adding that the war of aggression has meant "years stolen from our development".

Costs

Defence

The table opposite uses the average rate of exchange of metecais to US dollars for each year listed. The result of several devaluations is that while government expenditure has risen dramatically in local currency, the dollar figure has more than halved since 1986.

Mozambique considers normal defence and security expenditure to be 17 per cent of the national budget. This puts additional defence expenditure at over US$1 billion since independence in 1975.

Defence Expenditure as a percentage of National Budget*

Year	Govt Exp.	Defence/ Security	% of Exp.	Exp. on Defence at a normal ratio of 17%	Additional Expenditure
1989	200000(n/a)	80500(n/a)	40	46500(n/a)	34000(n/a)
1988	158851(344.58)	62700(136)	39	26146(56.72)	36554(79.29)
1987	91492(316.5)	41700(144.24)	46	5235(18.11)	36465(126.13)
1986	42358(1041)	12436(305.7)	29	5326(128.71)	7200(176.99)
1985	25490(590.32)	11031(253.84)	43	4333(100.35)	6698(153.48)
1984	23063(543.43)	10320(243.17)	45	3921(92.38)	6399(150.78)
1983	21794(542.41)	8327(207.24)	38	3705(92.21)	4622(115.03)
1982	19406(515.91)	6946(183.90)	36	3313(87.71)	3633(96.20)
1981	17346(490.69)	5741(162.40)	33	2949(83.42)	2972(78.99)
1980	14097(435.09)	4419(136.39)	31	2396(73.97)	2023(62.42)
1979	10676(326.38)	3826(116.97)	36	1815(55.49)	2011(61.48)
1978	10890(331.20)	2685(81.65)	25	1851(56.30)	834(25.36)
1977	8327(258.44)	1900(58.97)	23	1416(43.94)	484(15.03)
1976	7158(227.89)	1900(60.49)	27	1217(38.74)	683(21.75)
1975	6069(222.80)	847(31.09)	14	1032(37.88)	-185(-6.78)

Metecais unit: 1,000,000; US$ million, average annual exchange.

Source: Directorate of Statistics and Ministry of Finance.

However, in the authors' view, the 17 per cent norm is much too high; had there been peace and security in the region and in Mozambique, a maximum of 10 per cent of the national budget — possibly as low as the international norm of 5 per cent — should have adequately covered defence and security needs. Thus, the real additional defence cost to Mozambique is more likely $1.5 to $2 billion.

Even that statistic reveals only part of the picture for it does not contain expenditure on military hardware, bought on long term credit, or capital items such as military barracks, airports, etc. The figures for arms purchases are classified and it is difficult to determine an exact figure. However, analysis of statistics with supplier countries suggests that a conservative figure would be $4 billion and the actual figure is probably well in excess of that. While most this amount may be written off eventually by the suppliers, it remains at present a debt and an additional war cost.

These statistics also show that since Zimbabwe's independence in 1980 — after which Mozambique might have expected some respite — defence expenditure, again excluding armaments and capital costs, has averaged a staggering 38 per cent of the national budget.

If that is taken a step further to show defence and security as a percentage of government revenue, the picture is even more devastating. In 1985, for example, while defence and security accounted for 43 per cent of expenditure, these items accounted for 58 per cent of government receipts.

Economic and Social

In economic and human terms, no country in the region has suffered more from South African aggression, destabilization and sanctions. To have survived what it has, Mozambique has drawn on a special depth of resolve and, even without some of the economic and geographical benefits of other Frontline States, a special potential which began to be fulfilled in 1981 before South Africa decided otherwise.

A SARDC study prepared for President Machel in 1986 to identify and quantify the economic and social cost of South African destabilization and sanctions from 1980 to 1985 inclusive showed an economic cost of US$5.5−6.5 billion excluding military hardware and buildings, and a human cost of over 400,000 war-related deaths including direct war fatalities, victims of war-related drought, and adults and children who died as a result of the destruction of medical clinics and lost immunization, who would have lived had it not been for war.

These costs doubled in the intervening years, 1986 to 1988 inclusive. Two principal sources of foreign exchange income − rail/port fees, and remittance from migrant workers − have declined due to Pretoria's decision, as shown above, to cut back on the use of Maputo port and to speed up the repatriation of Mozambicans working in South African mines. Sabotage and destruction of economic and social infrastructure, and relief supplies and related infrastructure, have escalated sharply.

It is estimated that the cost of direct and indirect losses to Mozambique has now reached $11 to $12 billion, plus military hardware and buildings.

Environmental

The indiscriminate slaughter by MNR of wild animals in Mozambique's nine national parks and game reserves has caused a decline in the elephant population from 54,800 in 1979 to 16,600 in 1987, with the possible loss of up to half of the remainder in 1987 and 1988.

The wildlife conservation department in the Ministry of Agriculture says the country lost 20 per cent of its elephants in 1985-1986. Officials say that buffalos and antelope are also being killed, mostly for consumption, and zebra herds are being decimated for their skins.

Former MNR members who have returned to Maputo under the government amnesty often mention poaching and ivory smuggling. Paulo Oliveira, the former MNR representative in Western Europe, told of messages he had received referring to ivory smuggled out of Mozambique on MNR infiltration routes as "white material". Other former MNR members have described South African planes flying weapons supplies into MNR bases and flying out with ivory, precious stones and timber. This practice was continuing in 1988.

Areas reserved for national parks, game reserves, special protection, etc. total 96,700 sq. km — 12 per cent of Mozambique's land surface. The Department of Wildlife Conservation estimates that, in conditions of peace, this natural resource alone would bring in over $1 million in tourism.

Many other aspects of the regional environment have been affected by the war and the resulting movement of large numbers of people who are often crowded into limited land areas. Southern Malawi, with several hundred thousand displaced Mozambicans, is a case in point as the area is stripped of trees used for firewood and constructing shelter. Maputo's population of 300,000 displaced people must seek fuel firewood as far as 30 km from the city.

Human

As the main clandestine target of South Africa's total strategy, Mozambique is gripped by a vicious war in which the level of brutality is almost impossible to grasp. In addition, half of its population is threatened with hunger because rural farmers are afraid to till their land or have had to abandon it in fear of their lives, becoming "displaced" within their own country or just outside its borders; and recent estimates put war-related deaths at almost 900,000.

A Unicef report on the impact of apartheid, destabilization and warfare on children in southern Africa, entitled *Children on the Frontline* and updated in early 1989, says one Mozambican child in three will die before the age of five. The report says that 494,000 children under five have died in Mozambique in the period 1980 to 1988, children who would have lived had it not been for the war which has destroyed health clinics and food supplies, and disrupted immunization programmes.

"By 1988," the Unicef report says, "the number of Angolan and Mozambican children under the age of five whose lives were lost as a consequence of war and destabilization totalled more people than were killed by atomic bombs in Hiroshima and Nagasaki. The toll is still rising and will not fall until the conflicts have ceased. . . . Above all, the children of southern Africa need peace."

In addition to war-related child mortality, it has been estimated that over 175,000 older children and adults have died from health and famine-related causes. Mozambican authorities estimate 100,000 civilian and military deaths directly as a result of the war 1980-1985, and a report prepared for the US State Department in 1988 by Robert Gersony calculates what it says is a conservative figure of 100,000 civilians murdered by the MNR.

The number of Mozambicans fleeing into neighbouring Malawi

reached 20,000 per month by late 1988, UN officials said, swelling the numbers from 618,000 in November to over 650,000 in January 1989. An unenviable landmark was also reached, according to UNHCR statistics, with over one million displaced Mozambicans in neighbouring countries by November 1988: Malawi, 618,000; South Africa, 250,000 (estimated by South African Council of Churches); Tanzania, 72,000; Zimbabwe, 72,000; Zambia, 30,000; and Swaziland, 21,000. The true figure would be considerably higher when swelled by large numbers of unregistered or "spontaneously settled" refugees.

To this figure also must be added 1.7 million internally displaced, a further 2.9 million forced to abandon their land or unable to produce enough to feed themselves because of the security situation, and 3.1 million urban dwellers whose food needs are no longer catered for by rural surplus. At least 7.7 million people — half the population of Mozambique — are thus "affected" by war-induced hunger.

Mozambique's Emergency Appeal for 1989/90 requests almost $362 million, categorized as per the following chart, with the largest single item for emergency food. This total represents an increase of 9 per cent over the 1988 appeal, with an increase of almost 30 per cent ($54.2 million) for food aid.

Mozambique Emergency Requirements by Sector, 1989

Sector	Amount US$
Food Aid	237,600,000
Logistics	62,897,000
Road Maintenance	12,425,000
Agriculture	8,768,000
Health	4,913,000
Drinking Water	4,563,000
Primary Education	5,091,000
Relief and Survival Items	13,050,000
Programme Assistance for Returnees	5,816,000
Institutional Support	6,668,000
TOTAL	361,791,000

Source: Mozambique Emergency Appeal

A particularly important part of the appeal is logistical support — essentially for trucks, boats and aircraft needed to transport large quantities of food and other emergency supplies. In 1988 there was a critical shortfall in this category, and a net loss of trucks — almost twice as many trucks were destroyed by the MNR as were received from donors. Of 259 trucks pledged by donors at the emergency conference held in April 1988, only 23 had arrived by December. Yet 37 trucks were destroyed or damaged during 1988. Trucks moving food and relief supplies have been a particular target in recent years, and 20 drivers or assistants were killed in the 18 months to the end of 1988.

Behind those cold statistics, the appeal provides a further insight into Mozambique's reality. In a section on the Primary Education Emergency Programme, it is noted that: "Hundreds of thousand of children — both in and out of school — have been traumatised by the war. Many are orphans, others witnessed the brutal slaughter of family and relatives." As a result, Mozambique has been forced to give primary school teachers special training in dealing with war-traumatised children. The first of these courses occurred in 1988, when 635 teachers received special training reintegration of traumatised children into social and school life. During 1989 and 1990 5,534 teachers from all ten provinces will undergo special courses.

One of the most frightening aspects of this surrogate war is the use of child combatants, most in their early teens but some as young as 10 years old. The abduction of young boys in rural areas who are then forced to undergo military training is an established method of MNR recruitment which has been noticeable for some years, but the average age has dropped. One survivor of an attack on a school north of Maputo, in which 22 people were killed in November 1988, said the average age of the attackers was 14 or 15.

A 14-year-old youth captured recently in Gaza province said he had killed many people under orders and was told by his commander that "children can be made into good soldiers, but the adults should be killed because they are no use as soldiers." Another captured MNR recruit told journalists that there were more than 500 children serving at one base in Gaza province. The MNR prefers using children, he said, because the army "won't shoot children" and because "children do what we want them to do. Adults defect."

Two 11-year-olds relating their experiences operating as bandits in Inhambane province, said the Homoine massacre was carried out by an MNR group from a nearby base at Inhamungue and that some supplies and equipment came by helicopter. Another 11-year-old said he saw his family hacked to death with machetes, and less than two weeks later he was in training with the killers. He said he was afraid of guns, but those who refused were beaten. Another boy was made to watch while his grandfather was beheaded and the head paraded on a pole. The child was told that if he cried they would do the same to him.

UNICEF in Maputo has begun collecting these stories of brutalized children. One particularly awful one describes how some kidnapped boys are conditioned to kill: "First they kill a pig or a goat as a group. Then they kill as an individual. Finally, they graduate to a human prisoner."

When several MNR bases were overrun in Zambezia province in

1987, dozens of these children were found. They, and many others found since then, have been given special care. One centre in Maputo contains 35 children at any one time, under the care of social workers, doctors and psychologists. When they are able to leave, to be absorbed into family networks or orphanages, others take their place. They tell tragic tales of brutality, murder, mutilation, and drug abuse. One youth said, "they always give us injections, and some things to smoke when we go out on attacks."

"You can tell the ones who have killed," the director of Social Welfare in Maputo said. "When you speak they don't listen. They're always vacant." It is important to "note their conditions and behavior when they come in," she added. "Some always have to have a stick in hand as a weapon. Tantrums and fist-fights diminish over time, and depression is the long term problem. All of them are very tired and depressed."

In addition, over 250,000 children have lost or been separated from one or both parents. But it is not only the children who have suffered.

- A youth with a bandage over his left eye steps into the street at a traffic light in Maputo. As he passes, the realization that he has no ears, lips or nose is devastating.
- A young woman sitting on a bench at the airport has no ears.
- In Maputo's Central Hospital, a young mother with a mutilated face weeps as she tells of an attack on her village in Nampula province. She would like to return to her village and see her children, but she thinks she cannot live there again.
- An Australian doctor, at a village in southern Inhambane province, asks if there are any problems she might help with. "Yes," replies an elderly woman. How could they get the bodies out of the well where the "bandidos armados" had thrown them, and get clean water again?

The problem of resettlement and reintegration into society is a particularly thorny one, covering a broad spectrum of problems from physical to psychological. In many parts of the countryside the rural infrastructure has been destroyed, and traditional patterns of life disrupted. The social sector has been devastated and most aspects of the economic sector have been affected, including distribution of consumer goods through rural shops, transport and small-scale industry.

Rural Mozambique is not the Sahel or Ethiopia, the difficulties are not poor soil and desertfication. The main prerequisite for resettlement is the safety to till the land. Where security can be provided, there are normal requirements of seeds and implements, food, water, health and education facilities.

The psychological problems may be more difficult to handle. These displaced people are traumatized, having been uprooted from their homes and traditions. Most fled their villages after an act of brutality against a close relative or after belongings were plundered and dwellings burned. Many have been victims of, or witnessed, some atrocity. There are mothers and daughters who have been raped or have been forced to hurt their children in some way; families which have been scattered and separated from each other, often in circumstances of fear or brutality; men and young boys who have been forcibly recruited and made to kill, often hooked on drugs; people who have been mutilated and maimed; others accustomed to violence and theft. Those who have been forcibly recruited or detained against their will need reintegration into society, as will those who have been their captors. A large part of the population will need to be psychologically, as well as physically, resettled.

The day before the Songo meeting, a special document, prepared for the visit of the Pope five days later, came out with an unprecedented attack on South Africa. Referring to the Nkomati Accord signed in 1984 by the late President Samora Machel and P.W. Botha, the document, prepared for the Roman Catholic church, said, "South Africa has done very little to implement the letter and the spirit of the modus vivendi (way of living) and has thus effectively transformed it into a modus moriendi (way of dying)." Entitled "Mozambique Yesterday and Today", the church report described the perpetrators as "terrorist groups". These statements, coming from the Catholic church, and timed to coincide with the Pope's visit, added another powerful and influential voice to the mounting international awareness of what is occurring in Mozambique and to the condemnation of South Africa and its surrogates.

A few months later, in March 1989, the British Prime Minister, visiting a military training camp in Zimbabwe, said the British, Mozambican and Zimbabwean armies had one objective: "to defeat terrorism in Mozambique".

The US State Department report prepared by Robert Gersony, released in 1988, was based on interviews with displaced Mozambicans within and outside the country, and revealed in some detail the level of brutality against civilians by the MNR. The report said that many thousands of people are detained by the MNR against their will by such methods as food deprivation, so they are too weak to escape, or through fear after being forced to witness executions. Gersony's findings confirmed a high level of violence including rape and other physical abuse, murder and mutilation, abductions, forced labour in fields and as porters, systematic burning of villages and looting of possessions. "That the accounts are so strikingly similar by refugees who have fled from northern, central and southern Mozambique suggests that the violence is systematic and coordinated and not a series of spontaneous, isolated incidents by undisciplined combatants," the report concluded.

Commenting on Gersony's findings, a senior State Department official described the situation in Mozambique as "a systematic and brutal war of terror against innocent civilians through forced labour, starvation, physical abuse and wanton killing . . . one of the most brutal holocausts against ordinary human beings since World War Two."

2 ⬛ Zimbabwe

On 15 June 1987, a group of 100 armed men crossed the border from Mozambique and infiltrated 30 km into Zimbabwe's north-eastern Rushinga district. They burned whole villages and looted stores, abducted 70 people and wounded two others — a woman and a crippled child. On 5 July, 29 of the abducted villagers, along with 10 Zimbabwean fishermen abducted in a separate incident, were found massacred inside Mozambique where they had served their purpose as porters for the stolen goods.

This incident marked the start of an MNR offensive, which Zimbabwe's security forces had long expected, across the rugged mountainous 1,200-km eastern frontier. With it came the pattern of MNR brutality all too familiar in Mozambique — murder, mutilation, rape and arson. The following are four examples of the hundreds of cross-border incidents in the ensuing period:

- School children were forced out of their dormitories at gunpoint in an attack on a secondary school at Chipinge, in the south-eastern border area. Five were killed with bayonets and seven others were mutilated by cutting off an ear;
- Thirteen villagers were hacked to death with machetes in the Chiredzi district, further south;
- In the Burma valley near Mutare, a woman with her infant on her back was abducted to carry stolen goods. When she complained that she was tired, the child was snatched from her back, swung by the ankles and beaten to death on a rock;
- In Rushinga district in the north-east, and elsewhere along the border where there are regular hit-and-run attacks, villagers abandon their homes at night to sleep in trenches or in the open with no protection from the rain.

From 15 June 1987 to 9 April 1989, a total of 335 Zimbabwean civilians were murdered by the MNR just inside Zimbabwe, and 280 were wounded seriously enough to require medical attention. Another 667 civilians were abducted, usually to carry stolen goods; according to official records, 446 of this number remain unaccounted for and a considerable number of those missing are presumed dead.

During some of these incursions, pictures of Dhlakama were left behind with crude, barely literate, leaflets saying the attacks were carried out because of Zimbabwe's military support for Mozambique.

Total Recorded Cross Border Incidents
15 June 1987 to 9 April 1989

Total number of incidents recorded	375
Zimbabwean civilians killed[1]	335
Zimbabwean civilians wounded	280
Zimbabwean civilians abducted[2]	667
Abductees unaccounted for[3]	446
Soldiers and police killed	22
Soldiers and police wounded	44
MNR known killed[4]	29
MNR known wounded	5
MNR captured	45

1. *Figure for civilians killed includes only those whose bodies have been found. The actual death toll is certainly higher.*
2. *There is no doubt that the official figure for number abducted is well below the actual figure; in some cases, the exact number of people abducted in a recorded incident is difficult to quantify and in other cases there is no record.*
3. *Many of those abducted have been killed and where this is known they are included among the dead.*
4. *Ascertaining the exact number of MNR killed and wounded inside Zimbabwe is difficult because the dead are frequently buried or carried back over the border as are the wounded. The actual figure is certainly higher than that officially recorded.*

Source: Zimbabwe Government, April 1989.

Direct evidence that South Africa had ordered the eastern offensive finally emerged in early 1988, confirming what had been indicated by the timing and other circumstances. On 23 March, Paulo Oliveira, formerly the MNR representative in Western Europe, told a press conference that a brigadier in the SADF "gave the green light" for the MNR to begin military incursions into Zimbabwe.

The attacks across the eastern border from Mozambique are only the latest item on the agenda in Pretoria's intricate and multi-faceted programme against Zimbabwe. It encompasses a range of options, used separately and collectively, which include direct military action and sabotage, clandestine support for action by surrogates, assassination and indiscriminate terror bombings, propaganda and disinformation, and economic sabotage such as contrived freight delays, undermining of industry, and disruption of shorter and cheaper transport routes forcing greater dependence on South African ports.

Economic Sabotage

Transportation/Trade

In Zimbabwe, the planned reduction of economic dependence on South Africa is called "disengagement" and this was one of the earliest policy determinations of the Mugabe government after independence in 1980. The reasons for this policy are economic as well as political; and so are South Africa's responses.

In 1975, the year before Mozambique closed its border with the rebel Rhodesian regime in accordance with UN sanctions, almost all of Rhodesia's external trade transited the Mozambican rail/port system to Beira and Lourenco Marques (now Maputo). The illustration below indicates the geographic rationale for this policy, showing comparative rail distances to regional ports from the major centres in Zimbabwe, Zambia and Malawi.

**Major Centres to Regional Ports
Rail and Road Distances**

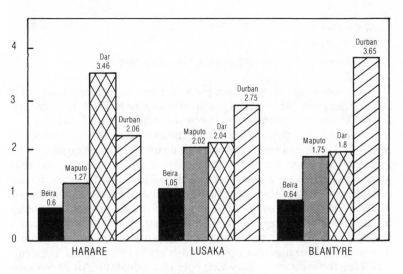

CITY TO PORT

Source: Mozambique Ports & Railways.

In distance/freight terms it makes no economic sense for Zimbabwe, Zambia or Malawi to use Durban. For Zimbabwe and Zambia, the route to Durban is over three times as long as the route to Beira; for Malawi it is five times the distance. For the same three countries, Maputo is also much shorter and cheaper than Durban. The cost implications for Zimbabwe can be seen in Illustration 2.3 which shows that containerized import traffic is 32 per cent – 50 per cent cheaper through Beira than through Durban.

Comparative Import and Export Container Prices

	Durban Z$	Beira Z$	Difference Z$	US$*
IMPORTS				
20-Foot Container				
Port Charges	502	576	+74	
Rail Charges	1843	1018	-825	
Carrier Haulage	31	31	—	
Total	2376	1625	-751	-412.64
40-Foot Container				
Port Charges	1005	1150	+145	
Rail Charges	3640	2036	−1064	
Carrier Haulage	31	31	—	
Total	4676	3217	−1459	−801.60
EXPORTS				
20-Foot Container	2370	1233	−1137	−624.72
40-Foot Container	4740	2467	−2273	−1248.90

1988 exchange rate

Source: Zimbabwe Ministry of Transport, November 1988.

The reopening of Mozambique's border with Zimbabwe after independence in 1980 offered the prospect for reducing traffic through South Africa, for disengaging within the objectives of SADCC, and returning the country's trade to its cheapest and shortest routes — which had been built for that purpose nearly a century earlier.

Before Mozambique closed the border in 1976, its ports and railways handled over 90 per cent of Rhodesian trade. The closure reduced traffic to nothing. From this position of zero traffic inherited in early 1980, the share of Zimbabwe's trade directly transiting Mozambique was increased to 52.8 per cent by 1983. By 1987, as a result of sabotage, direct traffic (excluding petrol, oil and lubricants) to and from Mozambique's ports had been reduced to 8.2 per cent. Including the indirect traffic which goes through South Africa to reach Maputo, the total Zimbabwean traffic through Beira and Maputo in 1987 was 22.2 per cent. Almost all of the remaining 77.8 per cent went through South Africa.

Zimbabwe's Ministry of Transport puts the annual additional freight bill at Z$200 million, taking an average over the years since independence. This is just over US$100 million per annum at the 1988 rate of exchange but would have been more in previous years when the exchange rate was higher. The additional freight costs since independence total Z$1.5 billion, or almost US$824.2 million at the 1988 rate of exchange.

Beyond the additional freight bill, there are other hidden costs to Zimbabwe. The destruction of the routes through Mozambique and of

Mozambican locomotives and wagons, coupled with the forced usage of longer routes through South Africa, have created chronic shortages of rolling stock. This has a ripple effect throughout the Zimbabwean economy. One example of this occurred in December 1988 when a sugar refinery was forced to close briefly, touching off a wave of panic buying, when it ran out of coal because there were insufficient wagons to haul coal from the colliery near Victoria Falls to Harare. The closure threatened other industries in the bottling, brewing and food sectors — as well as government revenues and the sugar industry's expansion plans.

In early November the Zimbabwe government had been advised that the locomotive requirement, to move an estimated 14 million tons of traffic each year for the region until 1995, was a minimum of 198 locomotives operational each day. The National Railways of Zimbabwe (NRZ) had 191 serviceable locomotives of which 126 were operational and a further 65 were inoperational because they required spare parts, which could have been purchased easily if it were not for the income that had to be diverted to defence or was lost for other reasons such as higher freight bills. With enough locomotives available, the internal turnaround time could be reduced from twelve days to eight, thus improving wagon availability by a staggering 33 per cent. In early 1989, government was able to allocate vital foreign currency to purchase the spare parts.

Meanwhile, NRZ has been hiring 10 locomotives from the South African Transport Services (SATS) at 1,500 rands per day each for an annual bill of 4.9 million rands (US$2.1 million). Wagon hire amounted to a further 6.9 million rands per year (almost $3 million) and normal interchange of locomotives and wagons cost a further 17 million rands per year ($7.3 million). All of this was payable in foreign currency, totalling 57.6 million rands since NRZ began operating on the Mozambican routes in January 1987 (US$24.8 million, Z$45.14 million at 1988 exchange rate).

Since the beginning of 1986, according to official government statistics, there have been 195 successful sabotages on the Beira to Mutare railway. These acts of sabotage have had a limited effect on usage of the Beira line, usually involving damage to a few metres of track taking 30 minutes to two hours to repair. No NRZ locomotives or wagons have been lost to date on this route.

Given the number of attempted sabotages of the railway from Beira to Zimbabwe, it is surprising how little success has been achieved in terms of disruption to Zimbabwe's shortest lifeline to the sea. In large measure, this is attributable to the presence of the Zimbabwe National Army along the Beira corridor — only one of whom was wounded (an army engineer defusing an anti-personnel mine) in the period detailed above. No ZNA or FAM soldiers were killed. One Mozambican civilian was killed, another wounded, and a third abducted.In the same period only one station along the line was attacked. Four trains were derailed as a result of sabotage in this period, all in 1986. Another detonated a mine and in another case two carriages were looted.

The final important point to emerge from a detailed study of the reported incidents since January 1986 is a change in the effectiveness of the MNR. In 1986, they frequently destroyed long sections of the track, in some cases up to 100 m. From 1987 the distance of track destroyed had moved from a scale of metres to centimetres, minimizing the delay to traffic from the hinterland.

Whereas 1986 records show explosives were used in most sabotages, in 1987 and 1988 mortar bombs, many of which were defused by army engineers, were more frequently used. However, records for the first half of 1989 suggest the saboteurs have been resupplied with explosives and a goods train was derailed with loss of life in June 1989.

Beira Corridor Rail Attacks and Attempted Sabotage
1 January 1986 to 19 February 1989

Year	Recorded Incidents	Successful[1] Sabotages	Repaired[2] Same Day	Repaired Next Day	Not Specified
1989 (7 weeks)	18	18	11	4	3
1988	66	60	32	n/s	28
1987	102	87	29	n/s	58
1986	30	30	n/s	n/s	30
TOTAL	216	195	72	4	119

1. *Successful sabotages refer to occasions when the line of rail was actually blown up or trains damaged as a direct result of sabotage. Derailments not attributed to sabotage are not included. Unsuccessful sabotage attempts are also excluded.*
2. *Prior to 4 February 1987, official statistics did not record the length of time taken for repairs. Thus, n/s (not specified) in this and the next column does not suggest that repairs took more than one or two days. This simply reflects the fact that official statistics did not record the time taken for repairs. Even after that date detailed statistics are sometimes lacking. In 1988, for example, where the amount of track destroyed was recorded, in 11 incidents the distance of track destroyed ranged from two cm to 1.1 m. On the basis of other detailed reports we are confident that all of these would have been repaired the same day. That would have been the case in many other incidents where detailed reports are not available.*

Source: Zimbabwe Government, April 1989.

All factors considered, the MNR has had little success, and is increasingly less successful, in preventing Zimbabwe and other land-locked countries in the region from using the routes through the Beira corridor, but the burden of defence cost is escalating.

The extent to which South Africa profits from its destruction of equipment and routes through Mozambique, and from forcing Zimbabwe to use the more expensive SATS routes, does not end there. Had Zimbabwe been able to afford the required spares to repair locomotives and wagons, had it been able to use its shorter and cheaper routes, had Mozambican railway stock not been destroyed, there would have been adequate equipment available to haul cargo without resorting to hiring from SATS. As in so many economic sectors, the ripple effect of South Africa's actions went a step further.

SATS informed NRZ in 1988 that it was not willing to hire out any more locomotives to meet Zimbabwe's shortfall. In early December the government of Zimbabwe was forced to accept a recommendation to purchase 20 second-hand steam locomotives from SATS at 30,000 to 40,000 rands each for a further foreign currency gain to South Africa of 600,000 to 800,000 rands (US$260,000 to $350,000). The steam locomotives have a life of only three years but will free internally-used NRZ locomotives to operate on the route to Beira.

Regarding road transport, 400 new trucks costing Z$48 million ($25 million) were required, and 660 new buses costing over Z$40 million ($21 million), as well as spare parts and tyres. Once again the cost of "total strategy" inhibited Zimbabwe's ability to afford minimal requirements. Short-term road requirements were adjudged to be in excess of Z$77 million ($42.3 million).

Direct road transport losses have not been systematically evaluated. These have occurred almost entirely on the Tete road corridor through Mozambique along which much of Malawi's trade has flowed since the Nacala route was sabotaged. The head of the Zimbabwe Transport Operators Association estimates that some 30 to 40 trailer units have been destroyed or damaged, or have required additional spares and maintenance because the security situation makes road repairs difficult. The replacement cost of a trailer unit with semi-trailer is about Z$400,000 ($220,000) which makes a total loss of Z$12-16 million ($6.6-8.8 million). Once again, this is largely a foreign currency cost.

As a result of the destruction of Zimbabwean-owned vehicles and the overall foreign currency constraints resulting from "total strategy", many haulage contracts have gone to non-Zimbabwean companies in the region which are subsidiaries of South African-owned companies, or Zimbabwean operators have been forced to hire equipment from South Africa. The roll-on effect is a further foreign currency loss to Zimbabwe and gain for South Africa.

While most damage to civilian trucks has occurred on the Tete route, there have been 241 recorded attacks on the Beira corridor road route since the beginning of 1986.

A senior MNR commander, Wiriam Erton, who accepted the government amnesty in late 1988, said the base he operated from at Mavonde, near the Zimbabwe border in Manica province, contained a

Beira Corridor Road Attacks and Attempted Sabotages
1 January 1986 to 25 March 1989

Year	Recorded Incidents	Incidents[1] Casualties	Civilians Killed	Civilians Wounded	Military[2] Killed	Military Wounded
1989 (3 months)	12	7	2	6	2	1
1988	42	11	10	9	2	15
1987	135	44	9	44	2	62
1986	52	21	8	11	7	26
TOTAL	241	83	29	70	13	104

1. *These statistics show that only one-third of the incidents involved casualties. Where there have been casualties, most have resulted from vehicles hitting mines, and most of the military casualties have involved only minor injuries. Rarely has the MNR taken on the ZNA in combat in any of these incidents.*
2. *Figures include both Zimbabwe National Army (ZNA) and Mozambique Armed Forces (FAM) casualties.*

Source: Zimbabwe Government.

special group of saboteurs, numbering 16 and trained in South Africa, whose main task was to sabotage the railway and pipeline in the Beira corridor. Erton also said the MNR did not maintain a presence in Zimbabwe, but crossed over, usually in groups of 5 to 15, to attack civilian targets and then return to Mozambique.

Zimbabwe confronts Pretoria with a dilemma which imposes constraints on how far South Africa can go in destabilizing Zimbabwe's economy. Zimbabwe's geographical position commands South Africa's trade access by land to the north. Two railways carrying this trade run through Zimbabwe, one direct to South Africa and the other via Botswana, and they are vital for the lucrative flow of the region's trade through the South African rail and port system.

While there were a few minor acts of sabotage on the line to Botswana in the early 1980s, it is no coincidence that the only regional railway not to be sabotaged is the one running directly through Zimbabwe to South Africa via Beitbridge. A different method of pressure on this route is customs delays, used to effect in holding up traffic in September 1986 after Zimbabwe participated in a Commonwealth mini-summit calling for sanctions against South Africa.

It is useful here to mention two previous sabotages in Mozambique which were related to Zimbabwe's early attempts to reduce dependence on South Africa and South Africa's determination to prevent this.

- In late 1981, the SADF headquarters in Pretoria announced that an officer, Lt Alan Gingles, had been killed on 15 October in the "operational area", a euphemism for the Angola/Namibia border area. At the same time Mozambique announced that unidentified

"Boer soldiers" had been killed trying to blow up the railway to Zimbabwe from Beira. This was dismissed as "lying propaganda" by South Africa. As is often the case, it was 16 months before evidence emerged showing that Gingles was one of those who died trying to sabotage the Beira railway. Born in Ireland and a former member of the British army as well as the Rhodesian Selous Scouts, Gingles had been based at the main MNR training camp at Phalaborwa in South Africa.

- On 5 December 1981, when Mozambican troops overran an MNR base at Garagua in Manica province bordering on Zimbabwe, they found a number of documents. These showed that the MNR commander, Afonso Dhlakama, had met senior SADF officers at Zoabostad, another MNR training base in South Africa, on 25 October 1980. Minutes from this meeting recorded the order for "the closure to traffic of the railway Beira-Umtali [now Mutare] and the traffic by road on the Inchope-Vila Franco do Save section. Regarding the increasing of our struggle, the South Africans suggested: interrupt the railway traffic Malvernia-Gwelo [now Chicualacuala-Gweru] . . .".

Petroleum

The Lonrho-owned oil pipeline from Beira to the Feruka refinery in Mutare, closed during the UDI years, resumed pumping in June 1982. It should have been feasible to resume pumping by the end of 1981 but on 29 October that year, a sabotage unit, now known to have been from the SADF, blew up the railway bridge which carries the pipeline over the Pungwe river, west of Beira.

As is so frequently the case with SADF covert operations against neighbouring states, it can be years before evidence finally emerges as to the perpetrators of the sabotage. In the case of the Pungwe river bridge, it was seven years before the truth emerged. Early in 1989, Mozambican authorities arrested a member of the SADF in Maputo where he was gathering information on ANC personnel and premises. During questioning he said he had served in the Rhodesian forces and, after Zimbabwe's independence, had joined the SADF, where he was an officer. He also admitted that, in October 1981, he had been a member of the SADF unit that sabotaged the Pungwe bridge.

Sabotage of the pipeline resumed soon after the oil began to flow and, on the night of 10 October 1982, the Maforga pumping station was extensively damaged. The Zimbabwe National Army (ZNA) was sent in to protect the pipeline, but on 9 December a SADF commando unit landed by sea and sabotaged the oil storage tanks at Beira with limpet mines, causing $20 million damage in destruction of facilities and lost fuel. This led to a critical fuel shortage in Zimbabwe, bringing road traffic to a virtual standstill by December, with queues of vehicles at petrol stations stretching several km. At one point there was only one day's supply of petrol and two days' supply of diesel in the country, and Pretoria limited the flow of alternative supplies, thereby exacerbating the crisis.

Recorded Sabotages and Attempted Sabotages of the Beira to Feruka Oil Pipeline
11 May 1982 to 5 April 1989

Year	Attempted	Effective
1989 (3 months)	7	2
1988	25	15
1987	37	26
1986	4	4
1985	2	2
1984	0	0
1983	1	1
1982	5	5
TOTAL	81	55

It must be noted here that officially recorded statistics for the latter years are more detailed than those for earlier years. This accounts for the apparently 100 per cent rate of effective sabotages from 1982 through 1986 as sabotage attempts which failed were not recorded in that period.

Also, 1987 and 1988, and the first quarter of 1989, show a new peak in sabotage against the pipeline, coinciding with the increased activity across the eastern border and against the road/rail links along the Beira corridor which could have reduced Zimbabwe's dependence on South Africa.

Source: Zimbabwe Government, April 1989.

South Africa has continued to use the fuel weapon against Zimbabwe. Supplies of base oils (lubricants), which cannot be pumped through the pipeline, have been delayed in South Africa forcing Zimbabwe to bring the lubricants through Beira in drums at an additional cost of Z$2.5 million ($1.37 million) up to November 1988. Jet A-1 fuel for the air force and commercial airliners has been delayed and on one occasion, during the 1985 Commonwealth summit in Nassau, the situation was saved only because the energy ministry had taken the precaution of ordering another shipment through Beira to coincide with one scheduled to come through Durban. The South Africans delayed the Durban shipment until they discovered that another one had come through Beira, and then released it.

The National Oil Company of Zimbabwe (NOCZIM) was set up in July 1983 to coordinate Zimbabwe's oil importation in the face of the growing threat. The ZNA presence along the Beira corridor reduced the level of successful sabotages to one that year and there were no further attempts until 29 January 1984. The next table shows fuel losses since then in quantity and value.

Fuel Losses by Product as a Result of Pipeline Sabotage
From 1984 to November 1988
(000 litres, 000 $)

Year	No. of Sabotage	Diesel litres	Value Z$	Petrol litres	Value Z$	Jet A-1	Value Z$	Total Z$
1988	16	2,847	772	1,194	348.6	562	155.7	1,276
1987	24	5,227	1,404	3,907	873.2	54	12.8	2,290
1986	4	1,141	225	1,922	414.4	—	—	639
1985	2	1,235	444	—	—	—	—	444
1984	5	576	182	229	64	—	—	246
Total	51	11,026	3,027	7,252	1,700	616	168.5	4,955
TOTAL US$[1]			1,815		1,008		93.3	2,916

1. *At annual rates of exchange.*

Noczim statistics do not coincide exactly with other officially recorded government statistics shown in the previous table; however the variation is of minor significance. For 1987, Noczim figures are slightly higher and for 1988 slightly lower, and they show more incidents in 1984. The years 1982 and 1983 are not available from Noczim as this pre-dated its creation.

Source: Noczim, December 1988.

Because of the war situation in Mozambique, insurance could not be obtained to cover the loss totalling, with amounts prior to 1984, well over Z$5 million. That figure, plus the additional cost of shipping lubricants in drums, represents a loss, all in foreign currency, of at least Z$7.5 million ($4.37 million). To this must be added the losses through damage and repair to the pipeline, additional expensive equipment which has had to be purchased to facilitate rapid repairs and extra staff needed to undertake these repairs. That figure is well over Z$3 million ($1.74 million). Thus the total loss to this one sector of the economy as a result of South African destabilization is over Z$10.5 million ($6.11 million at annual rates of exchange).

Other

Many other areas of South Africa's regional policy, and its ripple effect on the Zimbabwean economy, are more difficult to quantify:

- What additional level of foreign investment might Zimbabwe have gained if there had been peace and security in the region?
- How great are the losses to industry and commerce in Zimbabwe because their exports are less competitive as a result of higher freight bills?

- What has been the additional effect on Zimbabwean industry of South African tariff fixing?
- What has been the loss to the tourist industry resulting from overseas visitors cancelling, or not considering, visits as a result of what they read in their press?
- And what has been the effect on the ecology in Zimbabwe?

An important example of the latter two points is the Gonarezhou national park in south-eastern Zimbabwe. Largescale MNR infiltration into the park began in 1987 and the park was closed to the public in 1988 and 1989 because of the security situation. Thus the revenue from visitors was lost.

Beyond that, endangered species such as rhinos and elephants are being slaughtered. The park's most famous elephant, an old bull named Kabakwe, was killed and his substantial tusks advertised in a Johannesburg newspaper for US$100,000 each. During the Christmas period in December 1988, at least 17 black rhinos were killed in Gonarezhou and their horns removed. A few months earlier, a coalition of 14 environmental groups presenting testimony to a US Congressional sub-committee hearing gave evidence that ivory and tusks from the region are being smuggled out through South Africa.

Since 1987, Zimbabwean army bases in the area of the park have been attacked several times and a number of soldiers killed. Two park wardens have been killed in clashes with MNR and a third abducted. Villages in the area have been attacked so often that the Zimbabwe government decided in late 1988 to resettle 1,800 families away from park borders at a cost of some Z$3 million.

In the third quarter of 1988, military activities in Gonarezhou took on an even more sinister note. The park is located just north of South Africa's Kruger national park, which has been used for many years for MNR infiltration from South Africa into Mozambique. The geographical juxtaposition of the two parks has made it easy for South Africa to resupply its forces operating in Gonarezhou. Investigators studying the simultaneous sabotage of 886 electricity pylons in Mozambique, covering a 130-km distance less than 20 km from the Zimbabwe border, now believe that the sabotage was carried out by groups operating through Gonarezhou and that the park is being used by SADF as a base for attacks into Mozambique.

Sabotage, Espionage, Assassination

The first major post-independence sabotage operation against Zimbabwe occurred on 16 August 1981 when a massive explosion destroyed armaments worth Z$36 million ($52.2 million at 1981 exchange rate) at Inkomo Barracks near Harare. A former Rhodesian army captain, an explosives expert who had remained in the ZNA as commander of the corps of engineers, was arrested but later sprung from prison by a South African agent, a detective inspector in the police. The captain reappeared in the SADF.

Almost eight years later, the High Court in Harare was told that one of three men before it had been involved in that escape, part of an espionage/sabotage network that continued to do reconnaissance work for South Africa. The three in court were accused of involvement in the SADF attack on 19 May 1986, which had destroyed two buildings in the city and caused an abrupt end to the mission of the Commonwealth Eminent Persons Group.

Former members of the Rhodesian military and intelligence services, they were convicted of acting in common purpose with South African saboteurs to destroy the downtown offices of the ANC and a suburban residence. They were sentenced in June 1989, to an effective 40 years in prison each. The State alleged that two of the men had been recruited by the South African intelligence services in 1983 and that the third had been working for the SADF since 1981. A witness who knows the men well, now serving a prison sentence for failing to report the presence of South African agents, testified that one of the three had told him they were "working for South Africa".

Statements made to police by the three, which were ruled admissable as evidence, gave details of an operation involving 11 South African commandos flown to Zimbabwe, dropped on a farm near Bulawayo and ferried in several waiting vehicles to Harare, stopping on a hill nearby where they "sorted out guns and grenades". The three admitted playing various support roles, such as using lights to signal a landing strip for a South African aircraft carrying military equipment, but denied direct participation in the sabotage. The statements of the accused said that spikes were thrown on the road after the attack to delay follow-up and the commandos were airlifted out of the country by two helicopters which landed in a national park near the city. Propaganda pamphlets left behind said the South African army had attacked "ANC gangsters" and the SADF later confirmed responsibility for the incursion.

A ZNA explosives expert told the court that a total of 52 kg of explosives were used at the two locations causing the type of blast that suggested plastic explosives. He said the charges had been set to go off seconds after the departure of the bombers, to create a diversion, and the "method of initiation was either safety fuse, electronic delay or radio command", or a combination of the three.

One of the accused, Barry Bawden, following his arrest some 18 months after the attack, led police to a farm near Bulawayo where bombs, guns and parachutes were kept. From his house on the ranch, where he was manager, police recovered bottles containing explosive liquid, wire-cutters, black gloves and a black face mask. A large quantity of arms retrieved from the Bulawayo house of Kevin Woods, another of the accused, included pistols with silencers, radio equipment, grenades, plastic explosives and detonators as well as submachineguns, rocket launchers, rockets and ammunition.

A ZNA communications expert told the High Court that the radio devices were similar to those captured at a main MNR base in Mozambique in 1985. He testified that this radio equipment included a highly sophisticated transmitter-receiver normally used for clandestine operations. Called Syncal 30, it is manufactured by Milcom, a South African company which produces most of the SADF's military communications equipment. He said the ZNA has no equipment to intercept messages from the Syncal 30. A data transmission device, KY500, also manufactured by Milcom and found on the farm, can be linked to another by telephone or interfaced to a miniature printer. The KY500 can be used with Syncal 30 radios, and these devices were also found at the main MNR base in 1985. A PX1000 message decoder used for secure data communication via telephone, manufactured by Textel of Ireland, was also among the equipment found on the farm.

The third accused, Michael Smith, spoke of bombs he had had in his possession and of a container which had kept bombs used in a later attack, in May 1987, on a house in a central Harare suburb. "From August 1987 to December 1987, I was also in possession of the three remaining bombs which had not been used in the Lincoln Road attack," he said, adding that he had seen the bombs intended for use in an attack in early 1988 on a house in Bulawayo.

One man was killed in that attack, on 11 January 1988, and three others were injured by a car bomb large enough to cause damage 200 metres away. The dead man was the driver of the car, Obert Mwanza, a Zimbabwean hired from a labour exchange and paid Z$50 ($25) to drive the yellow Renault 5 to a house in the Trenance suburb and hoot the horn twice. The injured were South African exiles who stayed in the house at 16A Jungle Road. Mwanza was blown to bits and those who allegedly hired him — Woods, Smith and Philip Conjwayo, a former Rhodesian policeman — were charged with murder and two other counts covering terrorism. In November 1988 they were found guilty and sentenced to death, but have lodged an appeal with the Supreme Court.

Despite the random hiring of Mwanza from a labour exchange, Woods, who is a Zimbabwean citizen, claimed in mitigation that there was no intention "to sabotage Zimbabwe or injure any Zimbabwean. We are sorry that the man who died was not a member of the military wing of the African National Congress."

Sharpshooters patrolled the rooftops when the men were brought to trial, and the High Court was ringed with hundreds of police and troops, armoured personnel carriers and anti-aircraft guns. The accused in both trials were moved from Bulawayo to Harare under tight security after a rescue operation was exposed.

Details of the rescue attempt were made public at the trial in Harare of a South African national, Charles Dennis Beahan, who was handed over to Zimbabwe by Batswana police on 2 July 1988. He had fled back into Botswana when suspicious Zimbabwean customs officials at the Kazungula crossing near the Zambezi river had insisted on searching his car. Arms, ammunition, explosives and telecommunications equipment found in hidden compartments in the vehicle led to the unravelling of a scheme to spring the men mentioned above when they appeared in court for formal remand proceedings on 30 June.

Zimbabwe's security minister announced that the heavily-guarded van carrying the men between the court and prison was to be intercepted and the guards overcome. The five were to be transported to a stolen air force helicopter and then to a civilian Dakota at a remote airstrip in the Midlands province and flown out of the country. The rescue plan was aborted after Beahan's car was searched.

Those involved were former Rhodesians who had been active members of the South African Special Forces and were now on reserve for covert operations in Zimbabwe. The use of former Rhodesians gave Pretoria "deniability" should anything go wrong, as it did, and Pretoria denounced them as a "renegade group" who "once had links to South African authorities", claiming they had acted in their personal capacity. Given the cost of an operation involving an aircraft, a helicopter, sophisticated weapons and communications, several vehicles and a network of couriers, that seemed unlikely.

A defector from the Zimbabwean air force, Flight Lieutenant Gary Kane, took an Augusta-Bell helicopter from the New Sarum air base near Harare, landed at the Cleveland military rifle range, where he picked up a woman believed to have been Smith's wife, Eileen, and then flew to the remote strip to rendezvous with the Dakota. There Kane disabled the helicopter with gunfire, and shot dead a 10-year-old child who had wandered nearby.

The rescue attempt followed a foiled attack in Botswana 10 days earlier in which two South African commandos were arrested. Zimbabwean authorities were taking no chances on another escape plan, and Beahan was driven into the court yard for his remand hearing in an armoured vehicle. Facing a murder charge for complicity in the death of the child, Beahan changed his "not guilty" plea to "guilty" of the remaining charges and was sentenced to life imprisonment.

Between the August 1981 destruction of armaments and the January 1988 car bomb in Bulawayo, there were many other direct attacks and sabotage — against Zimbabwean people and property as well as against ANC members and supporters.

On 18 December 1981, an explosion ripped apart the Harare headquarters of the main political party, ZANU, killing six Christmas shoppers and wounding more than 100 others. Investigators traced the explosion to former members of the Rhodesian SAS regiment serving in the SADF. An attempt at about the same time to sabotage 30 tank transporters, tanks and armoured cars at the main Harare army barracks was discovered and prevented.

On 25 July 1982, five planes, with a replacement value of Z$30-$50 million ($39-$65 million), were destroyed on the ground and five others damaged by incendiary devices at the Thornhill air base near Gweru in the centre of the country.

On 18 August, a ZNA patrol ambushed and killed three whites in a group of South African soldiers who had entered Zimbabwe three days earlier. The SADF said they were on an "unauthorized raid", believed to be a mission to rescue a colleague who had been captured in Zimbabwe.

After this the SADF concentrated on arming some of the dissident elements operating in the south-west of the country and, when that option was exhausted, on cross-border raids by the MNR.

Another aspect of military aggression against the Frontline States are the attacks which directly target personnel or premises of the African National Congress (ANC). On 3 August 1981 the ANC chief representative in Zimbabwe, Joe Gqabi, was assassinated outside his Harare home, only a few months after a bomb attached to his car had been discovered and defused. Evidence later indicated that the assassination had been carried out by former Rhodesian Selous Scouts now serving in the SADF.

The house Gqabi had occupied, and the downtown offices of the ANC, were later destroyed in the attacks on 19 May 1986. A new ANC office in Harare was subjected to a rocket attack a year later, on 17 May 1987. And on 29 May, a young Zimbabwean woman, married to a South African, was killed in her Harare flat when she switched on a booby-trapped television set. A South African national, Leslie Johannes Lesia, accused of bringing the lethal television into Zimbabwe through Mozambique, has been charged with murder and refused bail.

On 13 October 1987, as the Commonwealth Heads Of Government Meeting began in Canada, a car bomb blast in a suburban Harare shopping centre injured a number of people, three of them seriously. The latter were Zimbabwean nationals, two of them anti-apartheid activists.

Related to these attacks are South African espionage activities in Zimbabwe, through strategically-placed cells recruited by South African intelligence services after the independence elections in 1980. The intelligence for Gqabi's assassination was supplied by one such group in Zimbabwean security, two of whom were arrested and charged with espionage and illegal possession of weapons. Immediately after their arrest, approaches were made to the Zimbabwe government through the South African trade mission in Harare in which it was admitted that the two were spies. South Africa proposed a prisoner swap but this was rejected. Other cases of active South African cells became public over the next eight years. One group was detained for supplying classified material about the telecommunications network. And a white South African woman was sentenced to 25 years in prison after pleading guilty to trying to infiltrate and spy on the ANC.

The following chart shows the pattern of these attacks.

Direct South African Attacks and Sabotage Since 1981

Date	Incident
3 Aug 1981	Assassination of ANC representative, Joe Qgabi, at his Harare residence.
16 Aug 1981	Destruction of armaments valued at US$52.2 million at Inkomo Barracks near Harare.
18 Dec 1981	Explosion at Zanu party main offices in Harare killing six Christmas shoppers and wounding more than 100 others.
Late 1981	Attempted sabotage of tanks and armoured cars at KG VI army headquarters in Harare.
25 July 1982	Five planes destroyed and five others damaged by incendiary devices at Thornhill air base near Gweru. Replacement value: US$39-$65million.
18 Aug 1982	SADF unit ambushed by ZNA in south-eastern Zimbabwe killing 3 white South Africa soldiers.
19 May 1986	ANC offices and residence in Harare destroyed by explosives planted during elaborate late-night attack in which attackers were flown clandestinely in and out of the country. SADF admitted responsibility, said target was ANC not Zimbabwe.
17 May 1987	Rocket attack on new ANC office in Harare suburb.
29 May 1987	Zimbabwean wife of South African exile killed in Harare flat when she switched on booby-trapped television set.
13 Oct 1987	Car bomb exploded in suburban Harare shopping centre seriously injuring 3 people, damaging several cars.
11 Jan 1988	Car bomb exploded outside house in Bulawayo suburb, killing one person, injuring three.
30 June 1988	Attempted "hot extract" of the suspects charged in the 1986 and 1988 attacks; rescue foiled after weapons and explosives found in false compartments of car at border post.
SURROGATE SUPPORT	
1982-1987	Arms supply to some dissident groups in south-western Zimbabwe.
15 June 1987	MNR, trained, armed and equipped by SADF, begin cross border raids into Zimbabwe: 335 Zimbabweans killed in eastern border area by early April 1989, 280 wounded, 667 abducted (446 unaccounted for).

Source: Zimbabwe Government and other reports.

Surrogate Forces

There is an abundance of evidence, including ballistics, to prove South African supply to some of the dissidents who killed 1,574 people in three provinces in the south-west of Zimbabwe from 1982. Although many refused South African offers of assistance, others admitted during questioning and subsequent trials to having receiving armaments and ammunition from South African agents whom they identified. The head stamps on ammunition found at some of the actions also provided evidence of South African supply, and similar head-stamps were found during operations across Mozambique. A detailed dossier of South African links to the killing of white commercial farmers in south-western Zimbabwe was presented to the South African authorities by Zimbabwe in early 1984. The inherent threat of embarrassing public exposure for targeting whites in Zimbabwe was enough to prevent further infiltration of armaments or armed personnel from South Africa for the next 17 months.

The late 1987 unity accord in Zimbabwe brought an end to the remaining incidents by dissidents, and an amnesty was declared on 19 April 1988. Thereafter there were no dissident activities in the south-west, and thus no cover for South African operatives, but it still left the ZNA fighting on two fronts — inside Mozambique and on its own eastern border.

Attacks across the eastern border, which were almost non-existent until 15 June 1987, had been expected to escalate for almost a year following a series of events in Washington at the time of the "Irangate" scandal when profits from the sale of arms to Iran were diverted to anti-government groups elsewhere, particularly in Nicaragua. Although no evidence has yet emerged to trace funds directly to southern Africa, three MNR representatives had a meeting in the White House in this period (August 1986) with the then Director of Communications, Patrick Buchanan.

On 17 August, the three MNR representatives and three representatives of Rev. Ndabaningi Sithole, discredited as a political figure in Zimbabwe, met in Washington and signed a "Friendship and Co-operation Agreement". The document itself was fairly innocuous. However, the first signatory for Sithole, Bruce Anderson, was head of a South African security company, and two other documents, which Sithole signed with Anderson two days later, were far from innocuous.

In one document, Sithole appointed Anderson as " my agent for Southern Africa", authorizing him to "recruit and employ all personnel that may be necessary to carry out the various duties as mentioned in the letter of Appointment to SACP Services (Pty.) Limited". The services to be provided were not mentioned. In a separate agreement, reference is made to a series of feasibility studies to be made by SACP Services — a security company with offices in Johannesburg — and the last part of the signed agreement reads:

"On completion of these long-term studies I undertake to pay on demand the sum of $100,000,000 Zimbabwean dollars.

Twenty percent of the aforementioned sum shall be paid in such currency and in any bank as may be directed by SACP Services (Pty.) Limited.

This agreement shall be secured by a bond of US$2.5 million, a copy of which attached hereto."

Few people in Zimbabwe took Sithole or Anderson seriously. In the British-administered pre-independence election in 1980, Sithole's party had received only 2 per cent of the vote and failed to win a seat in parliament. Sithole went into self-imposed exile in November 1983 in Maryland, outside Washington DC, and was subsequently granted political asylum in the US. Anderson, a former secondhand car salesman whose real name is Bruce Charles Anderson-Lynes, had moved to Rhodesia in 1978 from Britain, where he had a number of criminal convictions. Less than a year later, he was arrested for fraud by Rhodesian police, and he jumped bail and fled the country early in 1980.

While not taking Sithole or Anderson themselves as a serious threat, the Zimbabwean authorities knew that Sithole was in league with the South Africans and being used by them, and saw that the Washington agreements could foreshadow an offensive across the eastern border. The timing of these events in Washington coincided with early progress in the internal unity talks in Zimbabwe, and an expected agreement, ending dissident activity in the south-western Zimbabwe, would mean that it would not be viable for Pretoria to continue arming some of its own operatives in that area. Thus a new cover would be required for active destabilization of Zimbabwe. On 30 October 1986, 11 days after the plane crash that killed President Machel, Dhlakama announced that he was declaring war on Zimbabwe and the long-expected cross-border activity began the following June.

Refugees

By far the largest refugee population in Zimbabwe are those from Mozambique, numbering over 175,000, of which 100,000 are "spontaneously settled" and the remainder are registered with the United Nations High Commission for Refugees and resident in five camps. UNHCR briefing notes compiled at the end of 1988 said that, "Whereas at first most of those who sought asylum were victims of drought and famine, those who have entered Zimbabwe in the last four years have been victims of the banditry of the MNR and most come from areas of Mozambique bordering Zimbabwe."

The four camps along Zimbabwe's eastern border have rapidly become over-populated, necessitating opening of a fifth in 1988. The estimated total holding capacity for the four camps — Tongogara, Nyangombe, Mazowe and Nyamatikiti — is 25,000 people but by early 1989 they were accommodating three times that number, and work had begun on construction of Chambuta camp, in the south-east near Chiredzi, to accommodate a further 20,000. Due to a general land shortage, the camps are only for care and maintenance and cannot be self-supporting. The recommended camp population for viable agriculture in the four camps already in use is only about 4,000 people.

The presence of large concentrations of refugees who are not self-supporting is causing social and environmental problems in the areas of the camps. The incidents of stock theft near one of the camps dropped dramatically after the erection of a large security fence, but the destruction of nearby woodlands being cut down for firewood is more difficult to control.

Most international governmental assistance is channelled through the UNHCR, which committed over Z$5 million ($2.75 million) in 1988, double the amount for the previous year. For the four-year period 1985-1988, the UNHCR committed or dispursed a total of Z$9,709,815 ($5.55 million at average annual rates of exchange). A number of local and international non-governmental organizations provide additional refugee assistance.

As well as provision of the land and security for the refugees, the Zimbabwe government spent Z$2.1 million ($1.15 million) in 1988 on maintenance, infrastructure and administration. The total cost to government since 1980 can be estimated at US$8 million.

Defence Costs

One imponderable question for all of the Frontline States is how much money have they been forced to divert from development to defence to protect themselves from South African action, particularly against the regional transportation network.

In late 1982, following the attack on the Maforga pumping station on the oil pipeline from Beira, ZNA troops were first committed to Mozambique. Their task was to protect the route to Beira which includes the pipeline as well as road and rail access to the sea. This early commitment was increased in mid-1985 with the deployment of ZNA combat units in Mozambique's three central provinces of Manica, Sofala and Tete.

The following table details the resources allocated to defence expenditure in Zimbabwe's post-independence budgets and the defence percentage of each budget. With the exception of the immediate post-independence period in 1980/81 when it was necessary to integrate two guerrilla armies and the remnants of the Rhodesian forces, defence expenditure as a percentage of the total budget has remained relatively constant. However, in monetary terms, defence expenditure has risen by almost 300 per cent over the nine budgets since independence.

Zimbabwe Defence Expenditure Since 1980

Year	Total Expenditure National Budget Z$	Defence Expenditure Recurrent & Capital* Z$	Defence % of Exp.
1988/89**	6,052,263,000.	903,254,000.	15
1987/88	5,390.239.626.	787,291,000.	14.5
1986/87	4,837,263,860.	687,521,000.	14
1985/86	3,875,298,741.	519,659,000.	13.5
1984/85	3,568,378,248.	386,254,000.	11
1983/84	3,052,688,909.	425,636,000.	14
1982/83	2,935,559,565.	382,150,000.	13
1981/82	2,121,722,670.	329,882,000.	15.5
1980/81	1,627,534,995.	310,166,000.	19
TOTAL DEFENCE EXPENDITURE (Z$) July 1980 to June 1989		4,731,813,000.	
TOTAL DEFENCE EXPENDITURE (US$) at average annual rate of exchange		3,875,011,000.	

Includes Ministry of Defence budget and other capital expenditure by the Ministry of Public Construction and National Housing.
** Budget estimates*

Source: Ministry of Finance, Economic Planning and Development.

The increase in the defence statistic mirrors the demands on the ZNA on various fronts. After completion of the integration exercise, military expenditure dropped as a percentage of total budget in 1982, but went up in monetary terms when there was a dramatic increase in military activity in the south-west with 1,135 incidents recorded between 1 March and 31 August. This was also the year the ZNA was committed to guard the Beira corridor. Defence expenditure went down in 1984/85, after the Nkomati Accord between Mozambique and South Africa, but shot up again in 1985/86 when the ZNA entered Mozambique in a combat role in three provinces. Thereafter, defence spending has shown substantial annual increases in monetary terms, and, as a percentage of total budget, has crept up almost to its 1981/82 level.

An assessment of the amount of money that Zimbabwe would have had to divert to defence had the country and region been at peace is difficult, and requires answers to imponderable questions. In a peaceful situation, might the ZNA have had four brigades instead of six?

Would it have been necessary to purchase MiG-21s? The air force would say yes, but in a situation of peace the treasury may have been less amenable to the expenditure.

A further consideration is that the purchase of MiGs, armoured cars from Brazil and some other armaments, do not appear in the recurrent or the capital budget. They are purchased on long-term credits on soft terms. However, they must be paid for eventually and thus real defence expenditure is greater than shown above.

The figure for average additional defence expenditure generally used in official circles in Harare is approaching Z$1 million per day, or about Z$30 million per month. For the purposes of calculating costs relating to South African action, the years 1980/81 and 1981/82 can be excluded. Thus the period for calculation is the seven budgetary years from 1982/83, when South Africa escalated sabotage activity and support to surrogates, and when Zimbabwe committed troops to Mozambique. Estimates reaching Z$500 million per year are excessive, and the calculations contained here use a figure of Z$360 million per year. By this method, the additional defence expenditure over the seven-year period amounts to Z$2.5 billion.

The following table, showing excess defence expenditure above the 5 per cent norm, confirms this estimate, giving a slightly higher figure, also excluding 1980/81 and 1981/82, of Z$2.606 billion (US$1.85 billion at average annual rates of exchange).

Zimbabwe Excess Defence Expenditure Since 1982 (Z$ million)

Year	Defence Exp. Z$	Exp. %	Exp 5% Z$	Add.Exp. Z$	Add.Exp. US$*
1988/89**	903.254	15	302.613	600.641	330.022
1987/88	787.291	14.5	269.511	517.780	313.806
1986/87	687.521	14	241.863	445.658	268.468
1985/86	519.659	13.5	193.764	325.895	195.146
1984/85	386.254	11	178.418	207.836	158.653
1983/84	425.636	14	152.634	273.002	281.445
1982/83	382.150	13	146.777	235.373	305.679
TOTAL	4,091.765		1,485.580	2,606.185	1,853.219

* *Average annual rate of exchange.*
** *Budget estimate*

Propaganda/Disinformation/Threats

Another weapon in South Africa's considerable destabilization armoury is propaganda and disinformation, often combined with verbal threats against Zimbabwe. The South Africa Ministry of

Defence finds a pretext to threaten Zimbabwe every few months — over the purchase of new military hardware, a border incident, or merely over information emanating from Harare. This increase in verbal warfare, as well as the use of surrogates, would seem to be a response to constraints placed on Pretoria's actions by pressure from some Western governments over direct overt attacks and to increased Western military and other involvement in Zimbabwe and elsewhere in the region.

Most recently, the Deputy Defence Minister, Wynand Breytenbach, warned in February that South Africa would "take the necessary steps" should Zimbabwe proceed with acquisition of either British-made Harrier jump jets or Soviet-made MiG-29s. "Whatever necessary steps seem fit at the moment" would be taken if Pretoria felt it would "threaten our way of life or the stability of South Africa and the region", Breytenach said.

President Mugabe dismissed the threats as part of South Africa's campaign of destabilization that continues to "menace our territorial integrity, national sovereignty and peaceful development". He said South Africa could not be allowed to choose Zimbabwe's military hardware. A few days later part of the military shopping list for purchases from China was tabled in parliament, including a US$92 million air defence radar system, $8 million for aircraft and $4 million for missiles.

Although Breytenbach claimed the acquisition of advanced warplanes would "increase the level of tension in southern Africa", more to the point was South Africa's alarm at losing its air superiority over the region. Zimbabwe's forthcoming military purchases were seen in the local media as a signal to South Africa "that it can no longer expect to violate Zimbabwe's airspace unchallenged". In the wake of its lost air superiority over southern Angola and the bite of the international arms embargo, South African air force officials had already begun to speak of "repelling attacks" rather than "control" of southern Africa's airspace.

These threats coincided with editorials in government-supported South African newspapers describing Harare as "the anti-South Africa propaganda centre", criticizing Zimbabwe for hosting conferences aimed at condemning South Africa and "encouraging action to strangle it economically", and more particularly for being the venue of ANC meetings with various other South African groups of all races. These attacks were seen as a response not only to Mugabe's outspoken stance against apartheid and in favour of sanctions but his influential role in SADCC and leadership of the Non-Aligned Movement.

A few months earlier, in October 1988, the South African Minister of Defence, General Malan, had accused Zimbabwe of giving "terrorists a cloak of respectability" and assisting them with propaganda. Speaking at a military parade at Louis Trichardt, the SADF base nearest the Zimbabwe border, General Malan said "security comes first for South Africa" and reminded the Soutpansberg Commando of their responsibility to protect the country's northern borders.

In September, the SADF director of planning, General M C Botha, speaking at another military parade, had dubbed President Mugabe as "the foster father of terrorism in southern Africa". Botha described Mugabe as a "trained terorist" and said a new threat against South Africa was building up in Zimbabwe. This "threat" seemed to be Mugabe's outspoken stance against apartheid and in favour of sanctions, coupled with his influential role in SADCC and leadership of the Non-Aligned Movement. In addition, in some circles in South Africa, Zimbabwe's example of a non-racial society is regarded as a "threat".

The timing of this verbal aggression against Zimbabwe suggested that it was for internal South African consumption, as a counter-point to the agreement to pull out of southern Angola and to allow the UN to observe a ceasefire and elections in Namibia. It was also seen as a factor of Zimbabwe's determination to "disengage" from South Africa, reducing its dependence on the transportation system and seeking alternative markets and sources of import requirements.

The verbal temperature increased again in early February 1989 when two Zimbabweans were shot dead crossing the South African border near Beitbridge. Earlier threats, in late 1986 and early 1987, were generally related to the discovery of landmines in the border area.

Another aspect of disinformation involves sowing seeds of doubt about whites who had worked in sensitive areas in Rhodesia and who have continued to use their skills effectively for Zimbabwe. While there is adequate evidence that some who stayed on did so at the behest of South Africa, a blanket condemnation cannot be applied to all who remained, some of whom did so at considerable personal risk since their former colleagues who headed south after independence condemned them as "sell-outs". A Bulawayo police inspector who stayed on was murdered by former colleagues; others have been subjected to vicious smear campaigns.

A radio programme called "Radio Truth" is one of South Africa's weaker weapons in the post-independence propaganda war against Zimbabwe. As was the case with similar radio stations supposedly located in Mozambique and Angola, Radio Truth was said to be broadcasting from a location in Zimbabwe. Monitors in Zimbabwe first picked up Radio Truth in March 1983, broadcasting twice a day in the local languages of Shona and Ndebele, as well as in English. Communications experts traced the transmission to studios of the South

African Broadcasting Corporation at Meyerton, near Johannesburg.

Further confirmation came on 25 November 1983, when a tape carrying the introductory music of Radio Truth was switched with that of "Voz da Africa Livre" broadcasting to Mozambique. The tapes were switched back to their proper frequencies in less than a minute but the damage had been done, clearly revealing that the programmes were beamed from the same studio.

The disinformation campaign often has been more threatening. One early target was the Australian airline, Qantas, which replaced Johannesburg with Harare as the destination in southern Africa, diverting considerable foreign currency earnings to Zimbabwe by way of air crews and passengers. Soon after this occurred, the airline's manager in Zimbabwe received a letter threatening the safety of a visiting Australian cricket team. Other letters were posted from a London address to politicians, diplomats and individuals in Zimbabwe.

After the murder of a Malawian exiled politician in Harare, an anonymous letter was sent to senior government officials suggesting the involvement of two white security officers, with the obvious intention of causing suspicion within the Zimbabwean intelligence community. However, government did not accept the charges and when investigations revealed that this letter and the others had originated in the South African trade mission in Harare, one South African official was ordered to leave the country.

Quantifiable Costs

As occupant of the region's transport commanding heights, Zimbabwe confronts South Africa from positions of both weakness and strength. South African cannot destroy the rail routes through Zimbabwe without destroying its own regional trade. But it can, and does, destroy Zimbabwe's shorter and cheaper routes to the sea through Mozambique, thereby seriously undermining the Zimbabwean economy.

History and geography have left the economies of Zimbabwe and South Africa inextricably linked, although Zimbabwe's positive policy of disengagement, partly motivated by economic sense and partly by political reality, seeks to reduce this historical dependence. It embraces the fight to keep the routes through Mozambique open, to find new markets for Zimbabwean exporters and new sources of imports. However, disengagement is costly and requires specific international support including new markets on preferential terms, rescheduling debts, etc. as well as recognition of the costs of South Africa's deliberate actions in what amounts to the imposition of economic sanctions against its neighbours. These additional costs to Zimbabwe, without the areas which remain unquantified, total US$2.84 billion, more than the country's external debt.

The next table seeks to present some of this additional cost to Zimbabwe. However, it does not include a number of areas which cannot be quantified with any certainty: lost investment and tourism, increased prices of goods in Zimbabwe, less competitive exports, additional police and security costs, other incidents of sabotage. missed opportunity for development and so on. If these costs could be added, the total figure would be more than double that given below.

Some Quantifiable Costs to Zimbabwe* of South Africa's Total Strategy Since 1980

	Z$ m	US$ m**
Additional freight costs	1,500.00	824.20
Locomotive hire from SATS	45.14	24.80
Truck losses/costs	12.00	6.60
Fuel losses/pipeline costs	10.50	6.11
Sabotage (quantified)	66.00	91.20
Sabotage (estimated)	40.00	30.00
Refugee maintenance	14.50	8.00
Additional defence costs	2,606.18	1,853.22
TOTAL	4,294.32	2,844.13

* *Where estimates were given, the lowest figure has been used.*
** *At average annual exchange rates.*

3 Zambia

Zambia has been on a more or less permanent war footing since its independence 25 years ago — and no other Frontline State has confronted such a sustained external threat over such a protracted period and across so many frontiers.

The country's long-standing opposition to apartheid and its hosting of all of the main southern African liberation movements at one time or another in their campaigns for independence have made it a prime target for South African military and economic destabilization. So does its current position as chair of the Frontline States grouping, its membership in SADCC, and its determination to redirect its export traffic away from South African routes.

Zambia's geographical position makes it vulnerable to external pressures, as does its political position as host to the headquarters of the African National Congress (ANC) of South Africa. It seems likely that the quadripartite agreement on South African withdrawal from Angola and independence for Namibia, and the ANC's removal of its bases from Angola, while carrying the potential for peace in the Caprivi Strip on Zambia's border, may increase the vulnerability of Zambia to direct SADF attacks as it will remain the only consequential ANC location near to South Africa.

Landlocked and spread across the heart of the hinterland, Zambia borders on eight countries including both of South Africa's major regional military targets, Angola and Mozambique, suffering the resultant overspill, as well as on Namibia's Caprivi Strip where South Africa maintains the largest concentration of military strength in the region. Attacks and sabotage against Zambian targets have been mounted from South African military bases in Caprivi, and dissident groups have also been trained there to infiltrate and disrupt rural areas in western Zambia.

Five of the eight countries which border on Zambia's 5,000-km frontier have been used as bases for aggression by South African-supported colonial regimes or surrogate groups. Thus it is of interest to detail them here showing in each case the length of border to be guarded. Moving clockwise around Zambia, it borders on:

Zaire in the north	1,650 kms
Tanzania in the north-east	295 kms

Malawi in the east	645 kms
Mozambique in the east	430 kms
Zimbabwe in the south	710 kms
Botswana in the south	40 metres
Namibia in the south-west	185 kms
Angola in the west	990 kms

Assassination and Sabotage

Soon after the 1 April 1989 deadline for the start of the transition to independence in Namibia, a vicious campaign began against the ANC in Lusaka. The seeds of disinformation had been sown a few months earlier — before the ink was dry on the accords signed by the United States, South Africa, Cuba and Angola at Geneva, Brazzaville and New York — in stories emanating from London in the Africa specialist press, as well as from government officials in Pretoria. The objective was apparently to show dissension within the senior ranks of the ANC, and to blame later violence on this factor. However, the articles read like carbon copies of those written about the Zimbabwean liberation movements 10 years earlier, and the violence, when it came, was easily traceable to its source.

The opening salvo was on 15 April when two ANC members, including the farm manager, were shot dead at an ANC-operated farm near Lusaka. Witnesses to the double murder identified a recent arrival from South Africa as the man who shot the two while they were watching television at the farm. He was handed over to the Zambian government, who later charged him with murder.

A few days later, two ANC members died after sipping beer, which they said tasted peculiar. Two people who were drinking with them were arrested and charged. Another double murder in Lusaka, involving an ANC member and made to resemble a suicide pact, was soon followed by the death of two more ANC members in a landmine explosion in southern Zambia. All of these incidents occurred within a four-week period, during which time leaflets were circulated in Lusaka calling for the creation of "assembly points" in various countries to facilitate the return to South Africa of "disenchanted" members of the ANC. International radio stations broadcasting to Africa, such as the BBC, suggested that these events were causing a "rift" between the ANC and their host, the Zambian government.

A dramatic, but little publicized, incident occurred in mid-May, one month after the first killing in Lusaka and while Foreign Ministers of the 101-member Non-Aligned Movement were meeting in Zimbabwe. A planeload of ANC members being airlifted from Angola was subjected to an unsuccessful, but violent, hijack attempt as soon as it entered Tanzanian airspace.

A young white man was overpowered before the plane reached Dar es Salaam but after he had seriously injured one of the Soviet flight crew. The man, whose name was given as "Bradley Richard Stacey also known as George Hodges", was tried and sentenced to 15 years in maximum security prison in Tanzania. The court was told he had been carrying TNT, anti-personnel mines and detonators, and that he tried to divert the plane to Johannesburg.

After the events of the previous month, and the disinformation leaflets suggesting that ANC cadres should return home, it is not unreasonable to suppose that the plan called for the Aeroflot plane to land in Johannesburg amid much fanfare and to disgorge the first ANC "returnees" to an appropriate welcome, after which they would have been packed off for interrogation. One publication, *SouthScan*, suggests as much, saying that after the Law and Order Minister hinted at an amnesty for ANC members, "Pretoria would have had little difficulty in portraying it as the voluntary return of 150 ANC dissidents".

The ANC political offices in Lusaka have been a target for many years and bombs have been located near there on several occasions. The most recent incidents occurred in mid-June 1989 when three people were injured by a booby-trapped electrical appliance at an ANC welfare office, another ANC office was damaged in an explosion, and a person carrying a bomb was blown up with it some 400 metres from the main ANC offices near the city centre. These acts of sabotage against "soft" targets do not support South Africa's claim that it is destroying only "terrorist" bases.

Zambia itself has often been the target for clandestine bombings, which have damaged Zambian property and injured Zambian civilians, as well as disrupting the economy by hampering tourism and other related industries. Four Zambians were killed and 14 injured in three such incidents in December 1988 and January 1989. These three incidents occurred at hotels/bars open to the general public and the dead were all Zambians.

The following chart shows some incidents of this type of sabotage over a three-year period.

Known Incidents of Bombings and Other Sabotage
December 1985 to January 1989

Date	Incident
29 Jan 89	A bomb at the Bush Baby Bar near Livingstone killed a young Zambian women.
24 Jan 89	A bomb at Livingstone's Windsor Hotel killed one Zambian and injured another.
2 Dec 88	A massive car bomb exploded in a land-cruiser with Red Cross markings parked beside the crowded verandah of

a Livingstone tourist hotel, the North-Western, killing two Zambians and injuring 13. In the previous nine days, two civilians died in two other incidents: a car bomb outside a hotel in Lusaka and another bomb near a camp for South African refugees.

Aug 88	A powerful explosion ripped through another Lusaka suburb, Olympia Extension, injuring five people and damaging three houses.
June 88	A bomb exploded in a house in Libala, near Lusaka, narrowly missing a Zambian family of eight.
Sept 87	A Zambian postal worker was killed and 7 others injured when a parcel bomb exploded as they were offloading international mail onto a Zambia Railways wagon, destroying the truck and the mail. A second postal worker died later in hospital.
Sept 87	A bomb, planted under a parked vehicle near a bar in a Lusaka township, exploded injuring four people.
Feb 87	An explosion in a suburban post office caused extensive damage but no casualties.
Dec 86	Two explosions in Livingstone destroyed an electricity sub-station and damaged a railway office.
Dec 85	A letter bomb addressed to ANC headquarters exploded seriously injuring a party member.

Published sources and Ministry of Defence.

The above list of bombing incidents, which occurred mostly in 1988, and the events of the April/May 1989 mentioned previously, indicate a tactical shift to covert activities from the more overt actions of 1986 and 1987.

Direct Attacks

Zambia has been subjected to direct commando attacks by the South African military, near Lusaka and in the southern border town of Livingstone, which is very near Namibia's Caprivi Strip. The target for these raids has been Zambian civilians and property or South African civilians, although the victims are almost always presented in the South African press as a military threat. The attacks are timed for internal consumption within South Africa and often appear to be conducted on the basis of sheer terrorism.

On 25 April 1987, 11 days before a general election in South Africa, an attack in the southern border town of Livingstone signalled the start of an escalation of violence across the region. A small group of SADF commandos, apparently flown by helicopter from an airbase in the Caprivi Strip less than 50 km away and entering Livingstone on motorcycles, shot dead two unarmed watchmen at a central office building belonging to the Zambian National Provident Fund, then moved on to the nearby township of Dambwa. There they blew up a house, killing two Zambian brothers in their beds and seriously injuring a woman, a niece of the then Zambian Minister of Defence, General Malimba Masheke.

These facts went largely unreported in the severely restricted South African press which presented it as a victory over ANC "terrorists". SADF acknowledged the operation, describing it as a "reconnaissance patrol" which had encountered the "terrorists". Pretoria also claimed that a weapons store had been destroyed. None of the details of this version were borne out by local eyewitnesses, Zambian government or diplomatic sources.

The South African Minister of Defence accused the ANC of grouping forces in Zambia and Zimbabwe to infiltrate through Botswana to disrupt the elections, and said cross-border "reconnaissance" operations would continue. President Kaunda and other Frontline leaders described the operation as "pandering" to right-wing voters, and the attack was internationally condemned as an election ploy.

Namibia has been used as a springboard for this and other South African incursions into Zambia, from SADF bases in the Caprivi Strip which juts like a bayonet across Zambia's south-western border, separating it from Botswana. Thus, while Zambia does not share a common border with South Africa, it does in effect because of Pretoria's occupation of Namibia. It is no coincidence that the part of Zambia most affected by direct South African military actions is the area around Sesheke, close to the Namibian border, stretching north-west to the Senanga sector.

This area has been subject to tension from 1964 and, apart from espionage activities and the planting of landmines in Zambia which have killed civilians, there have been frequent ground, water and airspace violations of Zambian territory. The most serious and protracted incident occurred in early 1978 when South African forces occupied the area for five weeks before they were driven out by the Zambian Defence Forces.

The continuing tension in the area, and particularly the possibility of being confronted by the SADF or stepping on landmines, has disrupted local life. SADF domination of this part of the Zambezi river has also forced the suspension of cheap water transport from Katima-Mulilo to Mambova near Livingstone. However, direct South African aggression against Zambia has not been confined to the extreme south-west of the country.

During the first eight months of 1986, Zambian airspace was violated at least a dozen times, as shown by the chart below. This coincided with the presence in southern Africa of the Commonwealth Eminent Persons Group (EPG), which abruptly ended its mission after an open South African attack on three Commonwealth capitals in the region, including Lusaka, on 19 May. Two South African bomber aircraft, operating from a base in Caprivi, attacked a UNHCR refugee centre in the Makeni suburb of Lusaka killing two people, injuring five and causing extensive damage to property.

The attack was "vigorously condemned" by Washington and described as "a plain violation of sovereignty" by the British Foreign Secretary, "particularly deplorable". The EPG concluded that Pretoria had been planning these armed attacks even while meeting the group to talk about peaceful solutions, and that "apartheid South Africa poses a wide threat well beyond its borders."

Direct Attacks and Border Violations
March 1986 to March 1989*

Date	Incident
2 Mar 88	Speedboat armed with mortars and carrying 5 men in military uniform anchored in Zambian waters opposite Mwandi hospital.
12 Jan 88	SADF troop in Caprivi Strip shot dead 2 Zambian civilians and injured another suspected of illegal crossing.
20 Jun 87	Three SADF soldiers in a speedboat violated Zambian waters, shot dead a bull, wounded 2 cows near Kazuni village.
25 Apr 87	SADF soldier and his wife, both Portuguese nationals resident in Namibia, violated Zambian waters using a speedboat near Katimo-Mulilo and were apprehended.
25 Apr 87	SADF commandos raided Livingstone, killing 4 Zambians and wounding one.
1 Jan 87	SADF section in civilian clothes crossed into Zambia in Katongo area near Sesheke, wounded one man whom they abducted.
30 Aug 86	Helicopter violated airpsace near Mwandi.
25 Aug 86	SA jet fighter violated airpsace flying west to east at high altitude near Sesheke.
13 Aug 86	SA jet fighter violated airspace flying west to east at very high altitude near Sinjembela.
25 Jul 86	Two SA jet fighters violated airpsace flying from south to north near Sesheke.
20 Jul 86	SA jet fighter violated airspace flying west to east at very high altitude near Sesheke.
16 Jul 86	SA military aircraft violated airspace flying from east to west at very high altitude.
24 May 86	SA spotter plane seen flying around Senange Boma at high altitude, later flew west towards Angola.
5 May 86	Two SA jet fighters and spotter plane violated air-space flying east to west near Katima-Mulilo.
29 Apr 86	SA helicopter flew along Zambezi river from west to east near Katima-Mulilo.
10 Apr 86	SA jet fighter violated airspace flying from south to north at very high altitude near Sesheke.

| 5 Apr 86 | Two SA jet fighters violated airspace flying at very high altitude near Kazungula. |
| 24 Mar 86 | SA military aircraft overflew Sinjembela flying from north to south at very high altitude, and same plane was later seen landing in Angola. |

* The 1988/89 reduction in direct action against Zambia coincided with an escalation in covert activity such as bombings, espionage and disinformation. The drop in airspace violations coincidedwith an improvement in Angola's air defences, preventing South African aircraft from flying into that country's airspace.

Source: Ministry of Defence

Espionage

As well as the shadowy network of operatives currently being activated against the ANC in Lusaka and elsewhere, South Africa sometimes uses individual agents or travellers to glean information or prepare for sabotage. A spin-off effect of such action is that it acts as a sanction on tourism in the Frontline States and causes general suspicion. Following the May 1986 attack, several European tourists were arrested for questioning in Zambia, and, soon after the Livingstone attack, eight South African tourists were arrested in Zimbabwe while taking photographs of the Kariba dam. The following provides a few examples of suspected agents who have been caught.

In December 1986, after two explosions in Livingstone destroyed an electricity sub-station and damaged the railway station, Zambian authorities arrested a Briton, an Australian and a New Zealander on suspicion of being South African agents. The first two were released after two weeks but the third, who was arrested while assembling a nine-hour-delay time bomb in Lusaka's elite Kabulonga suburb, was sentenced to two years hard labour after pleading guilty to possession of the bomb.

Four young South Africans arrested after the 19 May raids in 1986, and released a year later, said they had been recruited by South African security after planning a holiday trip to Zambia. Another South African was arrested the same month, accused of being on a mission to blow up an ANC house.

Three members of the Zambian air force based at Livingstone air-base, and a businessman, appeared in court in July 1987 charged with spying for South Africa between September 1986 and May 987. This covers the period of the 25 April pre-election attack.

A self-confessed South African spy, Olivia Forsyth, whom ANC officials recognized very early on, was arrested in Zambia in mid-1986, soon after leaving South Africa, and transferred by the ANC to Angola. Forsyth, a dual citizen of Britain and South Africa, "escaped" two years later and sought refuge in the British embassy in Luanda for six months before being expelled from Angola in late 1988.

Three days before a meeting of the eight Commonwealth Foreign Ministers on Southern Africa in Harare in February 1989 — and the release of the preliminary version of this report identifying Ms Forsyth as an agent — the South African security police went public, confirming that she is one of their agents, "RS 407", and giving her version of her detention by the ANC. Admitting to be a captain in the security police who had infiltrated several campus organizations in South Africa, she stated that her main external mission had been to sow disinformation and dissent, and that the ratio of truth to fiction was about 30:70. The same could be said of her subsequent statement to the press, which was accompanied by demure photographs and read as if it had been written by a committee. One South African newspaper headlined the story, "The Forsyth Saga".

Surrogate Groups

The pattern of using surrogate groups against a sovereign government is repeated in Zambia, which is vulnerable on its western and eastern borders as well as its southern frontier with the Caprivi Strip. Furthermore, evidence of the training of dissidents for the purposes of destabilization dates back, as it does in Angola and Mozambique, to the Portuguese colonial days when some Zambians were given military training by the Portuguese in eastern Angola.

Zambia's western border with Angola, almost 1,000 km, is too long and too remote to protect from infiltration, and has been used on occasion as a supply route from South Africa for Unita. During the siege of Cuito Cuanavale in south-eastern Angola in late 1987 and early 1988, when Unita's supply routes by land from South Africa were disrupted, Zambian security forces were deployed in Western province to prevent its use as a supply route.

From 4 February 1986 to 19 October 1988 a total of 15 border incidents involving Unita were recorded by the Zambian Ministry of Defence. At least one Zambian was killed in these incursions, a number wounded or abducted and cattle rustled. In one incident in late 1988, a Unita group crossed into Zambia and addressed Angolan refugees. Many other incidents of abduction and harassment of civilians in remote areas go unrecorded.

During the Portuguese colonial period, Zambia faced two threats on this front. One was the incursions by Portuguese armed forces. The second came from a Portuguese surrogate movement, inherited by South Africa after the 1974 coup d'etat in Lisbon. This came to be known as the Mushala Terrorist Gang, named after its leader Adamson Mushala, a former game ranger from North-Western province.

From 1973 this group received some training and equipment from the Portuguese military in Angola who — like the Rhodesians in the case of the MNR — hoped to use them for intelligence gathering in Zambia.

Mushala's group was inherited by South Africa on the eve of Angola's independence, as was the MNR on the eve of Zimbabwe's independence five years later. They were given training at Zulu Camp in Namibia by the SADF and returned to North-Western province in 1976 where they carried out a campaign of banditry, terrorizing the local population until Mushala was killed by Zambian security forces in November 1982.

Zambian youths crossing into Namibia's Caprivi Strip to visit relatives or to look for work have reported being conscripted into the SADF-commanded guard force, and there has been evidence for well over a decade of South African military training of Zambian dissidents in the Caprivi Strip.

In October 1986, at the same time as the massive MNR offensive into the centre-north of Mozambique and a South African invasion of southern Angola, President Kaunda announced that the SADF was training 2,000 dissidents to invade the country. He said they had mobilized the remnants of the Mushala gang, and noted that the problem was serious and difficult to resolve, because it had taken eight years to corner Mushala. The Zambia *Daily Mail* said these revelations followed the formation of an underground political organization in South Africa calling itself the United Freedom Movement for Zambia. President Kaunda referred to this again a year later when, just before leaving for the Commonwealth summit in Vancouver, he accused South Africa of sending bands of trained Zambians into the country to overthrow the government.

South African-backed surrogates in Mozambique are also active against Zambia, and if their border crossings were accidental there would have been evidence of this activity several years ago. The MNR raids into Zambia's Eastern province began in March 1987, just three months before cross-border attacks into eastern Zimbabwe were launched on the orders of a South African brigadier.

Throughout 1987 there were minor cross-border raids and sightings, which involved molesting of the local population, abduction, cattle rustling, etc. by individuals or small groups armed with old-fashioned muzzle loaders or AK-47 assault rifles.

The first reported killing of a Zambian national occurred on 20 December 1987 when a large group of over 20 MNR attacked a border immigration post and a cooperative store, both in Chadiza district. The attackers, who on this occasion were well-armed, destroyed the immigration office, looted homes, abducted 8 people and set alight a landrover. The attack on the cooperative appeared to be the work of the same group, who were armed with light machineguns, AK-47 rifles and rocket launchers. The store was looted, money stolen, and a van and a motorcycle burnt. More than 100 people were abducted, as many as 1,000 left homeless, and 300 head of cattle were stolen, along with a quantity of maize. One man was shot dead. A poster of the MNR's leader, Dhlakama, was left near the body together with copies of an open letter to the Zambian government saying the attacks would continue until Lusaka stopped supporting the government in Mozambique.

These incidents escalated through 1988, following a similar pattern of theft of maize and cattle, destruction of housing, looting, abduction and murder. Women are often raped or abducted, and anti-personnel mines planted inside Zambia by the MNR have maimed several villagers. The Zambian security forces have lost only one soldier while the high figure of well over 100 captured MNR includes many suspected collaborators.

The Zambian government had faced similar incidents when Mozambique was still a colony and there were a number of incursions by Portuguese troops. However, the hope in Lusaka was that the independence of the Portuguese colonies in 1975 would remove these threats on its eastern and western borders. This was to prove a vain hope. Instead, another surrogate movement, the MNR, inherited by South Africa from Rhodesia, has become a new instrument of aggression against Zambia.

Recorded MNR Cross-border Attacks
March 1987 to May 1989

Year	Incidents	Dead	Wounded	Abducted	Huts Burnt	Cattle Rustled	Shops Looted
1989 (5 months)	21	44	12	13	152	121	9
1988	88	30	28	36	9	298	12
1987	24	1	1	122	—	419+	7
TOTAL	133	75	41	171+	161	838+	28

Source: Ministry of Defence.

The pattern of MNR atrocities against innocent Zambian civilians carries all of the hallmarks of brutality which have become all too familiar in Mozambique and along Zimbabwe's eastern border. This is illustrated by the following examples, of which there are many more:

- 18 August 1988: Five people were killed in three villages. One of the victims was a sick old woman who was tied and burnt in her hut. The other four, including a baby only a few weeks old, were axed to death. At another village nearby, 12 people, including children, had their heads smashed;

- 18 May 1988: Seven MNR bandits, armed with sub-machineguns and axes, axed 13 civilians. Eight civilians died immediately and the others were fatally wounded;
- 1 March 1988: Two MNR bandits and two MNR youth found Mr Cosmas James Mbewe of Chagumuka village. . . . They cut off his ear and sent him to report to the Zambian authorities.

The Zambian army conducts follow-up operations and has expanded its role in the area from defensive to offensive action. In May 1988, the Ministry of Defence said the army had pursued raiders 19 km into Mozambique's Tete province after an attack, killing 73 men and destroying two bases, the most extensive Zambian operation to date against the MNR.

Although there were a large number of incidents in 1988, many were sightings or capture of individual MNR collaborators. The attacks to date in 1989 are larger and more daring, resulting in a higher number of casualties, burning of more huts and granaries, looting of shops, etc. and escalating in a similar pattern to the attacks across Zimbabwe's eastern border. The number of deaths resulting from MNR attacks in the first five months of 1989 is already 50 per cent higher than the total for the whole of 1988, and the number of huts destroyed has increased 20 times.

It is noteworthy that the MNR in this remote area of Tete province used muzzle loaders and axes through 1988 and operated in small groups, except for one or two major attacks. Yet in 1989 the reports are substantively different, with attacks on military posts as well as villages. Witnesses often describe large groups of well-armed assailants carrying sub-machineguns and rocket launchers, suggesting a fresh supply of armaments.

Some examples are as follows:

- 13 February 1989: Attack on Chikalawa primary school by MNR group armed with small arms, rocket launchers, mortars and machineguns, killing 3 people including the headmistress, wounding her deputy and several others. A family with 5 children disappeared.
- 16 April 1989: In an MNR attack on Kafumbwe village in Katete district, they split into three groups to loot shops, a health centre, and attack a 10-man military post.
- 21 May 1989: Between 30 and 40 men armed with AK-47s and stick grenades attacked Chilowe village, burning 39 huts and 24 granaries, and exchanging fire with Zambian troops.
- 27 May 1989: During a raid on Kwenani village near Vubwi in which 6 people were killed, a villager shot dead one of the

attackers who had on him a sub-machinegun, 4 magazines and 99 rounds of ammunition.

Among the five neighbouring countries from whose territory Zambia has faced external aggression, the odd one out is Zaire. The border with Zaire is the longest and the most difficult to patrol. A piece of Zairean territory, called the Pedicle, punches hard into Zambia's vulnerable belly of the copperbelt.

The main supply road to some parts of northern Zambia must pass through this part of Zairean territory, where smuggling and violence are rife. Cross-border incidents have been largely a result of in-disciplined Zairean troops and widespread smuggling. Nevertheless, this has forced Zambia into a greater defence commitment on its longest and northern border, always with the potential for greater disruption.

In addition, the airbase in Zaire at Kamina, from which military supplies are ferried to Unita in Angola, is very near the meeting point of the borders of Angola, Zaire and Zambia.

The High Cost of Survival

Prior to Zimbabwe's independence in April 1980, Zambia's southern border marked the frontier between independent and settler-dominated Africa, a frontier that Olaf Palme, then Prime Minister of Sweden, called the "boundary of human decency".

Zambia has paid, and continues to pay, an awesome price for those 15 years of confrontation on its southern border, but quantifying this cost is not easy. It pervades every sector of the economy and every facet of human life in Zambia to this day, through foreign exchange constraints, high prices and shortages of essential commodities, and lost investment and development opportunities.

Only a year after Zambia's independence, and just prior to the Unilateral Declaration of Independence (UDI) by the British colony of Southern Rhodesia in November 1965, Rhodesia began to squeeze Zambia economically by blocking petroleum imports while building up its own stocks. High freight rates were imposed which Zambia had to pay in foreign currency, amid demands that a large percentage of Zambia's copper must transit Rhodesia in return for allowing imports through.

This economic pressure from Rhodesia forced Zambia to make three very costly decisions concerning diversification of its trans-portation routes. One of these decisions was the upgrading of the Tanzania-Zambia Highway to provide access by road to and from Indian Ocean ports in East Africa. The second decision was con-struction of the Tanzania-Zambia Railway linking Kapiri Mposhi to the port of Dar es Salaam. The third was construction of the Tanzania-Zambia oil pipeline.

The new railway cost almost US$500 million and repayment of the interest-free long-term loan from China is shared equally by Zambia and Tanzania. The 1710-km pipeline, constructed in only 17 months, cost 36 million kwacha, of which Zambia is responsible for repayment of two-thirds and Tanzania one-third. The pipeline carried refined fuel until a refinery was built at Ndola in Zambia and six storage tanks in Dar es Salaam port. This cost an additional US$25 million, and the pipeline now carries all of Zambia's fuel. There was also the cost of upgrading the Zambian section of what was then a dirt road to Dar es Salaam and the purchase of a fleet of trucks.

Added to this was the cost of the brief, but vastly expensive, airlift of Zambia's vital copper exports as well as petroleum and other imports, additional freight bills for hauling cargo to and from East Africa by road, disruption of economic planning, and expansion of the defence sector to cope with the threat from the south. It seems probable that the cost to Zambia as it was forced to respond to the Rhodesian settlers' rebellion was well in excess of US$1 billion by the early 1970s.

The first seven years after UDI were characterized by vast economic costs to Zambia against a backdrop of falling prices for copper, which accounted for over 90 per cent of exports by value — and the ever-present threat of Rhodesian aggression. A second cycle of economic and social cost began in December 1972 when, after a fitful beginning in the 1960s, the decisive phase of the Zimbabwean nationalist struggle began with an attack on a farm in north-eastern Rhodesia. Seven years to the day later, on 21 December 1979, the Lancaster House agreement ended the Rhodesian conflict, paving the way to Zimbabwe's independence.

Quantifying the economic and social cost to Zambia in this phase is as difficult as doing so in the first and third phases. Countries confronted by military, economic and social threats have greater priorities than keeping a daily record of the sort of statistical data that researchers subsequently demand. However, at the time of the cease-fire in December 1979, Zambia had survived 14 years of economic and military pressure from the South African-supported minority regime in Rhodesia, as well as the overspill of the liberation wars which began in Angola in 1961 and in Mozambique in 1964, one month before Zambia's independence.

After Rhodesia closed the border in 1973, UN officials estimated the direct cost to Zambia in the first two years was almost 200 million kwacha (approximately US$250 million), only 20 per cent of which was met by international aid.

This second phase took a considerable social and economic toll on Zambia, which faced direct military aggression for the first time.

Rhodesian cross-border raids and aerial attacks killed many hundreds of people, Zambians as well as Zimbabwean nationalists. The exact number of casualties is not known, nor is the economic cost of the destruction caused in this phase. Nevertheless, there are verifiable details which illustrate the cost.

The Rhodesians and/or South Africans destroyed 9 Zambian road bridges near the end of this period, of which the cost of repair was 9 million kwacha (US$11.42 million at the exchange rate of 1979). An important point about those sabotages, which is similar to South African sabotage of regional routes today, is where they occurred.

The most important sabotage, accounting for over half the total repair bill, occurred at the Chambeshi bridge in Zambia's Northern province. The repairs cost 4.82 million kwacha (US$6 million), and the attack cut Zambia's only independent route to the sea through Dar es Salaam. Five bridges were destroyed in Southern province in one night at the end of 1979, cutting links to the south during the Lancaster House conference.

The Lancaster Agreement, and Zimbabwe's independence in April 1980, marked the beginning of a third phase for Zambia, characterized by easing of some economic pressures and disruption of others. This marked the first occasion when the independence of a neighbouring country actually ended the cross-border raids which Zambia had been suffering. In theory, the long period of aggression was over, but in practice it resumed with a vengeance in other guises.

Transportation and Trade

Zimbabwe's independence meant the reopening of the route to Beira which had been unavailable since Mozambique closed its border with Rhodesia in 1976. Thus Zambia has access to two operational regional routes to Dar es Salaam and Beira, as well as those through South Africa, and has diverted all of its vital exports of copper and imports of fertilizer away from the latter.

This aspect has not necessarily been costly because these are the shortest routes to the sea for Zambia's trade — and normally the cheapest, in the absence of rate-cutting by the South African Transport Services (SATS). Furthermore, Zambian agencies can pay in kwacha for shipments by rail to Dar es Salaam, although those through Beira must be paid for in foreign exchange.

However, South Africa and its surrogates have targeted Zambia's other potential regional routes through Angola and Mozambique — and the Beira route is heavily defended by the Zimbabwe National Army. The route to Maputo, which is a few km shorter than Beira due to the connecting lines in Zimbabwe, has been out of operation since it was sabotaged in 1984. The railway to Nacala, which Zambia had hoped to reach by road link through Malawi, has also been out of operation since 1984 due to sabotage.

Distance to Port by Rail

Port	To/from: Lusaka	Kapiri Mposhi
Dar es Salaam, Tanzania	2045 km	1860 km
Maputo, Mozambique	2020 km	2205 km
Beira, Mozambique	2025 km	2210 km
Lobito, Angola	2679 km	2494 km
Durban, South Africa	2751 km	2936 km
East London, South Africa	2871 km	3056 km

The Benguela Railway

The Benguela railway through Zaire to Angola's Atlantic coast is the shortest route to Europe from Zambia's "copperbelt" and Zaire's mineral-rich Shaba province. But the railway has been unable to carry normal transit traffic across central Angola to the port of Lobito since 1975, due to war and sabotage.

Between 1967 and 1974, the freight traffic to Lobito from Zambia and Zaire rose 75 per cent to 1.59 million tons per annum, then ground to a complete halt after South Africa's invasion of Angola in 1975. The 1,400-km section of the railway within Angola was formally reopened to international traffic in 1978, but carried only a trickle and had stopped again by 1982. In 1985 the railway carried just over 260,000 tons of freight, all of domestic Angolan origin, just over 10 per cent of its pre-independence peak of 2.3 million tons.

The loss of the Lobito route has cost Zambia dearly in that it should be the shortest, fastest and cheapest route to Europe for exports of copper and other minerals. Since it is an Atlantic port, Zambia's copper exports would reach European markets several days earlier using this route, and Zambia would receive payment more quickly. Shipping agents in Lusaka say that Lobito could cut transit time for Zambian exports, and even some imports, by as much as 50 per cent and freight rates by 20-30 per cent. For the same reasons, one major shipping agent, hoping to offer an alternative Atlantic port, has plans for a truck route to Walvis Bay, which is 200 km shorter than Durban.

A major project in the SADCC transport sector is rehabilitation of the Benguela railway as part of a multi-faceted "Lobito corridor" programme. The cost estimate for this rehabilitation is US$ 280 million and it is expected to be funded primarily by the EEC and the owners of the line, Societe Generale of Belgium. The "Lobito corridor" programme is a three-phase project over 10 years with a total projected cost of $530 million, including modernization of the facilities at Lobito port, power lines, telecommunications and road works.

Despite the sabotage of its main trade routes, Zambia has made a concerted effort to redirect exports away from South Africa to regional ports. For the past two years, 80 per cent of copper exports have been sent through Dar es Salaam and 20 per cent through Beira. None have gone through South Africa. Non-regional imports also come via Dar es Salaam, representing over half of the total. In 1988, all fertilizer imports transited Dar es Salaam, although this may be diversified in future to prevent reliance on a single route.

In contrast to Zambia's purposeful diversion of its copper exports to alternative SADCC ports, mineral exports from Zaire's Shaba province continue to transit South Africa. In 1987, 43 per cent of Shaba's minerals used this route at an additional freight cost that must be substantial. The shortest route for these minerals from southern Zaire is also the Benguela railway to Lobito. The next shortest routes would be through Zambia to Dar es Salaam or through Zambia/Zimbabwe to Beira.

The Tanzania-Zambia Railway

Many, if not all, of southern Africa's railways were developed for political, rather than solely economic, reasons. The route through Ressano Garcia to then Lourenco Marques is a case in point. It was built 100 years ago to free the Boer Republics of dependence on railways and ports under British control.

The arch-colonizer, Cecil Rhodes, tried to prevent that railway being built by attempting to buy Delagoa Bay (now Maputo). However, his dreams of conquest lay elsewhere — in a Cape to Cairo railway linking the colonies of the British empire. According to his plan, part of this railway would be a line through Zambia (then Northern Rhodesia) to Tanzania (then Tanganyika) and onwards.

Sixty years after Rhodes's death in 1902, that part of the dream was revived by a then little-known nationalist leader, Kenneth Kaunda, who said in early 1963: "This railway is a political necessity. Even after Rhodesia wins majority rule, there will still be Mozambique and South Africa between us and the sea." A quarter of a century later — with Zimbabwe independent and Mozambique's rail routes devastated — the political, and economic, sense of this railway is ever more apparent.

Strenuous objections were raised against building the 1860-km railway from Dar es Salaam to Kapiri Mposhi. International consultants, UN agencies, the US and other Western governments, the World Bank, and others dismissed the proposal as a "white elephant". Zambia, they argued, should continue to depend on existing routes through colonized and minority-ruled Angola, Mozambique, Rhodesia and South Africa.

At the time, given Zambia's vulnerability, this seemed an extra-ordinary argument. With the wisdom of hindsight it was an amazingly blinkered and shortsighted view that failed to consider the probable, and now factual, realities of southern Africa's landlocked hinterland.

A 1965 report by the Washington-based Brookings Institute, prepared for the US Agency for International Development, stated: "No argument couched in economic terms has so far moved the Zambian Government to abandon its political goal of freeing itself from dependence on rail routes which run through countries at present dominated by white minority governments. Perhaps it is too much to expect any nation to remain vulnerable in such a fashion if any way can be found, however expensive, to avoid it."

Later that year, the late Chinese Premier, Chou En-lai, visited Dar es Salaam. His country, he said in private conversations, might be willing to help. Eight weeks later, a Chinese technical team of 12 people arrived to survey the proposed Tanzanian section of the railway. Kaunda and Nyerere continued to pursue the Western option and the British Prime Minister, Harold Wilson, and the Canadian government financed a parallel study. The Western argument con-tinued to be that the southern routes were adequate and secure, but if Zambia needed an alternative route (which they doubted), it should be a road — not rail — link to Dar es Salaam.

Finally, in the face of continued Western vacillation, Tanzania and Zambia signed an agreement with China in September 1967 under which Peking gave a 30-year interest free loan to build what becme known as The Great Uhuru Railway — The Freedom Railway — linking Dar es Salaam to Zambia's copperbelt. (The official name is Tanzania-Zambia Railway.) The agreement, China's biggest aid project anywhere in the world, was greeted with astonishment in Western capitals, leading to a campaign of disinformation which included a claim that the Chinese could not fulfil their promise.

The railway was completed in 1976, ahead of schedule, and pressed into service over part of its length the previous year after the failure of the Victoria Falls talks on Rhodesia, and the South African invasion of southern Angola, meant continued uncertainty for Zambia's main southern and western routes. South Africa's then Foreign Minister, Dr Hilgard Muller, described China's involvement, and the railway itself, as a "threat".

The line has not been without problems, caused by poor main-tenance, port congestion, and a shortage of rolling stock as a result of severe financial constraints a few years ago. However, action has been taken to improve these difficulties and, since 1984, Tazara has shown an after-tax profit. The upgrading of this line is a priority for SADCC and a 10-year development programme costing $157 million, approved in 1985, will focus on replacement of rolling stock, track improvement, training, and revision of tariffs and other financial structures.

The Great Uhuru Railway remains a vital contribution to Zambia's survival and, bearing in mind South Africa's role in the destruction of the region's transportation network, this is the sole route upon which the region can count for its survival.

Transport Diplomacy

South Africa has used the regional transport networks to exert economic pressure on Zambia, directly and indirectly, and this mixture of military aggression and what amounts to economic sanctions is characteristic of Pretoria's policy toward its neighbours.

As seen above, the indirect method, through use of surrogate groups to sabotage regional routes is an effective means of disrupting the region's trade, yet cost-effective for Pretoria, and also profitable in terms of the freight diverted to southern routes. The direct methods of transport pressure are more obvious, and often less profitable in that they may also disrupt Pretoria's income. The following are but a few examples.

Zambia, like Zimbabwe, remains vulnerable to provision of rolling stock for its railways, with an average of 2,200 South African wagons in use on the Zambia/Zaire railway system. In addition, there are 42 locomotives hired from the South African Transport Services. Threat of withdrawal or delays in provision are an subtle means of causing uncertainty from time to time.

Another form of economic pressure appeared in mid-August 1986, in retaliation for Zambia's anti-apartheid and pro-sanctions position at a Commonwealth mini-summit a few days earlier. South African customs introduced a levy on freight destined for Zambia, and demanded cash deposits from carriers. The Zambian Foreign Minister accused South Africa of imposing sanctions against its neighbours. Vital mining equipment, which was being repaired in South Africa, was held up, as well as imports. A similar deposit scheme on transit goods to the north was enforced by Pretoria in 1984 until early 1985.

South Africa has often threatened to retaliate by disrupting trade flows, and has backed this up with action by delaying shipments of maize and other grains, and also fertilizer at the critical planting time, thus disrupting Zambia's own production, causing it to import more food. Zambia took this action seriously enough to divert its fertilizer imports to other regional ports.

Although dependent on South Africa for as much as 40 per cent of imports by value, due to speed of delivery and attractive credit terms, alternative sources such as Zimbabwe are getting more orders from

Zambia as the business community slowly "disengages" from the apartheid economy.

Tourism

Livingstone, and nearby Victoria Falls, is Zambia's major tourist area, and government officials and private operators involved in this foreign-currency generating industry are in no doubt that recent attacks on two hotels and a popular bar in the area were calculated to undermine tourism.

Tourists are sensitive to media reports which suggest they could be in danger and simply remove such areas from their itinerary. Those who do come are discouraged by the sight of military roadblocks, necessitated by the regional security situation, particularly between Lusaka and Victoria Falls.

Soldiers, on the alert for would-be saboteurs posing as tourists, are, in the circumstances of southern Africa, insensitive to the bona fide tourist who innocently takes a picture of a strategic bridge. South African agents posing as tourists have been arrested in Zambia, Zimbabwe and Botswana. This has the dual effect of being a good cover because the host country does not wish to offend genuine visitors, and at the same time sowing suspicion about foreigners. Letters to the Zambia National Tourist Board from potential, or actually aggrieved, tourists illustrate the effectiveness of this strategy.

Statistics supplied by the Tourist Board show the impact of the regional security situation on tourism. Just after the end of the war in Rhodesia, when there was comparative peace in the region, the number of visitors to Zambia increased dramatically — from 86,931 visitors in 1980 to 146,649 in 1981. However, in 1982, with dissident activity in south-western Zimbabwe and an escalating war in Mozambique, the number fell to 118,627. That has remained roughly the annual figure, with the potential shown in 1981 not being reached again.

Zambia's tourist potential is inhibited by a further factor — poaching. A decade ago the Luangwa National Park contained 100,000 elephants. The park is famous for its "foot safaris" and still attracts tourists, but the number of elephants has dropped to 30,000, as a result of poachers seeking ivory. A key question about this plunder of natural resources is — who has been marketing the poached ivory? An answer began to emerge in 1988 when a South African citizen, Antonio Augusto Vieira, appeared in court in Botswana after customs officials discovered 700 kg of ivory and 94 rhino horns, together with some cobalt and copper, hidden in compartments of a truck travelling from Zambia to South Africa. Vieira told the magistrate that he had arranged delivery of the goods to two Johannesburg dealers, one with outlets in Hong Kong and Taiwan. The number of surviving rhinos has dropped to a few thousand and 94 horns represents a large haul.

Testimony to a US Congressional sub-committee hearing in 1988 by 14 American conservation groups produced evidence that South Africa is the funnel for tusks from the region — and for trophies of other endangered species stretching as far north as Burundi. Thus, another valuable resource and revenue generator is being destroyed, while the shortage of tourist dollars means a shortage of funds for combating poachers and preserving Zambia's physical and animal resources. So the vicious circle continues.

Refugees

In common with all of the Frontline States, refugees have placed an additional burden on Zambia, particularly those fleeing the South African-inspired wars on its borders. Statistics compiled by the Zambian Commission for Refugees and the United Nations High Commission for Refugees show the total number of refugees in Zambia at the end of 1988 as 143,000, and Zambian figures for the end of January 1989 show an increase of 2,000 over this number. The figures for January show that 107,000 of these were "spontaneously settled" which means they are not in camps but are scattered along border areas, although this is not encouraged for security reasons. Some 35,000 had been allocated land in refugee camps in eastern and western Zambia, and 2,660 are registered urban refugees.

Just over 93,000 of the total are Angolans, some of whom arrived before that country's independence and are now self-sufficient. A further 27,000 are Mozambicans, very recent arrivals. The remainder are from Zaire, South Africa, Namibia, Malawi, Uganda and elsewhere.

Refugees in Zambia by Country
December 1988

Country of Origin	Number	Location	Land Allocated
Angola	93,214	75,337 spontaneously settled	
		17,877 at Maheba, Mayukwayukwa	40,500 hec.
Other	791	also at Maheba camp	
Mozambique	27,000	14,144 spontaneously settled	
		12,856 at Ukwimi camp	12,000 hec.
Zaire	9,000	spontaneously settled	
South Africa	3,000	urban and rural	
Namibia	7,300	5,000 at Nyangu camp	
Other	2,660	urban, mostly professionals	
TOTAL	142,965		52,500 hec.

Source: Zambia Commission for Refugees and UNHCR.

Within the Frontline States, the policies and treatment of refugees varies, due in part to security considerations. In some cases, policies are geared towards preventing the refugees from thinking of themselves as permanent settlers as opposed to people who have been given temporary asylum until the security, or political, situation allows them to go home.

Within this context, Zambia has been particularly generous in its acceptance of them. A total of 52,500 hectares of land has been allocated formally to refugee settlements and a further 3,000 hectares has been requested by the commission for the 1989 expansion of Ukwimi camp for Mozambicans.

The earliest refugee arrivals in the late 1960s were allocated five hectares of land per family unit of five, double the standard UNHCR figure. In 1986, as a result of mounting land pressure and plans to resettle those along the border into camps for security reasons, this was reduced to 2.5 hectares per family, after a survey showed that some of the land was not being utilized. Today the figure for Mozambicans at Ukwimi camp is two hectares per family unit. Although the allocated land will revert to the state, if and when the refugees can go home, Zambia bears a number of other direct costs such as construction and maintenance of schools and clinics, payment of salaries for teachers and other personnel, purchase of medicines, etc.

The Commission for Refugees was established soon after independence in 1964, in the Ministry of Home Affairs, and by 1986 the office had a budget of half a million kwacha for water pumps, vehicles, liaison, administration, etc. Other costs involve as many as six different ministries and parastatals, and the difficulty of quantifying them is compounded by the fact that resources are shared. Zambia does not isolate refugees from the local population and at Maheba camp, for example, the secondary-school student population is 75 per cent refugees and 25 per cent Zambians.

Apart from the cost, the presence of large numbers of refugees brings other problems. One is security, protecting them from armed gangs such as the MNR which raid across borders seeking "recruits" and loot. This means that the refugees must be moved a safe distance away from the frontier. A further security problem is screening the genuine refugees from those who pose as refugees, seeking food or information.

There can also be health and environmental problems. Some of the refugees bring disease-carrying livestock with them from war zones where vaccination campaigns have long ceased. Furthermore, such large concentrations of refugees can have a devastating impact on the ecology where they are settled, leading to deforestation and soil erosion.

Defence Costs

Apart from the impact on the Zambian economy and social structures, the past 24 years of aggression and threatened aggression has necessitated considerable expansion in the security establishment. In 1971 the total strength of the Zambian Defence Force was 5,500, of whom 4,500 were in the army and 1,000 in the air force. Today the army has expanded to over 15,000 and the air force has tripled. This would not have been necessary were it not for Rhodesian and South African aggression.

Zambia has been forced to purchase an expensive air defence system, jet fighters, helicopters, transport planes, tanks, artillery and other hardware, all from limited resources badly needed for development. In addition, and in common with other Frontline states, Zambia has given military assistance to Mozambique through training and equipping a battalion in 1988.

Defence Expenditure as % of National Budget
millions kwacha (millions US$)

Year	Government Expenditure	Defence/ Security	% Exp.	Normal Exp. Ratio 5%	Additional Defence Exp
1988	8,303,145*	1,246,430	15	415.16	831.27 ($102.12)
1987	5,837,525	740,790	12.7	291.88	448.91 ($ 46.95)
1986	5,383,596	421,630	7.8	269.18	152.45 ($ 20.27)
1985	2,184,332	199,770	9	109.22	90.55 ($ 27.95)
1984	1,484,625	147,860	10	74.23	73.63 ($ 41.13)

* Budget estimate

Source: Ministry of Finance, Ministry of Defence.

As seen from the above table, Zambia's defence expenditure in local currency increased almost tenfold from 1984 to 1988, virtually doubling each year. This was in part a result of devaluations in the value of the kwacha, but an estimated 1,596 million kwacha — US$238.42 million, at average annual rates of exchange — over the 5 per cent normal ratio resulted from the need to improve and expand defences as a consequence of South African aggression and threatened aggression.

Overall Cost Equation

Zambia is suffering a severe economic crisis, in which its foreign debt including arrears reached over $7 billion in 1988, making Zambia's debt position per capita roughly the same as Brazil. In late 1988, the Minister of Finance announced that the annual budget deficit would reach 1,918 million kwacha (almost $200 million).

Yet 1988 was a good year for Zambia in economic terms, with 2.2 per cent growth as copper prices bounced back after years of decline and the weather cooperated with conditions for a bumper harvest. However, per capita income dropped, due in part to population growth but mainly because of the bottomless pit of years of additional defence, transportation and related costs. Failure to implement three National Development Plans and one interim plan after independence 1964 cannot be costed.

A senior official in the Ministry of Planning, who has been grappling for many years with the difficulties of non-implementation of national development plans, deserves mention for his eloquent presentation of the range of problems caused by lost investment and displaced resources. Even the earnings from copper exports cannot be used for development, he said, but must be used for survival — the extra costs of freight, imports of food and essential commodities, "and defence . . . always defence".

Development aid has had to be spent more on sustaining than on developing, he said. There are no new secondary schools, no expansion in education or health facilities, only lost opportunities. "How can we place a value, in any real terms, on the lack of growth and development when we are always running to catch up. The railway, pipeline, road, our transport infrastructure: all of our resources are eaten up to develop this and protect it. Shifting from one direction to another ate up our reserves."

Lost jobs, higher crime rate, inflation, over 25 years, are a result of so many years of moving backward, he said. "We are TWO DECADES BEHIND. How do you cost the frustration caused by this, the apathy? When people have lost the will to live, to work, can only cope with surviving?"

In this circumstance, sabotage or even accidents can strike a devastating blow to Zambia's fragile economy, contributing to higher costs, lost jobs and greater inflation — and it may not always be possible to determine with certainty the nature of such "accidents". Two recent, and very serious, examples occurred in early 1989.

Fire gutted a hydroelectric plant in the Kafue gorge in March, causing Zambia — which had been selling 350 megawatts of electricity to Zimbabwe for US$1 million a week — to become a net importer of electricity. Zambia must now purchase 130 megawatts per week from Zimbabwe and Zaire, paying in foreign exchange, while some Lusaka suburbs and industries endure blackouts. In May, a mysterious fire at the oil refinery disrupted supplies of petrol. Thousands of people were stranded as buses and taxis ran out of fuel, and desperate motorists paid exhorbitant sums for small amounts of petrol from youths with jerrycans. The causes of these "accidents" could be poor maintenance and lack of foreign exchange for spare parts, or economic sabotage, either way a result of Zambia's geographical and political circumstance.

The two major costs for Zambia over the past 25 years have been additional transportation and defence expenditure. But there are many hidden costs in lost investment, tourism, the higher cost of imports, less competitive prices of exports — and the human cost. The additional military expenditure for Zambia to defend itself against South Africa's onslaught since 1980 has been over US$ 1billion, and transport losses have reached a similar figure. Thus estimates of the quantifiable costs to Zambia of South Africa's regional policy from 1980 to 1988 *begin* at $2.5 billion, but, as with other Frontline States, variables such as the size of the army in peacetime are difficult to quantify and the cost may be higher.

With these variables and the cost of lost development included, the price to Zambia, which was strangled earlier because of its commitment to the Zimbabwean struggle, would be double that figure or higher from 1976. Since the uncertainty on its southern border had already cost Zambia $1 billion over 15 years ago, and given the escalation of costs in the intervening year, it is reasonable to suggest that the cost now may have surpassed $7 billion — the equivalent of the country's foreign debt.

Borrowing totalled almost $1 billion at the end of 1987, making Zambia the International Monetary Fund's largest sub-Saharan African debtor. The debt service ratio at that time was about 60 per cent of exports of goods and services, the fifth worst position on the continent. Zambia's limitation of its debt service payments to 10 per cent since May 1987 means that there has been a substantial growth in overall debt, with arrears to the IMF and world Bank approaching $1 billion.

Zambia's economic crisis, and the policies now being prepared with the IMF, can be seen as a direct result of the retaliation — both actual and threatened — by minority regimes for Zambia's commitment to the liberation of the sub-continent and to the ending of apartheid. These costs have been accumulating over a very long period of time, since independence, and cannot be solely attributed, as they often are, to poor management and the falling price of copper.

When the IMF tells us to cut the civil service, the planning official said, "They are looking at flowers, they are not looking at stems."

4   Botswana

Until 1977 Botswana did not have an army. A police force supported by a para-military unit numbering just over 200 was considered adequate security. There was a widely-held belief that the country's strength lay in its weakness — that no one would attack a country with no defences. Cross border raids from Rhodesia destroyed that philosophy and the Botswana Defence Force (BDF) was constituted in April 1977. The threat from Rhodesia ended with Zimbabwe's independence in 1980, but Botswana soon became a target for armed attacks and incursions from South Africa.

The aggression by Botswana's minority-ruled neighbours forced the country to create and expand a regular army and air force with the motto on its coat of arms, Thebe ya Sechaba — Shield of the Nation. At first it was a tiny force and, in theory, the ending of Rhodesian aggression should have meant it could stay that way. Yet from 1980 to 1989 defence expenditure rose by over 600 per cent, and since the financial year 1985/86 the annual recurrent and capital allocations have risen dramatically as a direct result of South African aggression.

A detailed chronology of South African attacks on Botswana follows in the next section. However, an analysis of direct attacks and bombings, other incidents involving SADF, and known air space violations provides an overview as to the necessity of expanding the defence forces.

BDF and police records show that from 13 February 1985 to 14 February 1989 there were 20 direct SADF attacks or sabotages, 37 lesser incidents involving incursions or cross-border shootings, and 23 known air space violations — the largest number of recorded incidents involving South African troops against any Frontline State in that period, except for Angola. After the third of these attacks, on 14 June 1985, in which 12 people were killed and six injured, the SADF chief, General Constand Viljoen, claimed that every effort had been made "to get at the enemy, and not at the Botswana police or members of the public or innocent members of the terrorists' families".

The statistics, however, tell a different story. Of 31 people killed in these SADF attacks only 10 were South Africans. And, of these, almost all were refugees. The remaining 21 victims included 19 Batswana and two foreigners — a child from Lesotho and a Dutch citizen of Somali origin. Only three of the 22 injured were South

Africans. Of the other 19, all except one Dutch citizen were Botswana nationals, including a young girl, Nthabiseng Mabuse, who was shot in the stomach and is paralyzed for life. Thus, out of 53 people killed and wounded in these attacks only 13 were of South African nationality.

Botswana nationals accounted for 70 per cent of the casualties, yet South Africa continues to claim that its war is not against Botswana.

BDF records list a second category of incidents involving the SADF. These are illegal crossings into Botswana, and cross-border shootings. From 3 January 1985 to 8 February 1989, a total of 37 incidents were recorded and others certainly went undetected. Of these, 22 involved illegal crossings into Botswana and 15 were cross-border shooting incidents. One Botswana national was wounded and 32 were kidnapped. Tourists visiting Botswana and game rangers were fired on by the SADF, incidents likely to discourage visitors to Botswana's parks.

The third category of BDF statistics records air space violations: 23 from 4 February 1985 to 9 August 1988. These include intimidating low level flights over villages by South African Impala jet fighters to SADF troops landed by helicopter in tourist areas. These figures are certainly much too low as most air space violations cannot be detected by authorities — the nearest monitoring equipment is in Johannesburg. For example, on 12 February 1989, a large group of journalists were flown from South Africa across Botswana to Unita's main base at Jamba in southernmost Angola. The journalists were able to identify their flight path clearly by distinctive landmarks such as the Okavango Swamps. A few days later a party of Republican members of the US Congress were flown to Angola on the same route. Neither of these air space violations are recorded in Botswana's statistics.

Botswana's problem in trying to monitor air space violations by South Africa is that its air traffic information is controlled through South Africa. Thus, instead of flying over Namibia to supply Unita in southern Angola, South African planes take the direct route across Botswana. Civilian planes, which are allowed overflight rights, are expected to seek clearance from Botswana but this is ignored by the South Africans. Military traffic does not have overflight rights but South Africa also ignores this, as the recorded airspace violations reveal. However, Botswana plans to install its own flight-monitoring equipment in Gaborone later this year and hopes these violations can be minimized by exposure.

South African aggression has also necessitated a considerable expansion of Botswana's police force. In 1985 the force numbered just over 2,000. Normal expansion should have been about 3 per cent per annum to keep pace with the birth rate while retaining the ratio of one policeman for every 500 people. However, by 1989/90, as a result of South Africa's attacks, the force will have increased to 3,500, an expansion of 75 per cent in four years. The increase in the size of the force means attendant capital expenditure on housing, vehicles, weapons, communications equipment and so on — more money diverted from development to defence.

SADF Military Action Against Botswana

Direct Attacks/Sabotage

South Africa's threats and attacks against Botswana resemble those of a bellicose neighbourhood bully, and raids across the lengthy frontier often coincide with other events in the region, as if to punctuate Pretoria's threats against its neighbours.

Botswana covers a vast, arid land area of 500,000 sq km, and most of its borders are shared with South Africa or South African-occupied Namibia. The tiny population of 1.3 million is settled along the line of rail and near the South African border. The capital Gaborone is particularly vulnerable, only 10 km from the border, and is often the target of SADF action involving direct attacks, planting of explosives and other sabotage.

In the early morning hours of 27 December 1988, the date of a meeting of Frontline leaders in Zambia and five days after South Africa signed a peace agreement with Angola, a 14-year-old boy, Tebogo Mohurutshane, died in a bomb blast in Gaborone. The boy's mother, father and brother were injured in the explosion that demolished the house while the family slept. Two other children escaped unhurt. The government expressed concern that South African aggression was continuing, despite an agreement to hold regular talks with Pretoria on security matters. The Chairman of the Frontline States, President Kaunda of Zambia, told his colleagues at the summit that the "barbarous" attack cast doubt on Pretoria's seriousness in regional peace efforts.

Two weeks earlier, a group of heavily armed men raided Ditlahrapeng village in Botswana, 1,000 metres from the South African border. They killed two men, burned two huts and demolished a two-roomed house. Local police said the assailants were SADF commandos who had crossed the border on foot and that footprints were traced from the scene back towards the border. The attack, in the early hours of 12 December, came less than a week after the External Affairs Minister, Dr Gaositwe Chiepe, held talks on security matters in Pretoria with her South African counterpart, Pik Botha, in a high-level meeting also attended by the South African Ministers of Defence, General Magnus Malan, and Law and Order, Adriaan Vlok. A SADF spokesman denied any involvement in "the alleged incident", which occurred four days after the sentencing in Botswana of two South Africans for an earlier attack.

The two, Corporals Theodore Hermansen and Johannes Basson, sentenced to 10 years in prison and eight lashes, were arrested in June 1988 after SADF commandos fired on a police patrol near Kgale, eight km south of Gaborone, wounding three constables. Five of the seven commandos escaped in their van, the two others were captured, and there was renewed pressure, reflected in the local press, for Botswana's police to be armed. On 21 June, the morning after the two men were captured, a powerful car bomb destroyed a vehicle and damaged a house in Gaborone.

In September, police foiled a plan to spring the two from prison in Francistown, arresting their Batswana lawyer and a black South African caught with a pistol and silencer, wire cutters, a two-way radio and 100 spikes. The spikes were apparently intended to be scattered on the road to puncture the tires of pursuers, an escape trick used in earlier attacks on Botswana and Zimbabwe in 1985 and 1986. Pretoria continues to press for the release of Hermansen and Basson, despite their conviction by a court of law.

Botswana offends South Africa by its very attempts to protect its sovereignty, and a Johannesburg newspaper, *The Citizen*, complained that people were "getting sickened by the sight of South Africans being brought to court in leg irons". The paper called for partial closure of the border or another military raid, while Pik Botha advised South Africans not to visit Botswana as it was not safe for tourists. A substantial reduction in Botswana's tourist trade in 1988 is traced to this statement, and the Foreign Ministry in Gaborone often receives letters from individual South African visitors giving details of their vehicle and itinerary and requesting safe passage.

Two more South African commandos were caught posing as tourists in a bizarre incident that occurred in early July 1988, shedding some light on covert operations in the region. As the case of Charles Dennis Beahan illustrates, South Africa tried to use Botswana as a springboard for an attack on neighbouring Zimbabwe. Beahan was part of a group sent to try to spring five South African agents arrested in Zimbabwe after a car-bomb attack in Bulawayo in January which killed a Zimbabwean driver hired from a labour exchange. The rescue attempt failed after it was discovered by Zimbabwean security and the perpetrators, including a white air force pilot, fled the country. Beahan, meanwhile, had been arrested in Botswana.

Together with another man, whom he named as Jimmy Maguire (the same surname as one of the accused in Zimbabwe), Beahan had driven to Kasane, on Botswana's north-eastern border with Zimbabwe near the Zambezi river. They were driving a vehicle with false compartments filled with weapons and, when challenged by Zimbabwean customs officials, the two fled on foot and crossed clandestinely back into Botswana. They went to a hotel in the nearby Chobe game reserve and flew in a private aircraft to Gaborone before taking a taxi to Tlokweng, near the South African border. Beahan was apprehended by BDF soldiers who spotted him walking through the bush toward the border; Maguire apparently escaped. Beahan was handed back to the Zimbabwean authorities.

A Johannesburg newspaper, *The Sunday Times*, suggested the bungled rescue attempt was the work of a "crazy gang" operating independently, however the cost of the elaborate operation and Beahan's professional background would suggest otherwise. Beahan holds a British passport and was a paratrooper in the British army until 1976 when he went to Rhodesia and joined the Rhodesian Light Infantry. Thereafter he joined the Rhodesian Special Air Services (SAS), an elite unit, as a member of the special forces. When Zimbabwe became independent in 1980, he went to South Africa and joined one of the special "reconnaissance" units of the SADF "special forces" which are used for covert action in the region. There is some indication over the past two or three years that many of the ex-Rhodesians in these "recce" units have been "demobilized" and have set up private security agencies which are used to carry out assignments with official, but clandestine, support from Pretoria. At the time of his arrest, Beahan (also known as Behan, or Henry Peter Coleman) said he was working as a security officer with an international hotel group in Sandton, near Johannesburg.

In the early hours of 28 March 1988, the SADF attacked Gaborone again, as anti-apartheid parliamentarians from Europe began a conference in neighbouring Zimbabwe. A commando group, driving a van with the licence plates removed, shot up a house in the northern outskirts of the city. Three women and a man were shot, doused with petrol and set alight in their burning house. Residents of the suburb of Phiring, where the attack took place, said they heard automatic gunfire and grenades then a period of quiet followed by another explosion. This is a pattern of attack often repeated in eyewitness accounts; the period of quiet represents a search for documents or planting of papers or booby-traps. The South African-registered van was abandoned nearby after being driven over a stump. Neighbours said they heard a helicopter but there was no other evidence of this.

Three of the four killed were Batswana women and the fourth was a man, a South African refugee. Announcing the attack, a SADF spokesman said the victims were "terrorists". The ANC representative in France, Dulcie September, was assassinated in Paris the following day, the second day of the parliamentarians' conference on "Southern Africa's Future: Europe's Role". A further significance of the timing of these particular attacks is that they took place 24 hours before a South African by-election for white voters in Randfontein, which the ruling party nevertheless lost to the main opposition which advocates stronger action against the ANC and neighbouring states.

Botswana demanded an apology and compensation for loss of life, while South African official radio commentaries stressed the importance of Botswana signing a formal non-aggression pact. One South African newspaper urged Botswana to sign such an agreement so "we can be truly good neighbours".

General Malan described the attack as a "pre-emptive strike", but the US State Department, which later criticized South Africa's "disregard for international law", rebuked Pretoria for making "no attempt to obtain the cooperation of the Botswana authorities to deal with a presumed security threat".

In 1987 there had been seven such attacks, in which the dead and wounded were all Botswana nationals. No South Africans were killed or wounded in these raids. Three people, including two children, died on 8 May as a result of a car bomb detonated by remote control. In another incident, a 72-year-old woman was killed and four members of the BDF wounded by a hand grenade. One, a Warrant Officer, later died from his injuries. The Botswana Book Centre, which could not have posed any threat other than the progressive literature on its shelves, was the target of a hand grenade on 11 December, as were three houses in or near Gaborone. A fourth was attacked three days later.

During the previous year there had been only two attacks. In one a Batswana woman was killed and a child injured. In the other, on 19 May 1986, Gaborone was one of three Commonwealth capitals chosen by the SADF for the attack that cut short the mission of the Commonwealth Eminent Persons Group (EPG). SADF helicopter gunships fired on the main BDF barracks at Mogoditshane village during the early morning attack, apparently to detract attention from simultaneous action against an adjacent civilian housing complex. One BDF soldier was wounded and a young Batswana man, Jabulani Masalila, was killed at the housing complex. Three people were hospitalized with injuries sustained during the raid.

In 1985 there were four attacks. On 16 November at Mochudi, north of Gaborone, a man, a woman and two children were killed by a car bomb which damaged the Deborah Retief Memorial Hospital. In May a South African refugee died when a bomb wrecked his flat, and in February two exiled South African journalists rapidly left the country after their Gaborone house was bombed.

The most serious armed aggression against Botswana to date was a bloody 45-minute raid on Gaborone, on 14 June 1985, in which 12 people were killed: 8 South African refugees, 2 Batswana, a Dutch citizen and a 6-year-old Basotho child. Six others were wounded: three South Africans, a Dutch woman and two Batswana. Four houses were destroyed, a fifth set on fire and others extensively damaged.

Eight locations were attacked, and at least three of the targets related to information and culture. The offices of an anti-apartheid news service were wrecked. Artist Thami Mnyele was shot dead, his artworks were plundered and some were stolen. A grenade was thrown into the house of trombonist Jonas Gwangwa — a well known musician who did the score for the film "Cry Freedom" — who was not at home. The SADF announced that they had destroyed an ANC "control centre" and that the dead were "key" activists. Only four of the 12 had any connection with the ANC and none had any military training.

The UN Security Council unanimously passed a resolution in September 1985 calling on South Africa to pay full compensation for loss of life, injuries and damage to property. The damage was estimated at US$20 million, but Pretoria refused to pay. An aid programme of $14 million was recommended to assist Botswana to improve its security capabilities and refugee facilities.

The raid silenced a vocal community of South African exiles, already the target of a spate of car bombs, and some of them left the country. The ANC representative was withdrawn for security reasons. The US ambassador in Pretoria said the raid made "it virtually impossible for President Reagan not to sign" the divestment bill then before Congress.

The following chart gives details of SADF raids and sabotage in Botswana 1985 to 1989 — and shows that 61 per cent of the dead and 82 per cent of those injured were Batswana.

SADF Raids/Sabotage
February 1985 to February 1989

Date	Incident
14 Feb 89	Explosion in men's toilet at Mphatlalatsane Hotel (Morning Star Hotel), Tlokweng. No injuries.
TOTAL:	1 incident
27 Dec 88	Explosion demolished house in Gaborone West in early morning hours as family slept, killing 14-year-old boy, injuring mother, father, brother, all Batswana.12 Dec 88 Early morning raid on Ditlharapeng village near SA border; two men killed, two huts burned and a house demolished.
8 Nov 88	Powerful bomb partially destroyed empty house in Gaborone suburb of Broadhurst.
21 Jun 88	Explosion destroyed vehicle at residence of Botswana citizen in Gaborone West.
20 Jun 88	Botswana Police patrol fired on by SADF commandos at Kgale, near Gaborone. Three constables wounded. Two SADF commandos, Theodore Hermansen and Johannes Basson, arrested, later sentenced to 10 years in prison, 8 lashes.

28 Mar 88	SADF commandos blew up house in Gaborone suburb of Phiring, killed three Batswana women and SA refugee by dousing with petrol and burning.
TOTAL 1988	6 incidents, 7 dead(1 SA, 6 Batswana), 6 wounded (6 Batswana).
11/14 Dec 87	The Botswana Book Centre and four dwelling houses in Gaborone and Tlokweng attacked with hand grenades. One boy injured.
8 Apr 87	Powerful car bomb detonated by remote control destroyed Toyota hiace parked outside house in Gaborone West, killed 3 Batswana sleeping inside.
1 Jan 87	72-year-old Batswana woman, Thero Segopa, killed when two gunmen bombed her house in Ramotswa. Four BDF men injured by hand grenade left at spot and one, a warrant officer, later died.
TOTAL 1987:	7 incidents, 5 dead (5 Batswana), 4 wounded (4 Batswana).
14 Jun 86	Gunmen killed a young woman, injured a man and paralyzed a child, all Batswana, at a house in Gaborone, Extension 2.
19 May 86	SADF heliborne attack on civilian housing complex in Mogoditshane village, near Gaborone, also fired on main BDF barracks. Young man killed at housing complex, 3 injured, BDF man wounded.
TOTAL 1986:	2 incidents, 2 dead (2 Batswana), 6 wounded (6 Batswana).
16 Nov 85	Car bomb at Deborah Retief Memorial Hospital killed man, woman, two children, and damaged hospital property including vehicles.
14 Jun 85	SADF commandos raided 8 locations in Gaborone, killed 12 people, injured 6, demolished 4 houses. Dead included 8 SA refugees, 2 Batswana, 1 Basotho and a Dutch citizen. Among the injured were 3 SA refugees, 2 Batswana and 1 Dutch national.
14 May 85	Car bomb exploded at Ext. 11, Gaborone, killed SA refugee, damaged neighbouring houses.
13 Feb 85	Bomb exploded in house at Ginger, no casualties but extensive damage to nearby houses and shops.
TOTAL 1985:	4 incidents, 17 dead (6 Batswana, 9 SA, 2 other), 6 wounded (2 Batswana, 3 SA, 1 other).

SUMMARY

	Incidents	Dead	Bats/SA/Other	Wounded	Bats/SA/Other
1989 (Feb)	1	—	—		
1988	6	7	6/ 1	6	6
1987	7	5	5	4	4
	2	2	2	6	6
1985	4	17	6/ 9/2	6	2/3/1
TOTAL	20	31	19/10/2	22	18/3/1

20 incidents
31 dead   (19 Batswana, 10 SA, 2 others)
22 wounded (18 Batswana, 3 SA, 1 other)

Source: BDF and Botswana Police.

Although the table lists SADF action against Botswana since 1985, there had been several incidents in the previous five years, including border violations from Caprivi, by aircraft and on the ground. These incursions often involved supply flights to Unita in Angola or game poaching in Botswana's northern wildnerness. Villagers in remote areas were sometimes kidnapped, as were South African exiles.

Incursions and Cross-Border Shootings

In addition to the SADF attacks and bombings listed above, there are other incidents involving SADF elements who cross over the border or fire on civilians or BDF patrols, and sometimes harass fishermen on the Limpopo river.

There were three SADF incursions in early 1989. On 1 February, South African soldiers questioned workers on a farm near the border, then returned to the area a week later and kidnapped a Batswana, Johannes Moshoba of Mathathane village. In January a BDF patrol had been fired on by two SADF soldiers whom they spotted on top of a hill near their camp.

In the period from 3 January 1985 to 8 February 1989, a total of 37 such incidents were recorded, including 22 incursions or border violations and 15 cross-border shootings. Some of the incursions involved river crossings in military patrol boats and, after one such incident, a para-illuminating bomb was lobbed onto the air strip at Kasane. Twice, in August and September 1987, South African soldiers crossed into Botswana in armoured cars.

SADF Border Violations and Cross-Border Shootings
Recorded in Botswana
January 1985 to February 1989

Date	Incursions	Cross-Border Shooting	Other
1989 (Jan/Feb)	3		1 kidnapped
1988	4	3	
1987	8	7	1 kidnapped
1986	5	1	
1985	2	4	30 kidnapped 1 wounded
TOTAL	22	15	32 kidnapped 1 wounded

Source: BDF.

These incidents have not so far resulted in casualties, although nationals of Botswana are often harassed. In one incident in 1985, 30 civilians including women and children, were kidnapped by the SADF while fishing on the Limpopo River. They were transported by truck to Messina and returned the same day. Another man, kidnapped on the river in 1987, was also taken to Messina. The fate of the man kidnapped in February 1989 is unknown. All are Batswana.

Airspace Violations

Botswana is within the Flight Information Region (FIR) located in Johannesburg, and its air space is controlled from there. All information pertaining to civilian and military air traffic over Botswana must therefore pass through Johannesburg control which is not obliged to give this information to Gaborone. Overflight rights are permitted for civilian traffic but not for military aircraft, which are supposed to seek clearance to overfly Botswana, although in practice they never do. SADF flights to and from its bases in Namibia's Caprivi Strip, which borders on southern Angola, do not fly around and over Namibia but take a short cut across Botswana. The SADF neglects to inform the authorities in Botswana about these flights, and they have no way of knowing what is overhead short of accidental discovery.

As far back as 1982, and even before, there was considerable tension along Botswana's northern border generated by overflights of South African aircraft near the Caprivi Strip. That situation continues to this day but there is very little that the government in Gaborone can do, short of protesting to Pretoria.

What follows is a list of 23 known, recorded violations of Botswana's airspace by South African military aircraft since 1985. However, these represent actual sightings of aircraft by BDF patrols or by civilians. Many more airspace violations go undetected and unrecorded.

Recorded Airspace Violations by SADF*
4 February 1985 to 8 August 1988

Date	Incident
1988	Three incidents recorded in March, July and August, all involving SADF helicopters overflying villages in the border area. In August, SADF troops were dropped at a farm in the Tuli Block, bordering on Zimbabwe.
1987	Eight incidents recorded involving 3 helicopters and 8 aircraft, seven of the incidents in the first half of the year.
1986	Seven incidents involving 11 helicopters and 4 aircraft, four of the incidents in the last quarter of the year. These included two massive airlifts on 19 and 20 October 1986. On 19 October, the helicopters dropped SADF troops near Tsetsejwe village. These troops were collected the following

morning, at 0600 hours on 20 October, by four helicopters. They fired one smoke bomb. At about 0200 hours on 20 October, a South African aircraft flew over a village coming from the south and returned to the west of Gobojango. It approached the area nine times from the same direction at an interval of 15-20 minutes. This lasted until 0500 hours.

1985   Five incidents in the first quarter, all involving military aircraft flying near Shakawe village, to or from Namibia.

* This list is a record of aircraft sightings by BDF patrols or by civilians, and is therefore incomplete. Since the Flight Information Region (FIR) covering Botswana's airspace is controlled from Johannesburg, Botswana has no means of monitoring civilian or military overflights.

Source: BDF.

Defence Costs

Botswana has not known a year of peace from South African aggression since 1985, and the BDF has been on full alert since May 1986. The government's growing concern at its military vulnerability has led to provision for a substantial increase in spending on the operations and development of the defence and police forces.

In the five years after Zimbabwe's independence in 1980, Botswana's annual defence expenditure rose by only l0 million pula, largely due to inflation. But since the financial year 1985/86 the total annual recurrent and capital allocation has risen by over 110 million pula, almost 400 per cent in nominal terms, as a direct result of South African aggression.

Much of the development expenditure in 1987 and 1988 was used forcapital items such as jet fighters, tanks and other hardware as Botswana rapidly improved its ability to defend itself. Plans for improvement of air defences include the purchase of more combat aircraft and helicopters, construction of an airfield and training of pilots, as well as anti-tank and anti-aircraft equipment to be supplied by the United States.

A British SAS regiment carried out a six-week training exercise for the BDF in Botswana in late 1986, and the US, India and Canada, as well as the UK, provide training to the BDF. The number of people serving in the army and air force increased considerably in this period, and in April 1988, eleven years after its creation, the force was reorganized into a conventional army structure.

In the 1988/89 budget, the BDF and police were allocated 63 million pula (US\$34.6 million), representing most of an expanded development budget allocated to the president's office. Security also received the largest share of the office's recurrent budget.

From l980 to 1989, Botswana's defence expenditure increased by 603 per cent in nominal terms, as shown in the following chart.

Recurrent and Development Expenditure on Defence Since 1980

Year	Total National Expenditure (pula)	Defence Exp. (pula)	Defence Exp. (US $)	Defence %
1988/89*	2,623,706,211.	154,829,060.	85,070,879.	6
1987/88	1,991,153,542.	140,003,760.	83,335,571.	7
1986/87	1,661,790,883.	69,367,010.	36,897,345.	4
1985/86	1,002,294,110.	41,434,520.	21,923,026.	4
1984/85	832,072,913.	35,883,690.	26,385,066.	4
1983/84	576,622,622.	27,919,097.	25,851,015.	5
1982/83	459,494,779.	23,614,376.	22,926,578.	5
1981/82	472,255,217.	26,171,716.	31,156,804.	5
1980/81	455,501,887.	25,653,515.	32,809,759.	5.6

* *Budget estimate*

Source: BDF, Ministry of Finance & Development Planning.

Threats, Espionage and Propaganda

In late May 1987, during a general escalation of South African-supported violence throughout the region, the SADF held its largest airborne exercise to date. In a massive exercise called Iron Eagle, 14 transport aircraft dropped 500 men and 50 tonnes of equipment near the Botswana border, demonstrating South Africa's capacity for air strikes into neighbouring states. Three South African aircraft flew over Sikwane village in Botswana during this exercise.

This was only a month after the heliborne commando attack on Livingstone in Zambia, and less than two months after a car bomb killed a woman and two children in Gaborone. The bomb followed within hours of a warning from Pretoria that the ANC was infiltrating through Botswana territory. Thus, a second warning three weeks later had the desired destabilizing effect without being followed by action. This occurred just before the whites-only general election in South Africa on 6 May 1987.

Later that year and through 1988, General Malan and other South African officials threatened Botswana verbally on several occasions. In October 1988, just before the whites-only municipal elections in South Africa, the Ministers of Defence, Security and Foreign Affairs addressed their constituency, heaping verbal abuse on Botswana. As the agreement with Angola on Namibia's independence neared fruition in late 1988, General Malan described Botswana and Zimbabwe as being "out of line" with the realities of the region, adding that they should not cry when South Africa strikes.

An escalation in verbal warfare, over the alleged failure of Botswana to check infiltration by armed groups, led one senior official from Botswana to remind the South Africans that there are two sides to the border and that SADF has more resources to effectively patrol its side than the tiny BDF. Pik Botha threatened Botswana and Zimbabwe again in early May 1989 after a mortar attack on a SADF radar station in the Western Transvaal.

South African espionage networks, which often provide information or material assistance to the saboteurs, are difficult to pin down. Some operate through certain sectors of the business community or with a false commercial cover. The difficultly in accumulating hard evidence means that suspects are almost always released. A resident of Maun, where Beahan is believed to have collected his weapons-filled vehicle before attempting to enter Zimbabwe, said, "I always thought they were here for the elephant tusks only, but now it seems they are diversifying."

Hermansen and Basson, the SADF commandos arrested in June 1988, were the first people charged under the National Security Act, enacted in 1986, which cites South Africa in the preamble as the main factor for the security legislation. They were also charged under the penal code for attempted murder of the three policemen.

The second group charged under the National Security Act, shortly after Hermansen and Basson, included two businessmen and a woman, charged with concealing information relating to the same commando attack. A supermarket manager was accused of communicating with Hermansen about his travel plans just prior to the abortive raid. One of his company directors and his domestic worker testified that Hermansen had previously stayed with the manager, himself a South African national. The other two accused were the manager of a firm dealing in wildlife products and his wife, who was accused of concealing and then setting alight SADF uniforms hidden in the company store.

At about the same time, another South African man, Ferdinand Prinsloo, was arrested while hitch-hiking in northern Botswana with only 14 pula ($8) in his pocket. He was believed to have connections with the Beahan-Maguire mission to release accused South African agents in Zimbabwe, and to have stayed with the other two at a lodge in northern Botswana. Prinsloo was deported to South Africa in mid-1988, where he made allegations of torture against the Botswana police, causing the latter to make public in August a statement he had written about alleged clandestine missions he had been involved in on behalf of South Africa, including training Unita to use US-supplied weapons in Angola and "training Renamo or MNR" in Mozambique. Less than a week later, an SABC commentary again carried a threat against Botswana, saying it had become the "major route for ANC terrorists".

Nine South African men, arrested in Francistown in late March 1989 and held for three days, were declared prohibited immigrants on the grounds of "insufficient means of support", after police found several discrepencies in their stories. They claimed to be salesmen marketing cleaning chemicals in northern Botswana, but they had no licence and lacked experience in the product they were supposed to be selling. A police spokesman noted that it was unusual for salesmen to travel in such a large group. Although there was insufficient evidence to prosecute them, he said "the security forces still have cause for concern." The group included both whites and blacks, many of whom said they had served in the SADF, and had handcuffs and a rocket flare in their possession when they were arrested.

Many international journalists covering southern Africa are based in South Africa, so Pretoria is often able to score a diplomatic or informational victory in lieu of a military one. Press briefings have been given at dawn on some occasions, immediately following an attack and before government leaders in Botswana have the details. Correspondents in South Africa are inhibited in what they can report by that country's censorship laws. South African radio and television also broadcasts Pretoria's viewpoint directly into Botswana.

The SADF attacks in June 1985 and March 1988 illustrate this point. In the March raid, in which three of the four people killed were Batswana, Pretoria was able to insert its version — that "trained terrorists" had been killed — into the daily press coverage and, even though officials in Botswana gave their account of the attack very quickly, most of the international media was already carrying the South African version. The June 1985 raid on Gaborone was presented by Pretoria as the destruction of an ANC "terrorist control centre" even though most of the dead had nothing to do with ANC and those who did worked in information and culture.

Allegations that the ANC is transiting Botswana to launch operations in South Africa are used to justify direct SADF intervention by commando units or "hit squads", generally resulting in damage to property and death of innocent civilians, as seen above. The Botswana government denies any knowledge of its territory being used as a springboard for attack and, despite considerable military and economic pressure, has consistently refused to sign a security agreement with Pretoria.

During the 1984 elections, an opposition party campaigned in favour of a security agreement after meetings in South Africa; and 1989 is another election year in Botswana.

Economic and Other Pressures

As well as the military pressure exerted through sabotage, aggression, or threat of aggression, South Africa exerts effective economic pressure on Botswana through its high degree of integration into the South African economy, its membership in the Southern African Customs Union (Sacu), and its geographical position.

Membership of Sacu was inherited at independence and ties Botswana into the South African economic system, as do historical and current patterns of investment. However, the government has managed to extricate itself from the rand monetary zone and establish its own fairly strong local currency, the pula (Tswana for "rain"). Botswana's economic strength is based on its mineral sector, and the country is one of the world's largest diamond producers, with output exceeding that of South Africa, but extraction and selling are reliant on South African investment and marketing.

Botswana has an open market economy, retaining substantial foreign exchange reserves from diamond production. Several years of drought have forced the country to import most of its basic foodstuffs, although a better yield is expected in 1989. As much as 80 per cent of Botswana's imports originate in South Africa and, while almost all exports are sold in Europe, beef and other non-mineral exports are shipped through South African ports.

Botswana has about 21,000 migrant workers in the South African mines, and only five times that number are in wage employment at home. Their enforced repatriation by South Africa, often threatened, would exacerbate Botswana's unemployment. In addition, the attacks and bombings create a poor climate for tourism and investment, and some companies which considered relocating to Botswana when disinvesting from South Africa, went elsewhere instead.

Security Agreement

Since the signing of the Nkomati Accord by Mozambique and South Africa in 1984, Botswana has been under considerable pressure from Pretoria to sign a security agreement and its refusal to do so has resulted in a kind of stalemate. Botswana government officials have stated their readiness to meet and discuss security problems, and there have been several such meetings. However South African officials have declined an invitation to go and see for themselves that Botswana contains no ANC military or transit facilities; and Pretoria has often tried to link important economic projects to the signing of a formal security pact.

In lieu of a formal security agreement, South Africa has demanded joint security mechanisms such as border patrols and exchange of information, but Botswana has refused. In April 1988, South Africa proposed installing a decoding machine in the Botswana Police headquarters so "secret" information could be exchanged between

Gaborone and Pretoria. When Botswana refused they were condemned for lack of cooperation. A South African request to open an
office in Botswana from which its security services could operate was
also refused.

In March 1989, Dr Gaositwe Chiepe, Botswana's Foreign Minister,
again told parliament that the government does not allow its territory
to be used as a launching pad for attacks against neighbouring states.
She said Botswana is not responsible for the turmoil in South Africa
and that attacks on Botswana would not solve South Africa's
problems. "For our part, we shall continue to talk to the South
Africans whenever it is necessary to address security concerns of the
two countries and economic issues of mutual concern," she said,
"because history has placed us together and we cannot wish each other
away."

Recognition of the "Homelands"

One of the goals of South Africa's regional policy is to force
recognition of the nominally "independent" homelands, of which
there are four — Transkei, Ciskei, Venda and Bophuthatswana. One
method of trying to do this is to force independent countries in the
region into agreements or situations which amount to de facto
recognition.

A main vehicle for this pressure is through Sacu, which groups
South Africa with Botswana, Lesotho and Swaziland in a common
trade area. Pretoria has tried for many years to include the
"homelands" in Sacu as separate entities, and has used various
pressures to try to encourage its Sacu partners to accept this.

The Sacu agreement allows for the common collection of customs
duty at ports of entry, i.e. South African ports, to be divided
proportionately at the end of each financial year. One means of
pressure on its neighbours has been to delay distribution of customs
revenue for up to two years. Another is to try to change the rules or the
proportion of revenue allocated to each country without joint
consultation.

In March 1988, the Finance Minister Barend du Plessis announced
to other members South Africa's intention to replace most excise
duties with a form of Value Added Tax in one year's time. Botswana,
Lesotho and Swaziland would not receive revenue from the new tax
and instead would have to pay tax on imported South African consumer goods. One clause of the Sacu agreement requires "consultation
and concurrence" before any member makes changes which would
affect the others.

The move is a transparent attempt to force renegotiation of the Sacu
agreement. Pretoria wants to cut down on the share paid out to other

member countries, and also to force admittance of the "homelands". However, Sacu income now accounts for less than 15 per cent of government revenue in Botswana, and although the country is reliant on South African corporations to mine its diamonds and fuel its transport, it is less vulnerable than Lesotho or Swaziland.

A joint water project to include Botswana in the supply of untreated water from the Molatedi dam in Bophuthatswana was signed in 1988 by the Water Utilities Corporation of Botswana and the South African Department of Water Affairs but, at the latter's insistence, the Bophuthatswana Department of Water Affairs was also a signatory — a pressure point South Africa may try to use in any renegotiation of the Sacu agreement. The first phase includes construction of storage and pumping facilities in Bophuthatswana and pipelines to Botswana, and costs over 25 million rands, to be financed by the South African-based Development Bank of Southern Africa and the Botswana Water Utilities Corporation.

Although the customs union agreement provides for the free movement of goods, services and people (without visas) across borders, the South African border has been used often to squeeze Botswana in what amounts to the use of economic sanctions by South Africa to pressure its neighbour.

In January 1988, South Africa ended a 40-day slowdown of border traffic at Tlokweng, the main border post, which had begun in December 1987, coinciding with a spate of of grenade explosions in Gaborone and seen as an escalation of pressure on Botswana to sign a security pact. The slowdown took the form of stringent security checks by South African police and security on the pretext of searching for ANC infiltrators, causing long delays and queues of up to 100 cars and trucks at the border post. The border squeeze was reminiscent of that which resulted in the coup e'etat in Lesotho two years earlier. It was the first incident of such proportion for Botswana, although Pretoria had threatened previously to close the border, and this action began during a major conference in Arusha, Tanzania, of international support for the ANC.

One year earlier, in January 1987, a South African-instigated attempt by Bophuthatswana to demand "visas" from Batswana and Zimbabwean railway workers backfired when the exchange of crews was removed to the Botswana side of the border, and when business in Bophuthatswana suffered from a sharp reduction in trade as a result of losing their regular shopping trips to Botswana. Seeking or acquiring visas from a "homeland" would imply recognition of its status as an independent state.

On that occasion, the Botswana delegation reminded the South Africans that the Sacu agreement allows "freedom of movement for people and goods". President Quett Masire blamed South Africa for a "clumsy attempt at a blockade of our trains".

South Africa's concept of a Constellation of Southern African States (Consas) with Pretoria at the centre included full membership for the "homelands" and regional recognition of their "independence". This plan was disrupted by the formation of the Southern African Development Coordination Conference (SADCC), a regional grouping excluding South Africa. Formed in 1980 to encourage regional cooperation and reduce dependence on South Africa, SADCC is headquartered in Gaborone and many of its goals were articulated by Botswana's first President, the late Sir Seretse Khama.

Transport and Trade

Insofar as the monetary value of Botswana's exports are concerned it has limited dependence upon South Africa's trade routes, much less than Malawi or Zimbabwe. Diamonds account for 80 to 85 per cent of exports and since these are small, the bulk-to-value ratio allows them to be flown out. The other principle exports are minerals such as nickel and copper as well as beef which together amounted to about US$280 million in 1988 against US$1.1 billion for diamonds.

In addition, there are alternative routes for Botswana's exports which are not necessarily more costly. On 18 March 1989, Botswana formally took over the 640-km section of the railway running through its territory from Zimbabwe. This was purchased from Zambia and Zimbabwe whose ownership was a legacy of the 1953-1963 Central African Federation. Four new railway projects were announced immediately by President Masire, costing 118 million pula (US$57.9 million). These include the purchase of 500 new wagons which can transport minerals and 40 refrigerated containers for beef exports as well as a workshop, signalling plant and repair of the track.

Both the Limpopo railway line and the Beira corridor through Zimbabwe and Mozambique are seen as alternate export outlets for Botswana's trade which presently passes through South Africa. The proposal for a railway across the Kgalagadi desert, shelved until Namibia's independence, would not in fact reduce Botswana's dependence on South African ports unless traffic is redirected away from Namibia's main deep-water port, Walvis Bay, which South Africa refuses to relinquish.

Botswana is contributing to the rehabilitation of the Limpopo railway line to Maputo and has pledged 5.8 million pula (US$3 million) in the form of concrete sleepers produced in a Botswana factory. The factory has no spare capacity — in fact Botswana can use every sleeper produced there for re-laying its own railway system — but the government considers the Limpopo line important enough to delay its own upgrading programme in order to speed up work in Mozambique.

All of Botswana's petroleum is imported through South Africa and, until storage tanks were built some years ago, it was subjected to delays in supply. Pretoria particularly wishes to retain this supply route to ensure that any tightening of oil sanctions would also effect neighbouring states such as Botswana, in the hope of discouraging such measures. Botswana could arrange to bring petroleum supplies through Mozambique and Zimbabwe by rail or pipeline, but is acutely aware of the vulnerability of those routes to attack, as well as its own storage tanks should they contain supplies imported via another route.

In contrast to its possibilities of reducing export dependence on South Africa, Botswana remains dependent upon the Republic for some 80 per cent of imports. But, as shown in the 1989 budget, efforts are being made to disengage through creating favourable terms for domestic self-suffiency by encouraging would-be investors.

Dependence and Disengagement

For the first decade after Botswana's independence in 1966, cattle ranching was the mainstay of the economy and beef accounted for as much as one third of export revenue. In this period, Pretoria could, and did, put pressure on Botswana by withholding refrigerated wagons and thus delaying export shipments. However, as a result of the discovery of the world's second largest kimberlite pipe — the source of diamonds — the mineral sector eventually surpassed beef as the main foreign exchange earner.

From 1982-1987, the value of exports increased fivefold, though the bulge in 1987 in part reflects the sale of stockpiled diamonds. By the end of 1988, Botswana had accumulated foreign exchange reserves over US$2 billion, enough to cover two-and-a-half years of import requirements. Botswana's diamonds account for 80-85 per cent of mineral production by value and contribute over half of government revenue through royalties and taxes.

Botswana's economic turnabout has been based largely on the development of its mineral wealth by the state in conjunction with South African capital, and government policy differentiates between private capital and the politics of the state in its relations with South Africa.

The South African conglomerate Anglo-American has an interest in the copper-nickel mine at Selebi-Pikwe and, through its De Beers subsidiary, joined government in the development of three diamond mines. De Beers's Central Selling Organization markets Botswana's diamonds abroad. The Botswana government and De Beers each have half of the shares in the De Beers Botswana Mining Company (Debswana) which controls the diamond mining. In mid-1987, Botswana reduced its five-year stockpile of diamonds in a complex business deal with De Beers in exchange for an undisclosed sum of cash, 20 million shares and two seats on the De Beers board.

Although the vital foreign exchange-earning sector remains highly dependent upon forces outside government control, under this agreement Botswana has acquired access to the decision-making process governing international diamond sales and, through De Beers's holdings in Anglo-American, in many sectors of the South African economy. Botswana becomes the first country in the region to own shares in a South African company, and one of very few developing countries to have purchased a substantial share in a parent company, not just a subsidiary.

The other major business development enterprise with South African capital is the Sua Pan soda ash project at the Makgadikgadi Pans, 600 km north of Gaborone, to be developed jointly with the South African chemical company, African Explosive and Chemical Industries (AECI). Together with Anglo-American and De Beers, AECI will hold 52 per cent of shares in Soda Ash Botswana. Vice President Peter Mmusi has said that the project, which will create 500 jobs directly and more indirectly, will help to reverse the dependence of Botswana because "South Africa will now become dependent on Botswana for something it needs very badly." Eighty per cent of the production will be shipped to South Africa, and the project could increase Botswana's export earnings by up to 10 per cent. Initially, the approval for this project from Pretoria was tied to the signing of a security pact, but the project was finally approved in 1987 without it.

For historical and geographical reasons Botswana has both strengths and weaknesses in its uneasy relationship with South Africa. In Gaborone two words — dependence and disengagement — dominate the debate about present and future relationship.

It is much too simplistic to say that Botswana is entirely dependent upon South Africa and is becoming increasingly dependent as a result of De Beers control of their diamond sales. Its Central Selling controls almost all of the world's diamond marketing, including that of the Soviet Union, and the dependency theory is not forwarded in other cases. It is true that Botswana is more dependent on diamond sales for export revenue than others producers, but De Beers has also become dependent on Botswana for some 50 per cent of all its profits and its international dominance would be severely threatened if an OPEC-style cartel were to be created which excluded South Africa.

Electricity supply is an important area of disengagement. The opening of the Botswana Power Corporation's Morupule Central power station in May 1987 enabled Botswana to produce almost all of the electricity needed for its own requirements, fueled by its own coal. Previously, local power station used imported fuel and Botswana depended on the South African Electricity Supply Commission

(Escom) for part of its supply, a dependence that increased for some five years during expansion of the mineral sector when up to 30 per cent of its needs came from Escom. The dependence on imported electricity has been vastly reduced and is now needed only for emergency back-up in the event of breakdowns. This is not expected to exceed 5 per cent of Botswana's needs.

The Morupule Central power station can supply 75 per cent of the country's needs with the remainder from the Selebi-Pikwe power station. Both operate on local coal, from the Morupule colliery adjacent to the power station. The Morupule project highlights both the fragility and complexity of Botswana's dependence and disengagement, since the colliery belongs to Anglo-American and and the contractors and supplies for the Morupule station were almost all South African.

Botswana is also becoming less dependent on tourists from South Africa which accounted for almost 30 per cent of total arrivals in 1986. In part the result of South African warnings to its nationals to stay away from Botswana, a new policy has been formulated. Botswana now seeks high-quality, low-volume tourism. a definite break with past policy where South Africans pre-paid their holidays in the Republic and little of the funds reached Botswana.

Geography and history have inextricably linked the economies of Botswana and South Africa. This position will remain unchanged once there is a democratic majority government in South Africa. And dependence is a two-way process which South Africa has clearly recognized in backing off its attempts to coerce the Botswana government into a joint security agreement by linking such a pact to Sua Pan and other agreements.

At the inauguration of SADCC, in April 1980, Botswana's President, the late Sir Seretse Khama, a leading advocate of the organization, sombrely warned that the struggle for economic independence was likely to prove more difficult than the struggle for political freedom. Since then Botswana has carefully weighed its options measuring dependence against the possibilities of disengagement. It has been a careful non-suicidal policy best summed up in a popular Swahili expression: Haraka Haraka Haina Baraka — Hurry Hurry Has No Blessing.

5   🌐   Angola

South African military involvement in Angola has been of a more conventional nature, over a longer period and on a larger scale, than anywhere else in the region. In addition, Pretoria has had considerable political and material support from outside the region for its Angolan proxy forces, particularly from Washington.

Since Angola has no common border and virtually no economic links with South Africa, unlike other states in the region, it has not been vulnerable to direct economic pressures nor has South Africa had to concern itself with damaging a profitable marketplace. Economic destruction has been achieved primarily through military action, and this potentially rich agricultural and mineral-based economy is shattered by war, the transport infrastructure destroyed, and almost 3 million people dislocated or affected by war-related famine.

South Africa has waged its war against Angola more or less openly for 13 years, directly as well as through material and strategic assistance to UNITA. There are similarities to the clandestine nature of its military-economic pressure on Mozambique in the training and equipping of terrorist squads for economic destruction and provision of sabotage units to assist them. However, the South African Defence Force (SADF) has also launched more than a dozen major incursions into Angola since they first entered the country in the second week of August 1975, and, after 1983, the war in southern Angola escalated into high-technology, high-casualty, confrontational warfare.

A massive battle in early 1988 became a turning point. South Africa lost its air superiority and technological advantage, due in part to the international arms embargo, and, facing sophisticated equipment and experienced personnel, could not batter its neighbour with impunity. Cuito Cuanavale, a tiny town in the remote south-eastern corner of Angola, became the battleground for a military test of wills between apartheid and its neighbours, a showdown of regional power over South Africa's aspiration to be recognized as the "superpower" of southern Africa.

The strategic importance of this tiny town is its airstrip and its use as a forward air defence base for southern Angola, but beyond that it became a bargaining chip for territorial gain and, to the region and beyond, a symbol of resistance to South Africa's military might.

"Not only a war against Angola," said General Olusegan Obasanjo, the retired Nigerian head of state, during a visit at the height of the fighting, "but a war against Africa."

The SADF deployed up to 9,000 troops in southern Angola including Namibian units and committed its most sophisticated military hardware in the form of long-range artillery, tanks, armoured cars and massive air force cover. The contest between South Africa's aggression and Angola's ability to defend itself resulted in severe casualties and loss of equipment on both sides but the heavily fortified town was held. The SADF, which does not announce black or foreign casualties, began sending home enough bodies of young white conscripts to disturb white public opinion. And, despite a visit by P.W. Botha and several senior cabinet ministers to a base in southern Angola (in a top-level violation of Angola's sovereignty), the SADF faced mutinies in its ranks, especially from black Namibian soldiers.

Crack Cuban combat troops were committed to the fighting in the south in late 1987, for the first time in 11 years. Previously the Cubans had been garrison troops, holding key installations in the rear and training government soldiers. They had not fired on the SADF since 1976.

The South African Defence Minister, General Magnus Malan, finally admitted openly that SADF troops were supporting UNITA but he refused to give details, and instead deplored Angola's failure to respond to South African offers to establish "joint security mechanisms" — a main objective of Pretoria's "total strategy".

These "mechanisms" came into being a year later, after a series of quadrapartite meetings involving Angola, Cuba, South Africa and the United States resulted in an agreement signed in New York on 22 December. That agreement, and previous "protocols", covered the withdrawal of South African forces from Angola, followed by the implementation of UN Security Council Resolution 435 for a UN-supervised transitional process to independence in Namibia commencing on 1 April 1989, and a phased withdrawal of Cuban troops from Angola by late 1990. An element of South Africa's "total strategy" agreed but unpublicized was the removal of ANC bases from Angola. Washington announced, before and after the signing, that it would not cease military aid to UNITA.

The peace process crept forward at a summit of 18 African leaders in June 1989 in Gbadolite, Zaire, when Angola's President Dos Santos shook hands with UNITA's Savimbi. However, Savimbi later denied that he had agreed to leave the country for a period as part of an arrangement to reintegrate his followers into national structures, and UNITA continued to breach the ceasefire several weeks later, with considerable damage and loss of life.

The following catalogue of 13 years of war in Angola illustrates the need for peace and underlines the finding of a UNICEF report,

Children on the Front Line, that "it is unrealistic to approach the challenge of protecting the children and people of southern Africa as a short-term matter, or as a problem readily amenable to the techniques applied to natural disasters. . . .

"Above all, the children of southern Africa need peace."

The Costs of War

An accurate quantification of the social and economic costs of the war in Angola since independence is not possible, but it is possible to illuminate, through known costs and estimates, the present and future implications of 13 years of war. UNICEF in Luanda gives five categories for classification of war costs, as follows:

- social upheaval and loss of life;
- undermining of social policy;
- direct damage resulting from attacks;
- disruption to the economy;
- diversion of government revenue, foreign exchange earnings and human resources into defence-related activities.

To these can be added a sixth classification:

- damage to the environment.

Social Upheaval and Loss of Life (The Human Cost)

The population of Angola, like that of Mozambique, has been massively disrupted by South Africa's war, with 1.5 million people displaced within and outside the country. Those displaced internally are dependent on humanitarian assistance, and a further 1.4 million people (over half the urban population) experience severe shortages of staple foods. Their suffering is not limited to displacement and hunger, many thousands of people have been maimed. Angola has a large artificial limb factory and hospital to cater for more than 40,000 people who have lost limbs, usually from land mines planted on paths to their fields.

In Angola, as in Mozambique, the farmers and rural infrastructure are an economic target of war, along with railways and other transportation routes, bridges, rural clinics and schools, teachers and health workers, foreign aid personnel and vehicles transporting relief supplies. The distribution of essential commodities is often hampered by the destruction of vehicles in landmine explosions. As well as the future implications of the loss of formal education and literacy programmes, malnutrition is rife and general health is affected by the destruction of clinics. The delivery and use of health services is declining, and immunization coverage is very low.

A visible consequence of rural insecurity has been the complete depopulation of some parts of the country, notably Cunene province in the south and Moxico in the east. The counterpoint of this is a massive migration of population to urban centres. The capital, Luanda, registered a population growth between 1970 and 1983 of 90 per cent. By 1988 its population had swollen to 1.3 million, causing the proliferation of sprawling shanty towns lacking the most basic sanitation and health services, and largely inhabited by destitute families with no means of support. The migration to cities in the south, such as Huambo, Lobito, Benguela and Lobango, is estimated by UNICEF to be even higher, due to their proximity to the war zones.

The war has disrupted rural production in the most agriculturally productive areas of the country, exacerbated on a few occasions by irregular rainfall. The subsistence type of agricultural production accounted for almost all the staple food supply of the rural population. The annual production of cereals (maize, sorghum, rice, wheat) has declined from 500,000 metric tonnes in the mid-1970s to 300,000 metric tonnes 10 years later, a drop of 40 per cent. Also disrupted is the rural-urban commercial supply system, so that any food surpluses do not reach urban centres.

The World Food Programme gives the population of Angola in 1989 as 9.5 million, with roughly one third inhabiting urban centres. According to WFP figures for 1989, 648,000 people are displaced, 447,000 are urban destitutes and 406,000 are rural affected.

Total Food Aid to Angola
1985 to 1988

April 1985/March 1986	61,664 metric tonnes
April 1986/March 1987	70,531 metric tonnes
April 1987/March 1988	110,487 metric tonnes
April 1988/March 1989	111,626 metric tonnes

Source: Food Aid in Angola From 1983 to 1989, *WFP.*

Part of this food aid is designated for refugees in Angola, which provides shelter to over 90,000 people from neighbouring countries. Almost 80 per cent of these are Namibians, now being airlifted home under the transitional independence process, with most of the remainder from South Africa and Zaire. The Angolan government has supplied land and other amenities for many years, through its State Secretariat for Social Affairs, while the international community provides agirucltural implements, transport, vocational training, and basic health and educational needs. Expenditure by the United Nations High Commission for Refugees (UNHCR) in Angola was just over US$3 million in 1988, with $5.2 million allocated for 1989.

At least 100,000 people perished in Angola during 1980-1985 through war-related famine and its effects; and, in the same period, almost 150,000 infants and children under five died who, but for the war, would have lived, according to a UNICEF report, *Children on the Frontline*. Deaths among the same age group were calculated at 173,000 for 1986-1988, assuming no further escalation in child mortality rates, already among the highest in the world (with Mozambique and Afghanistan). This means that the war in Angola claims the lives of 1,000 babies and young children every week.

Adding direct war casualties to the above figures — and assuming some overlap between the famine-related deaths and health-related deaths in other age groups — well over half a million Angolans have perished since 1980 as a result of the war.

War-Related Deaths of Infants and Young Children in Angola 1981 to 1988

Year	Dead
1981	10,000
1982	20,000
1983	31,000
1984	42,000
1985	55,000
1986	56,000
1987	58,000
1988	59,000
TOTAL	331,000

Source: Children on the Frontline, *UNICEF.*

Undermining of Social Policy

Angola's colonial legacy of social neglect, like that of Mozambique, included a population 90 per cent illiterate and 70 per cent out of the reach of any form of health care. The economy had been developed to serve the metropolis and the majority of Portuguese settlers left with the colonial flag, destroying part of the transportation system and disrupting the rural distribution network. However, unlike Mozambique, Angola has a mineral extraction sector that includes oil, diamonds and iron. Agricultural cash crops include coffee, cotton, timber, sisal, maize, tobacco and sugar. Oil and gas constitute almost all of Angola's export earnings, in joint ventures with several Western transnational companies. Prior to the collapse in oil prices, food was imported in times of shortage but the recent reduction in oil income has cut in half the country's ability to feed its people, also reducing imports of food and clothing, and cutting back on raw materials for factories.

The planned post-independence expansion of social infrastructure has always been disrupted by war, but nevertheless Angola had achieved 66 per cent primary school enrolment by 1982. Health policies implemented between 1977 and 1980 could have been expected to reduce infant and child mortality rates by 1985 to those of Tanzania. Post-independence health policies gave priority to primary health care and preventative medicine. Networks of health posts and centres were constructed in the rural areas, and mass vaccination campaigns were carried out.

By 1980, life expectancy at birth had increased to 41 years and the mortality rate for under-fives had been reduced to 260 per 1,000 live births. By 1986, however, the mortality rate for this vulnerable group had shot up again to 325/1,000. UNICEF links this deterioration in the standards of child survival directly to the war.

In an emergency-programme briefing note for 1989, UNICEF says that the aspect of the war that has had the greatest impact in undermining social policy is that of mass terrorism. "Crops have been burned, schools, health posts, shops, churches, mosques, indeed whole villages, have been pillaged and destroyed ruthlessly by insurgents. Teachers, health workers, agricultural technicians, engineers, local administrators and foreign aid workers have been killed or kidnapped, mutilated and maimed. In this way, the government's vigorous social policy, one of the greatest gains of independence for the rural population in particular, has been utterly sabotaged.

"The results are clear and tragic. The delivery and use of health services declined by 30 per cent throughout the country in 1985 alone. In that same year, at least 20 vaccination posts were destroyed, and an equal number of Food Distribution Centres were put out of operation."

Direct Damage Resulting from Attacks

Official Angolan figures in 1987 put the cost of the war at $12 billion since 1975. That includes $6.7 billion for the period 1975/76, a further $900 million to the end of 1981, and $4.4 billion to the end of 1986. These figures, include only damage to infrastructure and transport, industry and agriculture, lost petroleum income and other revenue. It includes some, but not all, of the destruction in the social sector to schools, hospitals and health clinics. And it does not include defence costs, which eat up half of Angola's annual foreign currency earnings as well as the vast local expenditure, or lost development and industrial expansion.

Two key economic sectors which have been major targets and have suffered considerable physical damage as a result of the war are petroleum and transportation.

Roughly half of the central government's annual revenue derives from petroleum taxation, and this sector is also the principal source of foreign exchange. Almost all of the sabotage to the petroleum sector has occurred since 1984 — with the exception of two very minor incidents in 1976 and 1979 costing less than $4,000 and the attack on the Luanda refinery in 1981. The most costly targets, in terms of repairs and lost fuel, have been the Luanda refinery, the storage tanks at the port of Namibe in 1986 and those at Huambo on the central plateau in 1987, with total costs/losses in the three attacks amounting to US$33.5 million.

The attack on the Luanda oil refinery, on the night of 30 November 1981, was by far the largest single act of economic sabotage to date. A South African commando unit landed by sea placed powerful explosives in strategic locations in the storage area causing an extensive fire, in an operation very similar to those carried out against oil storage tanks in Mozambique in 1979 and 1982. Documents, weapons and corpses as well as unexploded packs found at the site provided direct evidence of Pretoria's involvement.

The internationally respected and well-organized state petroleum company, Sonangol, gives the total cost of the damage to the Luanda refinery as $26.7 million. Repairs took three months and cost US$17.2 million, fixed costs for the repair period were $4 million, and the crude oil lost in the attack could have been refined and exported for $5.5 million. These official figures do not include lost production time during the repair period.

On 5 June 1986, South African marines attacked the southern port of Namibe, damaging ships and oil storage tanks. A launch carrying Scorpion missiles entered the harbour and fired on fuel storage tanks, destroying two of the seven and damaging a third, but missing the main fuel storage facility. Divers from the launch placed limpet mines on three ships at berth in the harbour, one of which was sunk and two damaged. Repair costs to the storage tanks in foreign exchange were $3.575 million and fuel losses (168 tons fuel oil, 850 tons gas oil) were valued in local currency at kz 1,401,000 — for a total cost and loss of just over $3.6 million.

Oil storage tanks in the province of Huambo were sabotaged on the night of 13 December 1987 with a repair bill of $3.06 million plus fuel losses of gasoline, gasoil and Jet A1 valued at kz 4,406,000, for a total of $3.21 million.

There have been several smaller sabotages at petroleum installations elsewhere in the country. One of these, at Galinda in the Kwanza area, took place in 1984 and the cost of repair was $130,000.

The repair cost of five sabotages at Quinguila in the Congo area in 1987-1988 reached $226,824. Damage to petrol storage tanks in Malange in March 1989 was estimated at 2 million kwanzas ($66,445).

Thus the minimum total direct cost to the Angolan petroleum industry of South African sabotage is just under $34 million.

A single event served to expose in some detail the facts of the campaign against Angola and its petroleum industry. On 21 May 1985, an army patrol foiled an attempt by a South African commando unit to sabotage the Cabinda Gulf oil complex, and captured the commander, Captain Wynand du Toit, a member of the SADF "special forces" based at Saldanha Bay in Cape province. Two of his men were killed and six others escaped. Du Toit said his unit came from an Israeli-built South African destroyer which lay off the coast while they landed at night in inflatable boats. South Africa initially denied that its forces were in Cabinda then adjusted this to say they were gathering intelligence on SWAPO and the ANC (neither of which has a presence in Cabinda).

Du Toit, who was released two years later in a prisoner exchange, said his instructions were to paint UNITA slogans at the scene of the sabotage. Among captured materials was a tin of paint which he said was to be used for this purpose as "part of the deception". He said he had participated in previous operations in Angola including sabotage of the Giraul bridge in Namibe province, which was claimed by UNITA. His revelation that UNITA often claimed responsibility for covert SADF operations shattered the credibility of other claims over the years. He said a successful attack in Cabinda would have shown that

Damage to the Benguela Railway
1976 to June 1987

Year	Mines detected detonated	Explosives attacks other	Derailments	Damaged locomotives wagons	Destroyed sleepers rails
1987	16	116	9	24	8,920
1986	47	138	22	54	5,819
1985	111	153	79	238	11,596
1984	180	195	108	292	3,592
1983	134	113	77	216	1,196
1982	176	82	84	296	971
1981	193	87	82	?	866
1980	141	209	56	?	2,033
1979	45	233	31	?	4,589
1978	14	137	16	?	2,402
1977	17	106	7	?	?
1976	8	143	13	?	?
TOTAL	1,082	1,712	584	1,120	41,984

Source: Benguela Railways and the Development of Southern Africa, *Editorial Vanguarda.*

UNITA was active in the north — and it would have damaged the petroleum industry, the mainstay of Angola's economy.

The other major economic target has been the Benguela railway which bisects central Angola, connecting the hinterland with the Atlantic port of Lobito. Over 3,000 acts of sabotage against the railway, involving landmines, explosives, attacks or derailments are known to have taken place over 11 and a half years from 1976 to June 1987 as shown by the table on page 129.

There were some 65 sabotage actions against railway bridges in this period, and some were damaged several times. Most of these bridges have been repaired but 12, between the centre of the country and the Zaire border, have not been repaired due to security.

The next table gives a breakdown of the direct costs of sabotage against the Benguela railway, totalling US$76.7 million.

Cost of Damage to the Benguela Railway, 1976 to June 1987 (000 kwanzas)

Electric diesel locomotives		637,780
Destroyed	452,600	
Damaged	185,180	
Steam locomotives, cars lounge cars, freight cars		260,950
Destroyed	208,200	
Damaged	52,750	
Rail cars, motorized cars, tow cars		4,470
Destroyed	2,900	
Damaged	1,570	
Cars		257,110
Destroyed	116,040	
Damaged	141,070	
Railroad		596,960
Damaged on the railroad	298,950	
Bridges and aqueducts	165,390	
Cost of derailment of locomotives, wagons	132,620	
Telecommunications		10,870
Damaged and stolen radios and related equipment	2,620	
Traffic central commands	5,750	
Telephone system	2,500	
Road vehicles		21,400
Destroyed	21,300	
Damaged	100	
Buildings, railway stations, etc.		184,690
Installations		80,500
Other		122,230
TOTAL		Kz 2,317,060

US$76.7 million at average exchange rate.
Source: Benguela Railways, *Editorial Vanguarda.*

In addition to the financial cost of the destruction on the Benguela railway, there is the human cost of keeping the trains rolling. The maintenance and upkeep of the railway has been a hazardous occupation. Almost 200 railway workers (local and foreign) died in the 11-year period to mid-1987, over twice that number were injured, and some 250 were listed as missing. The following illustration gives an annual breakdown which shows that the worst year for casualties on the railway was 1984, the year that the previous peace agreement was signed with South Africa.

**Benguela Railway Workers, Dead and Wounded
1976 to 1987***

	1987	1986	1985	1984	1983	1982	1981	1980	1979	1978	1977	1976
Dead	5	15	16	52	10	11	26	10	9	10	7	27
Wounded	24	40	49	47	33	18	57	38	32	15	25	38
TOTAL	29	55	65	99	43	29	83	48	41	25	32	65

Total local and foreign railway workers   killed 198
wounded 416

* *First 6 months, January to June.*
Source: Benguela Railways, *Editorial Vanguarda.*

Disruption to the Economy

A United Nations document on "The Emergency Situation in Angola: Priority Non-Food Requirements for the Year 1988" opens with a succinct notation:

"The main cause of the worsening emegency situation currently affecting Angola is war. Drought is no longer a significant determinant in this tragic situation. As a consequence of war, economic activity has been severely disrupted throughout the country. All sectors have been affected."

As with other elements of the cost of 13 years of war, the full impact on Angola's economy is impossible to quantify with any certainty. Areas in which an impact can be identified, but not realistically quantified, include production losses, shortages of goods, the rising level of imports, the deteriorating balance of payments and the massive depreciation in purchasing power of the local currency.

A main factor in the deteriorating balance of payments has been the loss of revenue from the Benguela railway, which has been closed to international transit traffic, effectively since 1975 and completely since the beginning of 1983. As seen above, this important railway has been a major target in South Africa's economic warfare against Angola.

Persistent attacks and sabotage of the railway over many years have several short and medium term objectives at national and international levels. At the national level, these aims include:

- disruption or prevention of supply from the coast to the population in central Angola;
- destruction of hinterland industries due to disruption of their communications;
- other ripple effects, such as the port of Lobito which has suffered for lack of international traffic;
- damage to the company itself (a joint venture of Belgian, British and Portuguese capital), not only directly to but through loss of revenue, especially in foreign currency;
- thus an important amount of currency was lost from Angola's balance of international payments;
- a negative reflection on balance of payments through expenditure of foreign currency to replace damaged equipment.

At the international level, neighbouring countries in central Africa, such as Zaire and Zambia, have been prevented from using Lobito for their exports and have been forced to use South African ports, thus paying transport costs to South Africa.

The Benguela railway was built just after the turn of the century specifically for the purpose of this traffic — to transport minerals from Zaire's Shaba province, then Katanga province of the Belgian Congo. Constructed over 26 years from 1903 to 1929, the railway had the additional advantage of opening up the hinterland of the then Portuguese colony of Angola. The distance of 1,301 km from the Zaire border to the port of Lobito remains the shortest trade route between central Africa and the coast.

Distance to Port
For Transit Traffic From Lubumbashi, Zaire

Port	Inside Zaire	Outside Zaire	Total
Lobito	759 km	1,301 km	2,107 km
Dar es Salaam	136	1,990	2,126
Beira	136	2,479	2,615
Durban	136	3,225	3,361
East London	136	3,325	3,461

Source: Benguela Railways, *Editorial Vanguarda; and SADCC documents.*

The Benguela railway earns considerable revenue from passenger transportation as well as freight, although it has carried only internal passenger traffic for 20 years; 1969 which was also the first year the number reached over one million. Passenger traffic has continued to rise on the basis of internal traffic, particularly between Lobito and Benguela, although long-distance trains from Lobito inland to Huambo/Bie/Luena and Luau were suspended for safety reasons in December 1975. Passenger trains continued to operate along parts of the route until December 1983. The following chart shows pre- and post-independence freight and passenger levels. Most of the transit traffic shown is for Zaire and Zambia.

Benguela Railway: Freight and Passengers Transported*
1965 to 1986
(000 tons)

Year	Passengers	Freight		Total
		National	Transit	
1986	4,118.3	249.5	—	249.5
1985	3,871.2	261.7	—	261.7
1984	3,557.6	202.4	—	202.4
1983	4,049.4	186.4	—	186.4
1982	3,926.4	253.6	5.7	259.3
1981	3,232.3	390.0	11.4	401.4
1980	2,470.2	313.1	11.9	324.0
1979	2,405.0	391.3	5.5	396.8
1978	1,927.3	488.3	—	488.3
1977	1,955.9	266.2	—	266.2
1976	1,309.4	229.5	—	229.5
1975	1,635.2	359.2	848.2	1,207.4
1974	1,983.1	789.9	1,593.3	2,383.2
1973	1,590.6	927.1	1,639.9	2,567.0
1972	1,412.8	833.7	1,066.8	1,900.6
1971	1,214.5	833.3	1,229.3	2,062.6
1970	1,143.2	816.7	1,121.7	1,938.4
1969	1,018.7	865.8	959.1	1,784.9
1968	906.2	841.1	1,075.4	1,916.5
1967	846.9	903.4	909.1	1,812.5
1966	864.3	876.7	861.6	1,738.4
1965	850.9	1,011.4	776.7	1,788.3

* *Excluding service traffic.*

Source: Benguela Railways, *Editorial Vanguarda.*

Estimates of the cost per annum of interrupting the operations of long-distance passenger trains, reducing merchandise transportation at national level, and suspending international traffic, are shown in the following illustration.

**Benguela Railway Annual Revenue Losses through Reduction in
Passengers and Freight***

	000 kwanzas	US$
Long distance passengers (national traffic)	190,680	6,311
Merchandise (national traffic)	415,770	13,761
Traffic from Lobito — 232,915		
Traffic to Lobito — 182,855		
Inter-African traffic	50,660	1,677
Transit: Zaire	994,460	32,914
Traffic from Lobito — 254,170		
Traffic to Lobito — 740,290		
Transit: Zambia	1,034,240	34,230
Traffic from Lobito — 332,000		
Traffic to Lobito — 702,240		
Estimation of Annual Revenue Loss	2,685,810	88,893

* *These estimations are based on the premise that Benguela railways would
have transported the same number of long-distance passengers as in 1974, the
year prior to Angola's independence, with regard to national and international
traffic. Rates used are those for 1987.*

Source: Benguela Railways, *Editorial Vanguarda.*

In a Declaration of Intent in April 1987, the Presidents of Angola,
Zambia and Zaire agreed to rehabilitate the Benguela railway. with
international participation, and operate it for the transportation of
civilians and civilian goods. Rehabilitation costs are estimated at
US$280 million and this is expected to be funded primarily by the
European Community and the Societe Generale of Belgium, owners
of the railway. It is anticipated that, if security conditions improve, this
rehabilitation project could enable the return to pre-independence
levels of national traffic within a few years and that Zaire's export
traffic could be won back fairly quickly. However, Zambia would be
expected to continue diversification of its export traffic through Dar es
Salaam and Beira, as well as Lobito.

The railway is one component of a SADCC rehabilitation plan for
the Lobito Corridor, approved at a special donors' meeting in Luanda
in January 1989. The three-phase plan contains several other components in addition to the railway. Among these are the harbour,
hydroelectric dam, telecommunications, additional capacity for road
and sea transportation, improvements to the cement factory at Lobito
and to the city's water supply. This 10-year development plan encompasses three phases at a total cost of $530 million.

All other sectors of the economy have also been disrupted by the
war. According to estimates contained in the UNICEF briefing note

for 1989, the diamond industry has been losing approximately $30 million per annum since a particularly serious UNITA attack in early 1984. A further $30 million in manufacturing production has been lost each year since the sabotage of power plants and electricity transmission lines to Huambo and Benguela in 1983. The agricultural sector was already disrupted by the flight of large commercial farmers and bush traders at independence, but the spread of destabilization has reduced much of the remaining rural infrastructure — making self-sufficiency a struggle.

Based on the statistics shown above, the cost of damage and lost revenue due to sabotage of the Benguela railway since 1975 amounts to some $1.25 billion, excluding port and other charges. Sabotage to the petroleum sector has caused damage valued at almost $34 million. Five years of $30 million losses in the diamond industry and six years of roughly the same amount of loss to the manufacturing sector total $330 million. Thus a minimum cost to those four sectors alone amounts to $1.6 billion.

Diversion of Resources to Defence

Recurrent expenditure on defence and security more than doubled between 1982 and 1985, reaching US$1.15 billion in 1985 — just over 35 per cent of total government expenditure but almost 45 per cent of total recurrent expenditure — and 43.7 per cent of government revenue. Military expenditure accounted for over 50 per cent of imports that year. Although data for recent years is incomplete, the enormity of the problem can be established from statistics to 1987, taking into account the massive escalation of conventional warfare in late 1987 and early 1988, including Cuito Cuanavale.

Coupled with the diversion of economic resources to defence is the necessity to divert scarce human resources. A significant proportion of the country's technical and professional labour personnel are serving in the armed forces, increasing the effectiveness of Angola's defence infrastructure but exacerbating the chronic skill shortages in other economic sectors.

Defence Expenditure since 1980
Recurrent[1]
(millions of kwanzas)

Year	Total Govt Revenue	Total Expend. (Recur)	Defence Expend. (Recur)	% Defence Expend.	5% Def. Exp.	Excess Defence	US$[2]
1987	70,600.	75,204.	32,100.	42.7%	3,760.	28,340.	960.68
1986	71,205	75,737.	32,630.	43.1%	3,787.	28,843.	964.33

Year	Total Govt Revenue	Total Expend. (Recur)	Defence Expend. (Recur)	% Defence Expend.	5% Def. Exp.	Excess Defence	US$[2]
1985	78,556.	78,390.[3]	34,306.	43.8%	3,919.	30,387.	1,015.95
1984	74,556.	69,735.	31,943.	45.8%	3,486.	28,457.	944.16
1983	55,589.	58,056.	23,295.	40.1%	2,903.	20,392.	675.00
1982	50,656.	54,386.	18,275.	33.6%	2,719.	15,556.	514.93
1981	73,708.	57,472.	18,505.	32.2%	2,874.	15,631.	561.46
1980	60,143.	58,769.	16,821.	28.6%	2,938.	13,883.	507.42

TOTAL recurrent defence expenditure in US$ 6,143.59

1. *Does not include capital items of budget expenditure or defence expenditure.*
2. *Annual average rate of exchange.*
3. *Estimate based on per cent recurrent of total expenditure.*

Sources: Ministry of Finance, World Bank.

The above chart shows that the excess recurrent expenditure on defence and security (after allowing for a 5 per cent international norm for expenditure on defence) totals over $6 billion to the end of 1987, and has been running at almost $1 billion per year since 1984. With 1988 expenditure the total figure since 1980 would reach well over $7 billion — and that excludes all military hardware and buildings, which are not reflected in the budget. So the true figure would be at least double, and possibly higher.

The above chart also shows that government revenue covers only recurrent expenditure. Capital costs, representing about 20 per cent of total expenditure (excluding most capital items for defence), are deficit financing. Just over 40 per cent of government revenue was drawn from petroleum taxation in 1986 and 1987, and in previous years (before the 1986 drop in international oil prices) it was most often a higher proportion — over half of government revenue.

All of the above charts, showing damage and lost revenue in various sectors, give an insight into the present and future implications for Angola, and it is easy to see how cost estimates including war damage, economic losses and defence spending begin at $20 billion. Revalued to current rates of exchange and replacement values, these estimates range to $27 billion. By comparison, Angola's foreign debt in 1987 reached only $4 billion, five times less than the minimum cost of the war.

With a fraction of that sum to spend on development instead of defence, and with peace instead of war, Angola's population of 9.5 million could live in relative prosperity rather than the squalor of displacement. What these figures cannot reflect, of course, is the human costs of bereavement, malnourishment, loss of education, psychological and physical resettlement, amputation and rape.

Damage to the Environment

One effect of the war in southern Angola that often goes unmentioned is the long-term environmental damage. A US conservation group recently presented a dossier to Congress accusing South Africa of hosting a massive international ivory smuggling operation. The report by the Conservation, Environmental and Animal Welfare Consortium said at least half of the great elephant herds that roamed the plains of southern Angola in numbers exceeding 200,000 — once the largest elephant population in Africa — have been systematically annihilated.

A secret ten-month investigation by the US attorney-general confirmed that SADF members in Angola and Namibia "have been actively engaged in killing and smuggling of wildlife species — including rhinos and elephants — for personal gain and profit". Three US citizens have been charged with smuggling rhino horn and other wildlife trophies into the US, and formal requests have been made for the extradition of three South African nationals, including two SADF officers, to face charges.

Satellite pictures show the decimation of the great teak forests of southern Angola. And the UNITA leader, Jonas Savimbi, told a reporter from the French magazine, *Paris Match*, in 1988 that UNITA was ordered to pay for South African assistance with ivory and teak.

A survey of the international ivory trade for 1988 shows that 50 tons of elephant tusks originated in South Africa, yet the country's official records account for only 14 tons of legally exported ivory — 7 tons from animals culled in the Kruger National Park and 7 tons from ivory imported legally from other countries. Since culling of elephants is strictly controlled in South Africa, it is reasonable to assume that the excess was smuggled from neighbouring countries.

An official of the Endangered Wildlife Trust in Johannesburg, which revealed the illegal trade, writing in the conservation magazine *Quagga*, said: "A number of discoveries have made it clear that South Africa is guilty of harbouring some big-time criminals who have been making a huge profit by dealing in rhino horn and ivory. . . . The fact that these people have probably been operating for a number of years is a serious indictment of our government conservation departments . . . (and) of our police."

An international expert on the trade in rhino horn, Bradley Martin, recently exposed South Africa as the major source of rhino horn being sold in Taiwan. He said Taiwanese traders had told him that they import the horn on the regular flights between Taipei and Johannesburg. A Johannesburg dealer with close business links to Hong Kong has been named in the South African press recently as a major clandestine importer and exporter of illicit ivory and horn from the region, via South Africa. The rhinocerous population in Africa has dropped to 3,500 and is said to be declining at a rate of 100 a month.

A Historical Perspective

South Africa's War Front Since 1975

South African military involvement in Angola began in the second week of August 1975, less than two months after the independence of Mozambique had removed a buffer state on the other side of the continent. SADF troops crossed the border from northern Namibia and took up positions around hydroelectric installations on the Cunene river at Ruacana and Calueque. A week later, on 22 August, a SADF battalion supported by armoured cars and helicopters attacked and destroyed Ngiva, the capital of Cunene province, and occupied a strip of border territory 50 km deep. A SADF officer and 18 military instructors were sent further north to the central plateau in September, to UNITA bases in Kuito and Huambo. In early October this group was reinforced with combat troops and armoured cars and the operation, known as Foxbat, became the eastern prong of the pre-independence invasion of Angola.

On 16 October, a combined force of about 2,000 men from UNITA, the small FNLA group and the SADF, wearing green Portuguese army uniforms and accompanied by 50 armoured cars and artillery batteries, crossed into Angola at Oshikango and moved north-west toward the coast. This was the other prong of the armoured columns which began moving toward Luanda in the pincer movement of Operation Savannah, in a bid to prevent the MPLA from declaring independence on 11 November. Their instructions were to take as many towns as possible before reaching Luanda. By early November, this second column, known as Zulu, had taken seven urban centres including the ports of Namibe, Benguela and Lobito, and installed proxy administrations. South African-led forces in the south numbered about 6,000, a figure which doubled shortly after 11 November.

To the north, a combined force of FNLA, European mercenaries and 11,000 Zairean regular soldiers, assisted by SADF officers and artillery, were halted at Kifangondo, 20 km north of Luanda, after a fierce ground attack in early November and Luanda was under fire from the artillery. Oil-rich Cabinda province, separated from the rest of Angola by a thin strip of Zaire, also faced an invasion, assisted and supplied by the CIA.

South African and US involvement in this period is well documented by John Stockwell, former head of the CIA Angola Task Force, and others, and much of what followed is well known. Cuban military instructors numbering 480 arrived in October and, in early

November, Cuba decided to respond positively to a request from MPLA for combat assistance, sending in the first 650 troops of Operation Carlota on the eve of independence, when Portugal ceased to be the administering power. Yugoslavia supplied arms and equipment, and the Soviet Union resumed supplies to the MPLA after a 20-month suspension.

The mercenary-led forces in the north were routed and a small force of Angolans and Cubans held Cabinda. Fighting broke out in the south between the FNLA and UNITA, and the rapid South African advance was turned back 100 km south of Luanda when confronted by Cuban and Angolan forces. The FNLA fell apart and the scattered UNITA forces reverted to acts of banditry. South African troops finally left Angola on 27 March 1976, destroying bridges and other infrastructure as they went, plundering vehicles, machinery and cattle. The Angolan government estimated the quantifiable war damage in this period at US$6.7 billion, and the social fabric of the southern part of the country was left in tatters.

Members of the US Congress, angered by revelations of covert operations in Angola and the CIA cover-up, banned military aid to anti-government forces in Angola without congressional approval. The Clark Amendment was passed in early 1976 and remained in effect until it was rescinded nine years later, in 1985. However, the US Secretary of State, Henry Kissinger, sent a message to UNITA saying that the United States would continue support as long as there was a capacity for effective resistance to the MPLA, and Washington escalated economic and political pressure on the government in Luanda. There were attempts, successful for a short period, to block Gulf Oil's payments and stop the pumping of oil, and to prevent the delivery of two Boeing aircraft.

On the political front, Stockwell records, the United States "launched a major political effort" to prevent recognition of the MPLA government. The January OAU vote was split, but Angola finally became a member in February, largely as a result of opposition to the South African invasion, particularly by Nigeria. However, the Ford administration vetoed Angola's admission to the United Nations, and this had to wait until after President Carter took office in 1977. The US then abstained, and Angola joined the UN, but the government of Angola has never been formally recognized by Washington, despite its oil exports to the US and its good relations with US business interests.

1976 to 1980

In April 1976, less than a month after the withdrawal of South African forces, Angola and Cuba agreed on a programmed reduction of Cuban forces, which were reduced by more than one-third in less than a year. Renewed South African aggression stopped the withdrawal, and a further decision in 1979 to reduce the number of Cubans was again followed by an escalation of SADF military operations in southern Angola.

Several new SADF bases were established along the Namibian border for the purpose of regrouping and training the remnants of FNLA and UNITA. FNLA members were incorporated directly into SADF, mostly in 32 "Buffalo" Battalion based at Rundu. UNITA was reorganized in Namibia, where Savimbi had been evacuated, and entered into a surrogate relationship with the South African military who, bruised by their experience in Angola, were reformulating their approach to a new regional and international environment.

This approach culminated in changes to the power structure in Pretoria involving more military influence at the strategic and administrative levels. Prime Minister Vorster was forced to step down in 1978 to be replaced by the Minister of Defence, P.W. Botha.

During this period, the five Western members of the UN Security Council — Britain, Canada, France, West Germany and the United States — had set up a "contact group" to negotiate a settlement in Namibia. Through shuttle diplomacy involving the Frontline states, Nigeria, South Africa and SWAPO, an independence plan was agreed by all parties and its implementation demanded in Security Council resolution 435 of 1978.

Pretoria, while stating publicly that it agreed to the plan "in principle", found various pretexts for not implementing it, and escalated its undeclared war against Angola throughout 1979, culminating in June 1980 with Operation Smokeshell, when ground and air forces penetrated 140 km into the country. It was US presidential election year again, and Pretoria was waiting for Carter to be defeated.

The largest attack of this period was on 4 May 1978 when 612 Namibians were killed and about the same number wounded in a massive South African ground and air attack on a camp at Kassinga in Huila province sheltering primarily refugees. A nearby transit facility was also destroyed. Of the dead, 167 were women, 298 children and 147 men. Fragmentation bombs and paralyzing gases were used in the six-and-a-half hour attack, and all access routes to the camp were mined. A health centre and other buildings were destroyed, as were 100 head of cattle and 160 hectares of crops. In another large attack on a similar camp ten months later, conducted jointly by the Rhodesian and South African air forces, 198 Zimbabweans were killed and 600 wounded.

Although South African incursions into southern Angola became more aggressive as SWAPO became more successful and were presented as in "hot pursuit" against SWAPO guerrillas, most attacks of consequence in this period were against targets which damaged the economy of Angola. On the morning of 26 September 1979, four South African jets bombed Lubango, capital of Huila province, damaging 11 factories including a sawmill and two flour mills and destroying a furniture factory, Madeiras da Huila. Twenty-six people were killed, 41 seriously injured and many jobs were lost. Estimated damage was over $12 million. An hour later, six South African jets attacked the southern town of Xangongo, killing 30 people, wounding 100, destroying a primary school and a food store.

On 28 October, South African troops landed by helicopter in the Serra da Leba mountains to sabotage the Lubango-Namibe railway line, destroying 15 metres of track and mining another 20 metres. A railway tunnel was damaged and several bridges blown up. The cost estimate for the infrastructural damage, not counting lost revenue, was over $33 million.

Estimated human loses in Angola from the "end" of the war in early 1976 until the end of 1980 were over 1,900 dead and 2,500 wounded, with an unknown number of people kidnapped or missing. Material damage during the same period — caused by ground and heliborne attacks, bombing raids and occupation of towns — was assessed at approximately US$530 million. This covers damage in the following sectors: agriculture and livestock production, construction, transport, fisheries, industry, education, health, commercial and administration/ public service. Unquantifiable losses result from the forced exodus of people from war areas, interruption of schooling and disruption of social services, unemployment caused by destruction of economic targets and unfinished development projects, nutritional and material shortages, and the psychological damage caused, especially to children.

1981 to 1983

The UN conference on Namibia held in Geneva in January 1981 was the first attended by delegations from both SWAPO and South Africa. But South Africa stalled, waiting for president-elect Reagan to take office, and stepped up its aggression against Angola during the conference. After 1981, the SADF occupied parts of southern Angola almost continuously until its most recent withdrawal in 1988.

The new administration in Washington linked Namibia's independence to the withdrawal of Cuban troops from Angola, and the pressure on South Africa to end its illegal occupation of Namibia was replaced by pressure on Angola to accept "linkage". The various pretexts previously used by Pretoria for refusing to implement Resolution 435 had never included the presence of Cuban troops in

Angola. By taking the Namibia negotiations out of the ambit of the UN, the Reagan administration caused the demise of the "contact group" and President Carter's two conditions for recognition of Angola — withdrawal of Cuban forces and sharing power with Savimbi — became conditions for Namibia's independence.

Documents on US-South Africa talks, leaked to the *New York Times* in June 1981, included a memorandum on talks in Pretoria in April which said:

"South African Government (SAG) sees Savimbi as a buffer for Namibia. SAG believes Savimbi wants southern Angola. Having supported him this far, it would damage SAG honor if Savimbi is harmed. . . . Malan declared SAG view that Angola/Namibia situation is number one problem in southern Africa. Angola is one place where US can roll back Soviet/Cuban presence in Africa. Need to get rid of Cubans, and support UNITA."

From the beginning of 1981, there was a marked increase in South African aggression against Angola, with the following operations recorded in the first eight months of the year: 1,617 reconnaissance flights, 100 bombing raids, 50 strafing incidents, 26 ground reconnaissance operations, 67 troop build-ups, 4 paratroop landings, 34 ground attacks, 7 shelling operations, 9 mine-laying and other mining operations.

South African attacks and sabotage, occupation, shelling and mine-laying centred on the southern provinces of Kuando Kubango, Cunene, Namibe and Huila, a vast area with a scattered population of just over one million. These regions, however, are of special economic importance because of their agricultural and livestock resources, industry and fisheries. Basic foodstuffs of maize, beans, sorghum and millet are grown in this area, which also contains the largest numbers of cattle and pigs, and the Kassinga iron mines. Industry relates to the processing of agricultural and livestock products, and Namibe is the centre of the country's fishing and fish processing industry.

The seeming contradiction of increasing military action against Angola while calling for a Cuban withdrawal indicated that insistence on "linkage" was a way of easing pressure on South Africa to proceed with Namibian decolonization, while enabling presentation of the problem in terms of global East-West conflict. The Cuban presence suited the South Africans because they could be seen to be an active ally of the West against the Soviet Union.

In July 1981, the Angolan authorities announced that 40,000 South African troops were massed on the Namibian border with a vast quantity of equipment, and on 23 August the SADF launched Operation Protea, a massive invasion of southern Angola involving three armoured columns, long-range artillery and bombing raids on urban centres in the south. There was fierce fighting on the ground but South Africa's superiority in the air proved decisive. A large quantity of captured equipment and ammunition was recycled to proxy forces. The SADF occupied most of Cunene province as a buffer zone, protected by air and ground patrols, ambushing and mining access routes and allowing UNITA to infiltrate its forces further north, while a publicity campaign was mounted in support of Savimbi. On 30 November, while Savimbi was in Washington, a South African commando unit sabotaged the Luanda refinery.

The general assessment of damage for 1981, including relief for 160,000 people displaced by the conflict, was just under $400 million. Over 1,000 soldiers were listed as missing in this period, with 206 killed and 389 wounded, 158 civilians killed and 265 wounded.

The occupation of southern Angola continued through 1982 and 1983 despite South African denials, but the balance of military power improved for the government as the army was reorganized and better equipped to deal with a conventional confrontation. Commando units newly trained to handle guerrilla warfare mounted an offensive to drive UNITA out of vantage points handed over to them after the South African invasion. The deterioration in UNITA's military situation in this period caused deep divisions within the ranks of the organization, and some key figures disappeared (foreign secretary Sangumba, military chief Chiwale, and Vakulukuta, once secretary of the interior).

1984 to 1986

On 6 December 1983, the SADF launched its biggest military operation of the period, surpassed only by the offensive against Cuito Cuanavale four years later. Cloaked in the verbal disguise of the time as "hot pursuit against SWAPO terrorists", Operation Askari was more about consolidating bargaining positions during a US presidential election year and was designed to expand the occupied area. It failed to do so, and South African generals conceded that they had not expected such fierce resistance, making it the costliest SADF operation in Angola in terms of South African losses since 1975-1976.

South Africa's air superiority, which had proved decisive in previous operations, was still a factor but, to their surprise and dismay, the Angolan army was better prepared this time. What had escaped South African military intelligence, or been ignored by SADF commanders, was the appearance of sophisticated Soviet defence equipment, including helicopter gunships equipped with rockets and cannons, surface-to-air missiles and a new radar system. This prevented the invaders from sending ground troops too far ahead or attacking by air. Cuban troops were not involved in this fighting and remained garrisoned further north, deployed to protect strategic installations, freeing Angolans for combat.

The failure of Operation Askari, South Africa's economic crisis to which the war in Angola was adding an estimated US$2 million a day, and the Reagan administration's desire for a foreign policy victory before the presidential elections, were the main reasons for South Africa's participation in the Lusaka Accord of 16 February 1984 and the agreement to withdraw its troops from Angola. Another factor which cannot have passed unnoticed was a tripartite meeting in Moscow with the Angolans and Cubans at which it was agreed to strengthen Angola's defence capability. Under the terms of the Lusaka Accord, Angola would ensure that SWAPO forces did not enter areas vacated by the SADF during the period of withdrawal, and a Joint Monitoring Commission (JMC) was set up to oversee this. South African delegations visited Zambia, and SWAPO was optimistic that a settlement was near. South Africa, however, neither withdrew its forces from Angola nor moved toward implementation of Resolution 435.

Angola presented a detailed programme for Cuban withdrawal, with the precondition that South Africa must begin implementing Resolution 435 and withdraw all of its troops from Namibia except the 1,500 stipulated in the UN plan.South Africa responded with a counter-proposal that all Cubans leave within 12 weeks, that the Angolans provide a detailed list of Cuban personnel in the country, and that the withdrawal should be monitored by a commission, to include South Africans, free to move anywhere in Angola.

Far from ending its occupation of Namibia, Pretoria was proposing further violation of Angolan sovereignty. A US statement declared that there was no basic difference between the two positions, the only problem remaining was to "bridge the gap". Press reports said the difference was a "clash over time limit for pull out of Cuban troops". These manipulations managed to hold the situation at a plateau while Washington was occupied with its elections and until the administration was re-elected at the end of 1984.

In late 1984, a planeload of journalists was flown from Pretoria to the UNITA base at Jamba, in the south-east corner of Angola near the border with Namibia's Caprivi Strip, where Savimbi announced, as he had a year earlier, that he would take Luanda by Christmas. His stated aim was "to make the inclusion of UNITA in the negotiations a precondition for settling the Namibian issue".

In April 1985, more than a year after the agreement to withdraw troops from Angola, South Africa finally announced that it was doing so, leaving two companies at the hydroelectric dams on the Cunene river. Despite a much-publicized and much-photographed "withdrawal of men and equipment", the SADF maintained a powerful force on both sides of the border. At the same time, Pretoria announced the installation of an "internal" government in Namibia. By the end of 1985, the South Africans had openly rescued their surrogates and were again occupying parts of southern Angola.

The transition from destabilization to diplomacy and back again was so sudden that one South African magazine likened it to a Transvaal thunderstorm.

Soon after South African troops withdrew, the US Congress moved to repeal the Clark Amendment banning open US military aid to anti-government forces in Angola. A public relations firm was hired on a $600,000 contract to "sell" Savimbi to the US public. A Reagan adviser on national security affairs, Christopher Lehman, left the White House to join the firm.

A single event that served to expose the facts of the campaign against Angola was the unsuccessful attempt in May 1985 by a South African commando unit to sabotage the Cabinda Gulf oil complex, which resulted in the capture of Captain Wynand du Toit and the publicity which surrounded his story of SADF sabotage activity in Angola. Four months later, SADF confirmed reports that one of their military doctors had been killed in Moxico, in the centre-east of Angola near the Benguela railway but gave no explanation as to what he was doing so far from the border area. A South African magazine, quoting intelligence sources, said that South African military aircraft had flown UNITA troops and equipment to Moxico province on two occasions in September, and local residents confirmed that South African transport planes regularly ferried equipment to the area.

Bills were tabled in Congress authorizing aid to UNITA but these did not pass, nor did a proposed trade embargo against Angola, and President Jose Eduardo dos Santos told the UN that Angola remained Washington's fourth largest trading partner in sub-Saharan Africa, and that financial relations with US banks in the first half of the year amounted to more than $100 million.

In December, the SADF advanced over 30 km into Cunene province, near the devastated provincial capital of Ngiva which it had occupied for three years from August 1981 to February 1984. This invasion involved five battalions with tanks, armoured cars and air support, including the Buffalo Battalion as well as SWATF units from Namibia. SWATF had first been used by SADF in southern Angola in 1981, although the use of Namibian specialist units goes back to 1978.

In January 1986, Savimbi again visited Washington where he was given all the protocol of a visiting head of state, including an audience with the President. An Angolan-Cuban-Soviet meeting in Moscow the same month confirmed their "readiness to undertake concerted actions in defence of the independence, sovereignty and territorial integrity of Angola". In February, the US State Department announced the administration's decision to provide covert military assistance to UNITA, bypassing Congress, and other reports indicated this amounted to $15 million, including shoulder-fired surface-to-air Stinger missiles.

Angola responded by suspending talks with the United States. In a letter to the UN Secretary-General, President dos Santos said the US had not fulfilled the terms of a previously unpublicized agreement, the Mindelo Act, with Angola providing for the cessation of acts of aggression including support for UNITA.

On 3 April, the Angolan air force shot down a C-130 Hercules transport aircraft overflying the centre of the country at midnight. The unidentified and unclaimed aircraft, which exploded in mid-air and spread wreckage over a wide area, was believed to be transporting arms to UNITA. A second Hercules was damaged but limped out of Angolan airspace with a third.

From 19 to 26 May 1986, the SADF launched attacks deep into Angolan territory, with helicopters, armoured cars and heavy artillery, escalating a month of such attacks. This was widely seen as part of a general escalation of South African military aggression across the region to coincide with the presence in Pretoria of the Commonwealth Eminent Persons Group, including the 19 May raids on Botswana, Zambia and Zimbabwe that caused the EPG to suspend its mission. On 5 June, South African marines attacked the southern port of Namibe, damaging ships and oil storage tanks. The two largest incursions of this period were into Cunene province in early November and again three months later near Mongua, some 70 km from the border, both of which SADF claimed were "pre-emptive" strikes against SWAPO guerrillas making a rainy season advance.

1987 to 1988

In June 1987, South Africa budgeted a massive 54 per cent increase to air force operations and later the same month its warplanes bombed army positions in southern Angola. Angola reported to the OAU at the end of July that eight battalions numbering 7,000 South African troops were in southern Angola and that two battalions were stationed in the south-east corner of Kuando Kubango province near the UNITA headquarters. The report said the Namibe railway had been sabotaged again in May. A strategic bridge over the Kuito river was sabotaged by South African divers in August.

In early August, Angolan government troops began an offensive to retake Mavinga, the nearest town to the UNITA headquarters. The Afrikaans press reported that SADF was "definitely involved" in the fighting, and General Malan announced a few days later that SADF was in Angola assisting UNITA. Savimbi promptly denied this. Both sides suffered heavy casualties and loss of equipment, and government troops were halted at the Lomba river, 50 km north of Mavinga.

It was announced in Luanda in late November that the South African regular army was massing more troops on the Namibian border with large quantities of equipment including heavy artillery, and that the Eighth Mechanized Division was advancing under full air cover and fully equipped having disembarked its equipment at Walvis Bay in Namibia. These forces entered in two prongs, one through Cunene province and the other from Rundu base in Namibia directly into Kuando Kubango. About 360 men from SADF Battalions 101 and 102, mostly black Namibian soldiers, were detained in Namibia when they refused to fight in Angola.

In December 1987, SADF escalated their attacks on army positions at Cuito Cuanavale with air strikes and long-range artillery, ignoring a UN Security Council resolution demanding their withdrawal from Angola by 10 December and their own claim, on 5 December, that their forces were being withdrawn. Strong anti-aircraft defences made the loss of irreplaceable aircraft costly for the South African air force, and armoured cars were stopped with anti-tank missiles. The SADF offensive continued primarily by battering the town with G-5, G-6 and Valkyrie heavy artillery, causing heavy damage. The G-5 and G-6 can fire further than any other gun currently in use and the first G-5s were imported from the US in the late 1970s. From 10 January, 170-200 shells per day fell on or near the town.

A UNITA spokesman outside Angola claimed incorrectly on 22 January that the town had been taken, which would have secured the heavy duty runway and the strategic main roads to the north. There also was one announcement from within that a provisional government had been declared, and government sources in Luanda believe that this would have been the intention after moving UNITA's headquarters deeper into country.

As well as the shelling of Cuito Cuanavale, about 300 km into Angola, there was heavy fighting at Munhango, some 590 km from the border, along the Benguela railway. Sabotage of the line soon after independence reduced transit traffic to virtually nothing, although some sections continued to operate internally. Its functioning was further reduced in 1987 when the railway was a target of regular economic sabotage in Moxico and Bie provinces. Over four months, there were 100 actions against the line including mining, acts of sabotage and ambushes, resulting in the destruction of locomotives and carriages and damaging several km of track. Repairs were carried out and specialized units kept the line open over some stretches, but in late December commandos destroyed a bridge over the Kwanza river, cutting off the east.

The South African offensive against Cuito Cuanavale allowed

UNITA to concentrate its attention on towns along the railway, and journalists taken to the area in early March were shown equipment captured from UNITA which included South African-made vehicles. Some UNITA forces were engaged in action along the railway while others were moved to a new base at Quimbele in the far north of Angola near the border with Zaire, across which there is extensive infiltration into the northern provinces and into the enclave of Cabinda. They were supplied with arms flown from Kinshasa in a plane marked Santa Lucia Airways to an abandoned Belgian air base remodelled by the US military at Kamina in Zaire's Shaba province.

SADF's unsuccessful offensive in mid-January 1988 against Cuito Cuanavale, was followed by another in mid-February from 20 km east, apparently with the aim of destroying the town's airstrip and its anti-aircraft missile-linked radar sites. The loss of Cuito Cuanavale would have been a severe setback for the Angolan army, making another assault on UNITA strongholds strategically difficult. Cuito Cuanavale is the last in a line of bases stretching east from the Atlantic coast, each one with a fighter airfield, a radar system, and anti-aircraft missiles. Their perimeters overlap, providing an unbroken line of cover.

The artillery bombardment of the town escalated again on 16 March, followed by a bloody retreat on 23 March after SADF units tried to break through the minefields and other defences using tanks and armoured cars. These battles marked a turning point, with both sides holding position and some SADF units partially cut off from their means of retreat.

As is often the case with high profile regional action, the assault on Cuito Cuanavale coincided with important internal events in South Africa, in this case three by-elections in February and March 1988. Also in March, the US State Department was able to resume its shuttle diplomacy when the Assistant Secretary of State for African Affairs, Chester Crocker, held his first meeting with Pik Botha in two years. Angolan talks with the US had resumed at a meeting in Brazzaville a year earlier, and Crocker began shuttling again in July.

Sources assessing military traffic in northern Namibia say the SADF military build-up coincided with this diplomatic activity, beginning in early 1987 with nightly flights of heavy military transport planes into the northern Namibia base at Rundu coupled with an increase in military ground traffic to the base, which was substantially built-up with the extension of the runway and other facilities. Military flights to Rundu increased in July. Three military bases in the Western Caprivi Strip were also substantially developed, and roads in the border area were upgraded.

This high-tech, high casualty battle over a tiny town in southern Angola was costly for all of the states involved, directly or indirectly —

South Africa, Angola, Cuba, the United States and the Soviet Union — and they all participated in intensive negotiations that let to formal agreement in December 1988.

South Africa views these international contacts as further recognition of its role as regional superpower, but wishes its neighbours to see it the same way. Regional acceptance of such status would ensure their survival through military and economic domination, and would enhance their future ability to resist pressure — even from their allies.

During the massive South African offensive in late 1983, when Soviet officials summoned their South African counterparts at the UN to an unprecedented meeting to warn them that "aggression cannot be left unpunished", Pretoria took it as recognition of South Africa's role as the region's superpower. "South Africa is to southern Africa what the Soviet Union is to the world at large," said an SABC commentary. "The Soviet Union is a super power; South Africa is a regional superpower. This reality merits acknowledgement by the governments of southern Africa."

6   Tanzania

On 22 October 1959, Julius Nyerere addressed the Tanganyika Legislative Assembly in a speech which has since become known as "A Candle on Kilimanjaro".

He stressed Tanganyika's desire for peaceful constitutional progress, reflecting the Ghandi approach of those of that era in southern Africa who were seeking majority rule without bloodshed.

"I have said before elsewhere that we, the people of Tanganyika, would like to light a candle and put it on the top of Mount Kilimanjaro which would shine beyond our borders giving hope where there was despair, love where there was hate and dignity where there was before only humiliation."

Nyerere went on to say: "We cannot, unlike other countries, send rockets to the moon, but we can send rockets of love and hope to all our fellow men wherever they may be. . . ."

While Nyerere's message at that time was addressed primarily to the British colonial rulers of his country, it had a far broader meaning.

A little more than two years earlier the Soviet Union had begun the exploration of space with the launching of Sputnik I. John F. Kennedy was President of the United States, speaking of "brave new frontiers". The "wind of change" was blowing across Africa bringing with it hope where there had been despair, dignity where there had been hatred and humiliation.

That burning light from Africa's highest mountain was an inspiration for those who, then, believed that their liberation from humiliation could be achieved by non-violent means.

When Nyerere made that speech, most of today's Frontline parties who were later forced into liberation wars did not even exist.

When they emerged on the region's political chessboard they believed, as did Nyerere, that the democratic values and laws promulgated by their colonizers were a sufficient force to achieve the goals their people sought.

For those whose privilege it has been to know such gentle and reluctant warriors as Eduardo Mondlane, Agostinho Neto and Robert Mugabe over the 30 years since Nyerere's remarks, what followed, and what is contained in the preceeding chapters, is a travesty of the values they adhered to.

Decolonization

The British colonial empire withdrew quietly (more or less) from absolute political control, but apartheid, Rhodesian settler domination and Portuguese fascism remained south of the Zambezi river challenging the young men and women of those days and leading directly to the bloodshed which continues to this day.

Even before his Kilimanjaro speech, Nyerere had begun to enunciate the thinking of those who were to become the region's future leaders. When he was a student at Edinburgh University from 1949 to 1952 he wrote an article, entitled "The Race Problem in East Africa", which reflected the non-racial approach of the region's leaders, then and now. The organization he wrote it for refused to publish it.

"We reject the principle of equal racial representation on the same ground on which we condemned that of European domination," he wrote. "It is a principle which in spite of its deceptive name assumes the principle of racial superiority. If equal representation is unfair in the USA and New Zealand where the whites are in a majority, it is still unfair in Africa where they are in a minority. . . ."

Throughout this early period Nyerere spoke out vigorously against violence. "Don't be provoked into violence. Be as calm and as good-humoured as you have always been. The Enemy is bound to lose," he wrote in *Sauti Ya Tanu* (Voice of TANU) in 1958 in an article for which he was later tried and convicted of criminal libel.

In March 1961, nine months before his country's independence, Nyerere wrote an article for the London newspaper *The Observer*, entitled "The Commonwealth, South Africa and Tanganyika". It was his earliest important contribution on the international stage which he has occupied ever since.

"The policies of apartheid now being practised in the Union of South Africa are a daily affront to this belief in individual human dignity. They are, in addition, a constantly reiterated insult to our own dignity as Africans about which we cannot be expected to remain indifferent, and which could inflame our own passions if not otherwise dealt with.

"To be successful in building up a good society in our country we must therefore make our detestation of the South African system apparent in every action. The Tanganyika government cannot afford to have any relations with the South African government, and it must, within the bounds of international law, lend support to those who struggle against the system of apartheid."

He continued: "If the Commonwealth is, as we believe, a voluntary association of friends, a 'Club', we do not see how any country like ourselves, committed to policies based on the dignity of man, can be a member at the same time as South Africa is one."

That article was deliberately timed to coincide with the Commonwealth Prime Ministers' conference in London where a central issue was South Africa's application to remain a member after becoming a Republic. It was a great influence in forcing South Africa to withdraw the application rather than face certain refusal.

Tanganyika became independent in December 1961, the first of (what were to become known as) the Frontline States to attain that goal. Nyerere, then and still a prolific writer and thinker, wrote an article which was published that month in the *Journal of the Royal Commonwealth Society.*

"Tanganyika's desire to join the Commonwealth hardly needs explanation. Our nationalism is not exclusive; we seek to promote African unity, but not African isolation. We want to be a member of the community of nations. . . . The Commonwealth is an association of equals, having no struggle among its members for domination. In other words the Commonwealth is in practice a great champion of the principles of the UN charter."

Developing his theme, Nyerere went on to speak of the contribution that countries like his could make to the Commonwealth — then perceived as the "British Commonwealth" — and of the special relations that could be developed with other states which were not eligible for membership.

Nyerere, then comparatively unknown, was enunciating values which he and other southern African leaders were to build upon as the the cornerstone of political philosophy for their young nations. Further, these statements reflected the loathing of violence by Nyerere and his peers, who considered armed struggle as a last resort, to be used only if there was no alternative and after all peaceful methods to achieve decolonization and democracy had failed.

Liberation

On 25 June 1962, only six months after Tanganyika's independence and with the encouragement and support of Nyerere, the Frente de Libertacao de Mocambique (Frelimo) was formed in Dar es Salaam, marking the beginning of a long and deep national commitment to the liberation of southern Africa. On 25 September 1964, after the Portuguese colonial regime had rejected any form of negotiation, Frelimo launched their liberation struggle in Mozambique with the support of Tanzania. (The country's name had changed after the union with Zanzibar in April that year.)

As a result, Tanzania was the first of the Frontline States to be subjected to destabilization, albeit on a much lesser scale. However, those early days provide a familiar pattern to some of today's events:

the establishment of espionage networks, use of surrogates and political malcontents against the government, cross-border attacks, killing of innocent villagers, and political assassinations.

In the late 1960s the Tanzanians broke up a large Portuguese spy ring in Dar es Salaam. Under questioning the agents said they had been recruited at the time of independence by a man who carried a Belgian passport and said he was a shoe salesman. There the trail ended and the recruiter could not be identified. Some years later in Lisbon he told his story to the authors. The Portuguese military had foreseen the possibility of Tanganyika supporting a liberation war across its southern border and had decided to set up an intelligence network. Ironically, the recruiter was Major Vitor Alves, later a key figure in the Portuguese coup d'état. Another key figure who slipped through the Tanzanian net was a lieutenant-colonel in Portuguese military intelligence whose cover was assistant manager on a tea estate in southern Tanzania, located close to Frelimo's main training camp at Nachingwea.

Tanzania was also the first Frontline State to be subjected to surrogate warfare. In 1967, the former Foreign Minister, Oscar Kambona, went into self-imposed exile in Britain. A few years later he surfaced in Lisbon at the side of Jorge Jardim, a godson of the Portuguese dictator, Antonio Salazar, and a man with powerful business interests in Mozambique. In December 1971 and July 1972 pamphlets were dropped from a Portuguese aircraft over Dar es Salaam in support of Kambona. The Portuguese also set up a military training base for Kambona in north-western Mozambique commanded by a Portuguese major who admitted his role to one of the authors in Lourenco Marques (now Maputo) soon after the Portuguese coup d'état of 25 April 1974. There were a few inconsequential incursions into south-western Tanzania but Kambona, with no support at home, quickly faded into oblivion.

There were a number of Portuguese cross-border attacks into Tanzania during the Mozambican struggle, mines planted in the rural areas which killed or maimed a number of Tanzanians and frequent air space violations.

Tanzania was the scene of one of the earliest assassinations of a liberation movement leader. On 3 February 1969, Frelimo's first President, Eduardo Mondlane, was killed by a book bomb at a beach house where he was working just outside Dar es Salaam (a Swahili name which means "haven of peace"). With the help of Scotland Yard the bomb was traced back to Lourenco Marques and specifically to the Portuguese secret police, the International Police for the Defence of the State (PIDE). Thus Portugal, a member of the alliance with Rhodesia and South Africa, set the stage for what is today called destabilization.

Rhodesia's Unilateral Declaration of Independence (UDI) in November 1965 was of massive consequence for Tanzania. Zambia, to the south and landlocked, desperately needed lifelines to the sea for its survival. Dar es Salaam was the only viable alternative. A massive air and road rescue operation was imperative and trucks ploughed through seas of mud from Dar es Salaam to Zambia to get that country's imports and exports in and out.

However, such a costly operation could be sustained only for a short period of time and long term alternatives had to be found, alternatives the region may benefit from in the future. The most important of these was the building of the railway linking Dar es Salaam to Kapiri Mposhi in Zambia, funded by China after several Western countries refused to assist. The cost to Tanzania and Zambia was US$500 million, of which Tanzania agreed to pay half. Despite the generosity of a Chinese interest-free loan, it is a debatable point whether the railway would have been built had it not been for UDI.

A pipeline had to be built, at a cost of about $36 million, to ensure Zambia's fuel lifeline. Tanzania was responsible for one-third of this. The highway linking the two countries — which to Nyerere's irritation became known as the "Hell Run" — had to be rapidly upgraded and Tanzania was responsible for half of the cost. Hundreds of trucks had to be purchased and, again, Tanzania bore half the cost.

In those early days, Dar es Salaam was the crossroads of southern Africa's emerging liberation movements, all of whom had their headquarters or offices in the city. There was a continuous flow in and out of Tanzania of liberation movement leaders and international figures who came to meet them, ranging from Che Guevera to Bobby Kennedy. It was logical, therefore, that when the Organization of African Unity (OAU) decided to set up a Liberation Committee, the headquarters should be in Dar es Salaam, where it remains to this day.

Tanzania has never attempted to quantify the total cost of this enduring commitment which, in addition to its OAU and other regular contributions, has amounted to several million dollars a year for over 25 years — a remarkable sum for a nation of such modest means. This commitment is demonstrated by the population, as well as their leadership, and ordinary Tanzanians have frequently contributed many millions of shillings from meagre incomes to support liberation movements. During the Mozambican struggle, Tanzanians shared what they had with Frelimo, committing large sums of money, food or even bicycles.

Destabilization

Despite its geographical position in East Africa, Tanzania has always been in the forefront of the opposition to apartheid, as seen above.

Although the independence of Mozambique in 1975 removed the decolonization process in southern Africa from Tanzania's borders, the escalation of South Africa's surrogate war through the MNR after 1980 brought it back.

In 1984, when South Africa was seeking an alternative route of supply for the MNR after signing the Nkomati agreement with the government of Mozambique, the clandestine search shifted to southern Tanzania.

If direct assistance from South Africa to the MNR across the Mozambican border was to be curtailed for a period, then alternatives had to be found, if only as a smokescreen. Supply by sea increased in this period, and some equipment may have been diverted via the Comoro Islands, virtually a South African satellite and ideally situated for access to northern Mozambique and southern Tanzania. Later on, a massive MNR invasion was launched from Malawian territory, which continues to be used as a supply route. However, in the months immediately following the signing at Nkomati in early 1984, some exploration was carried out in southern Tanzania close to the Rovuma river border with northern Mozambique.

On 26 August 1984, four Portuguese men, who had entered Tanzania ostensibly for a hunting trip in the Selous game reserve, were arrested after Tanzanian authorities noticed that there was little hunting going on and that the "hunters" were occupied with map-making and surveying — as well as constructing a clandestine bush airstrip. Three of the four were related, from a former settler family in Mozambique with close links to the MNR.

Adelino Serra Peres (Senior) had been since colonial times a close associate of the wealthy businessman and newspaper proprietor, Jorge Jardim. Adelino Peres (Junior), was a former member of the Rhodesian army in the notorious Selous Scouts unit which had been disbanded after Zimbabwe's independence. Carlos Cardeano, the third member of the Peres family arrested, had been in South Africa the month before his arrest for talks with Evo Fernandes, appointed MNR secretary-general after his predecessor, Orlando Cristina, was assassinated in South Africa.

The Peres family used its links with Portuguese political figures in the government of Prime Minister Mario Soares to press for and secure the release of the detainees, thus embarrassing the foreign ministry in Lisbon which continued to deny any connection with the MNR. Soares's Deputy Prime Minister, Mota Pinto, has often been named as the source of a telephone call to Fernandes in Pretoria a few months later, after which peace talks with Mozambican government officials were suspended.

Defence and Other Costs

Tanzania has no economic links and no common border with South Africa and is usually excluded from the cost analysis of destabilization. The economic and social costs to Tanzania of opposing South Africa's "total strategy" are in some ways difficult to quantify. However, there are areas to which attention can be drawn.

In June 1985, the leaders of Mozambique, Tanzania and Zimbabwe met in Harare to discuss the deteriorating military situation in Mozambique. Mugabe, then Prime Minister, offered to increase Zimbabwe's commitment from a force guarding the Beira corridor to encompass a combat role with deployment in three provinces against the MNR. Tanzania, one of the world's 25 poorest nations, was in a more difficult economic position. Nevertheless, President Nyerere offered military training facilities at Nachingwea in southern Tanzania. Given Tanzania's economic constraints, that was a considerable and costly gesture.

The cost of that training to a country where the most desperately short commodity is foreign currency has been US$3.5 million to date. That may not seem a large sum to richer nations, but in Tanzanian terms it represents a consequential amount — and is almost certainly an underestimate by the government.

In September 1986, just prior to the plane crash that killed President Machel and several senior officials of the Mozambican government, there was a dramatic escalation of the war. Mozambique was confronted with a massive invasion in the centre-north of the country which Machel publicly stated had come from Malawi. Large groups of armed men swept through the fertile central province of Zambezia in an apparent attempt to cut the country in half and declare a provisional government in the provincial capital, Quelimane. The economic destruction was vast. Towns were occupied and destroyed, as were mining and agricultural complexes.

Recognizing the gravity of the new situation in Mozambique, Tanzania increased its commitment and, despite considerable economic constraints, sent a brigade group of 4,000 soldiers who were stationed largely in Zambezia province. Their primary task was to hold the towns and villages, freeing the Mozambican army to regain control of the countryside. Of those 4,000 troops who went to Mozambique about 60 are now buried in that country, a figure very much lower than the MNR claims but a commitment in blood by Tanzanians.

The initial request was for three months but it was not until two years later, in November 1988, that Tanzania was able to withdraw its military units. The number of lives lost and the dollar cost of this commitment have not been announced, however senior government officials say the cost is over US$120 million.

Tanzanian support for Mozambique against South Africa's surrogates has involved additional hidden costs and implications.
Although on a minor scale when compared with Zambia or Zimbabwe, Tanzania has been forced to strengthen its southern border
defences to deal with the threat of raids across the Ruvuma river. The
military cost of this is put at US$10 million. There are also the costs of
providing shelter and sustenance for 72,000 Mozambicans displaced
across the border in Tanzania, and the number of Tanzanian nationals
killed or damage done in MNR cross-border incursions. From late
1987 to April 1989 there were five MNR incursions in which one
Tanzanian was killed, 68 were abducted and large amounts of
property, food and money were stolen from poor border area villagers.

The people of Tanzania responded to Mozambique's needs at a
personal level when a solidarity fund, launched through the cities,
towns and villages, drew donations of anything from a few shillings to a
bull. Villagers, national service camps and others donated monies and
livestock. By late 1988, well over 20 million shillings had been
contributed to a "people-to-people" fund.

There are several areas of cost to Tanzania to consider. The railway,
highway and pipeline from Zambia to Dar es Salaam, and the port
facilities, have had to be upgraded as an alternative route for the
region and insurance against South Africa's possible blockade of other
routes. It is also necessary to take account of the improvement of the
land route to Malawi and increased use of the port by that country
since the Nacala railway in Mozambique was sabotaged in 1984.
Tanzania continues to host the OAU Liberation Committee, as it has
for 25 years, and throughout the organization's history has been a
reliable contributor to the liberation fund.

Until his retirement as Tanzania's President in 1985, Nyerere was
the chair and driving force of the informal grouping of six independent
states known as the Frontline States. The role of this group, both
regionally and internationally, has been pre-eminent for well over a
decade. Other countries and international organizations including the
OAU, the United Nations and the Commonwealth have taken their
lead on southern African issues from the six.

Historically and in many other ways, Tanzania has played a pivotal
role in the southern African region, in the deliberations of the
Commonwealth and the international community. Geography has not
yet removed Tanzania from the Frontline, and its principles and
support for justice and equality in southern Africa are, despite its
limited means, as firm as they have been for over a quarter of a
century.

As the earliest Frontline supporter of the liberation movements and
the first to experience the price of destabilization for that commitment, Tanzania provides a fitting postscript for this report to the

Commonwealth Heads of State and Government meeting in Kuala Lumpur in October 1989.

Almost three decades after his speech to the Legislative Assembly on 22 October 1959, and with total consistency 30 years on, Nyerere wrote in the foreword to a recent book: ". . . millions of people, including many in leading or responsible positions in democratic Western countries, are unaware of what has been happening — and what is still happening — in southern Africa. . . .

"Some of them may genuinely not know that the apartheid regime they abhor is threatening the very existence of the states whose independence they welcomed a short time ago."

Returning to the the candle of hope he had spoken of 30 years earlier, Nyerere offered his congratulations to the people and governments of the victim states "who have kept the beacon of freedom alight by their endurance, their courage, and their absolute commitment to Africa's liberation."

Summary and Recommendations

After 1980, South Africa began to effect coordinated interventionist policies toward neighbouring states, under the rubric of "total strategy". The specific objectives are: regional economic dependence, formal security agreements, and acceptance of the "homelands". The general goal is to create and maintain a zone that will be politically submissive and economically lucrative, and act as a bulwark against international sanctions to bring pressure for an end to apartheid.

To achieve these objectives, and to bully neighbouring states which are unwilling to cooperate, Pretoria has resorted to illegal and violent measures which have had an enormous social and economic cost for the region. Those states have had to forego considerable development potential and economic growth in order to defend themselves.

The combination of tactics that South Africa uses against each of its neighbours depends on their individual political, economic and military vulnerabilities, from open military aggression against Angola and a surrogate war in Mozambique to sabotage of regional transportation routes and industrial equipment, congestion at border posts, withholding railway rolling stock, customs delays and rate manipulation as well as direct attacks, sabotage and car bombs in Botswana, Zimbabwe and Zambia, economic pressure, assassinations and kidnappings in Swaziland and Lesotho. Through these methods, South Africa is in fact using economic sanctions against its neighbours.

Despite Pretoria's presentation of itself as the region's "peace-maker" and "stabilizer", these goals remain in place and diplomatic forays involving international negotiations and discussions are part of the same process, giving recognition to to South Africa's aspirations as the regional "superpower".

In dealing with South Africa, things are never as they seem, and neighbouring states have considerable experience of this over the past eight years. An allegorical description of South Africa's relations with the region is the common police interrogation technique in which one administers the blows while another offers the sweets.

This "total strategy" also encompasses the internal situation in South Africa through preparations for sanctions-busting and military self-sufficiency, tough repression of popular political leaders and co-option of others for the process of apartheid's "reform". From Pretoria's point of view, this strategy has enabled it to weather 10 years of increasingly severe internal and international pressure, while strengthening its defence capabilities, improving its technology, and employing more sophisticated tactical responses to the region and the international community.

In the case of Mozambique, there was a vicious and widespread escalation of military activity — directed at economic and human targets — after the Songo meeting in September 1988 between P.W. Botha and President Chissano, coupled with mounting evidence of South Africa's involvement in the supply and direction of this "contra" activity. The most senior officials in the US State Department made public pronouncements on this during the first half of 1989.

A tripartite meeting of Mozambique, Portugal and South Africa, to discuss the repair of Cahora Bassa electricity transmission lines was told two months earlier that 524 pylons were in need of repair from previous sabotage. A discussion of reconstruction costs was based on this figure. However, by the end of 1988, a further 900 pylons had been destroyed in the south of the country, most of them after the Songo meeting. The estimated cost of repair trippled after the Songo meeting and, in January 1989, Mozambique openly accused South Africa of responsibility. Since the earlier sabotage, soon after the signing of the Nkomati Accord, Mozambique has been forced to spend valuable foreign currency importing electricity from South Africa.

Mozambique's main railway systems have been closed to regional transit traffic since they were sabotaged in 1984, adding billions of dollars to freight bills for landlocked countries whose trade must transit the longer routes through South Africa. The only railway operating along its full length is that through the Beira corridor, which is defended by the Zimbabwe National Army, vastly inflating Zimbabwe's defence costs. Transportation is a priority of the nine-nation Southern African Development Coordination Conference (SADCC), formed in 1980 for the purpose of increasing regional cooperation and reducing dependence on South Africa, and these lines are now being rehabilitated.

Armed attacks from Mozambique across the eastern borders of Zimbabwe and Zambia, which began in 1987, increased through 1988 causing several hundred civilian deaths, destruction or theft of property, and further escalation in defence costs. Reports of new massacres, the funerals of the victims and angry statements by government officials were appearing almost daily in Zimbabwe's national press in January 1989. In one such incident in mid-January, the victims were five children aged 5, 7, 9, 11, and 13, all from one family, and two adults aged 50 and 60.

Zimbabwe has committed troops to Mozambique, and Zambia has

been involved in training Mozambican soldiers as well as protecting its own borders. Tanzania has had to pay the price of defending its southern border, training Mozambican soldiers and sending a brigade to assist in the defence of key installations in Mozambique. Botswana is subjected to cross-border raids and bombings which kill or maim Batswana nationals as well as destroying property. Mineral-rich Botswana, which maintains large foreign currency reserves, is also contributing to the defence of Mozambique and the rehabilitation of its railways.

In Angola, South Africa's military action has been overt, with a full-scale invasion in the southern part of the country, halted in a dramatic battle for the tiny town of Cuito Cuanavale, which saw the first entry into combat by Cuban troops since 1976. The battle for the town, held by Angolan and Cuban forces, was seen in regional and continental terms as an African battle against South African aggression and its aspirations as the region's "superpower". Although South Africa has the most modern and effective long-range artillery, its military limitations particularly show in its lost air superiority. It is an important comment on the UN arms embargo, how it works and how it could work more effectively if fully applied.

If any further military message to the region was required — juxtaposed with the Angola/Namibia agreement and the prospect of talks in Mozambique — it came with the test launching by South Africa in early July 1989 of an intermediate-range ballistic missile, developed with the help of Israel and capable of delivering a nuclear warhead as far north as Angola and Tanzania.

South Africa's "total strategy" has cost its neighbours in the Frontline States a minimum of $45 billion since 1980, and some estimates range up to $60 billion at current rates of exchange. The suffering has been enormous with almost half the population of Angola and Mozambique threatened with hunger, and some four million displaced within or outside national boundaries. The war-related death toll in the region has risen to 1.5 million through direct military action, disruption of the delivery or production of food, and destruction of health facilities and immunization programmes. The psychological effect of war and the lost educational opportunities through destruction of schools and murder of teachers bodes ill for future development in those two countries. A generation has been scarred and many of these scars are permanent, as are the ecological scars on the region's environment.

In the case of Namibia, while accepting an independence process in exchange for an honourable withdrawal from southern Angola, South Africa already has in place the structures for economic and military destabilization. Walvis Bay itself provides South Africa with a military base in the heart of Namibia, and control over trade through the country's only deep-water port. To reinforce the point, South Africa held its biggest ever naval exercise off Walvis Bay in September 1988.

Peace and stability are vital to human and economic recovery in southern Africa and there can be little sustainable growth or development in the region until the end of apartheid in South Africa. An integrated international response involving several components is required:

- Pressure for an end to apartheid must be increased by all possible means. The effect of sanctions, particularly financial, is beginning to show on the South African economy, and has forced Pretoria to be more responsive to the international community. This is not the time to reduce that pressure, when results are beginning to appear, but rather the pressure must be continued and increased through determined widening and tightening of sanctions until the recommendations of the Commonwealth Eminent Persons Group are fully implemented.

- Any application of sanctions must be accompanied by positive compensatory measures to fortify, strengthen and develop the economies of the SADCC states and thus to assist them in their efforts to reduce their dependence and disengage from South Africa and withstand any retaliation.

- A detailed report on South Africa's military and economic action against its neighbours should be presented to governments and international organizations and to the UN Security Council. This report should be updated on a regular basis, to keep governments and institutions fully aware of South Africa's ongoing aggression, to assist in determining the compensatory measures mentioned above, and to provide a basis for reconstruction should hostilities cease.

- Formal denunciation of South African destabilization and sanctions against its neighbours as a contributory factor to southern Africa's economic crisis should be sought, and special efforts initiated to relieve economic pressure through debt relief, import cost reduction and assisting the SADCC states to find alternative markets on preferential terms to further their efforts to disengange from South Africa.

- Emergency and development assistance to the SADCC region should be increased and should take account of the security situation in the region through governments recognizing the need to provide suitable support to protect and rehabilitate economic targets.

- Provision of all assistance should take into account the need to strengthen national economies of the region, where possible purchasing within the region, thereby enhancing regional trade, and transportation routes other than those through South Africa.

• The broadest circulation of accurate information about the region's reality is of paramount importance to increase awareness in the international community and to counteract South African disinformation and propaganda. There is also a need for greater awareness within the region as to the importance of information. The Commonwealth has a special role to play in disseminating information about the region's realities, and should consider establishing a fund to assist in visits to the region by journalists, policy planners and others, as Nordic countries do.

• All efforts must be made to ensure "free and fair" elections in Namibia, a stable transition to majority rule, the recognition that Walvis Bay is an integral part of Namibia, and to assist Namibia to strengthen its economy and disengage from South Africa.

Secondary Sources

Material contained in this volume is largely from primary sources, but the following list offers selected secondary sources for background and further reading.

Books

Children on the Front Line. The impact of apartheid, destabilization and warfare on children in southern and South Africa (1989 update), UNICEF, 1989.

Operation Timber, Basic Books, US, 1988.

Frontline Southern Africa: Destructive Engagement, P. Johnson, D. Martin (eds), Ryan Publishing, UK; Four Walls Eight Windows, US, 1988.

Mission to South Africa. The findings of the Commonwealth Eminent Persons Group on southern Africa, Penguin, 1986.

Beggar Your Neighbours, J. Hanlon, James Currey Publishers, UK; Indiana University Press, US, 1986.

In Search of Enemies, J. Stockwell, Andre Deutsch, UK: W.W. Norton, US, 1978.

Periodicals

Mozambique file, Mozambique News Agency (AIM), Maputo.

Mozambique News Review, AIM, London.

Southern Africa Dossier of African Studies, Eduardo Mondlane University, Maputo.

Emergency Mozambique, National Executive Commission for the Emergency, Maputo.

ANGOP News Bulletin, Angola News Agency, London.

Front Line States Destabilization Calendar, SARDC, Harare.

World Campaign Against Nuclear and Military Collaboration with South Africa, Oslo.

CSIS Africa Notes, Centre for Strategic and International Studies, Washington DC.

Articles, Studies

Southern Africa: The Security of the Front Line States, O. Obasanjo, Commonwealth Secretariat, 1988.

Summary of Mozambican Refugee Accounts of Principally Conflict-Related Experience in Mozambique, R. Gersony, US State Dept, 1988.

Southern Africa: Challenges and Choices, M. Clough, Centre for Foreign Relations, US, Summer 1988.

Victims of Apartheid, P. Johnson, D. Martin, UNHCR/OAU, 1988.

Struggle for Southern Africa, R. G. Mugabe, Foreign Affairs, US, Winter 1987/88.

The Emergency Situation in Angola, UN Office for Emergency in Africa, 1988.

Angola Emergency Programme Briefing Note, UNICEF, 1988.

The Rise of the South African Security Establishment, K. W. Grundy, South African Institute of International Affairs, SA, 1983.

Total Strategy in Southern Africa. An analysis of south African regional policy since 1978, R. Davis, D. O'Meara, Journal of Southern African Studies, April 1985.